Deadly Odds 5.0

Allen Wyler

Deadly Odds 5.0

Other books by Allen Wyler (fiction)

Changes
Deadly Odds
Deadly Odds 2.0
Deadly Odds 3.0
Deadly Odds 4.0
Ringer
Dead Ringer 2.0
Dead End Deal
Dead Wrong
Deadly Errors
Dead Head
Cutter's Trial

Other books by Allen Wyler (nonfiction)

The Surgical Management of Epilepsy

Deadly Odds 5.0 ©2022 Allen Wyler, All Rights Reserved

Print ISBN 978-1-949267-92-1
ebook ISBN 978-1-949267-93-8

Visit Allen online at www.allenwyler.com

Cover design by Guy D. Corp
www.grafixCORP.com

STAIRWAY≡PRESS

STAIRWAY PRESS—APACHE JUNCTION

www.stairwaypress.com
1000 West Apache Trail, Suite 126
Apache Junction, AZ 85120 USA

CHAPTER 1

NOT THAT IT was chump change by any stretch—not by a long shot—but the profit wasn't remotely the issue. No question, he could put it to good use, but what he viscerally ached for was hate-fueled, ego-satiating vengeance.

With a grin, he tapped ENTER, then melted back into his padded leather gaming chair, eyes on the business alerts and stock prices scrolling across the bottom edge of CNBC, awaiting the opening act of *Swift and Complete Retribution.* It took several minutes before the bulletin he'd anxiously been anticipating appeared.

CURCHFIELD TECHNOLOGIES DENIED FDA APPROVAL.

Ramesh Singh punched air.

"*Yes!*"

Whistling his favorite *Carmen* aria, he turned to the right-hand screen, logged into the Schwab account. Curchfield Technologies was currently bid at $16.41 on low volume, up $0.125 for the day. Thirty seconds later, on rapidly escalating volume, it slid south of $13.25. In another three minutes it had plummeted past $10.05 on what was becoming an explosive dumping frenzy. An hour later a handful of bottom feeders continued to peck away at shares oscillating around $0.235, give or take a fractional penny.

Perfect.

Singh bought ten thousand shares, covering his short position, which—not that it mattered—netted a tasty profit of $150,000 (plus change). Although he certainly had no intention of sneering at the delightful addition to his bank account, it paled in comparison to the joy permeating his chest. Not only did he flawlessly orchestrate a beautifully intricate scheme, a *tour de force* of brilliance and ingenuity, a precisely executed complex plan.

No need for modesty, just total objectivity.

Phase I of *The Revenge* had struck with the precision of a drone-guided missile. Phase II would see the bastard punished for what he'd done. The righteous prick, playing all high and mighty with a network that wasn't even his.

Three hours of intense focus on three glowing monitors was now officially over.

Enough.

He rolled back the chair, stood with fingers interlaced behind his head and arced his back to the fringe of balance working out the muscle knots that such prolonged sessions provoked. The results, however, certainly trivialized any fleeting discomfort.

One Month Later

Carlos Lopez loved his job. Most of all, loved the freedom of working from home unsupervised. His boss's only proviso— which really wasn't unreasonable—was that he complete assignments on schedule.

Hey, no problem.

Positioned on the introverted end of the personality spectrum, this arrangement served him brilliantly. The Starbucks directly across the street from his condominium was a major-league benefit too.

Yes, life was good.

That was, until loud banging on the front door jarred him awake at five AM. Though he didn't know it yet, this was the moment his copacetic life would turn to shit *al a flambé*, and the curtain would go up on the opening act of *The Nightmare*.

Yawning, padding barefoot to the front door, knuckling sand from his eyes, he wondered who the hell would be out there at this godforsaken hour.

"Yeah, yeah, coming," he yelled at the insistent pounding.

He opened the door to a tall, lanky, freckled dude with military-short blond hair dressed in black tac pants and a polo shirt with FBI across the chest in reflective yellow letters.

"Carlos Lopez?" the dude asked in a no-nonsense tone that matched his posture.

"Uh, yeah?" Carlos answered, still groggily confused.

Fisher held up an identification wallet with some sort of official-looking ID.

"FBI Special Agents Gary Fisher and John Chang."

Only then did Lopez notice the other guy, a shorter Asian dude dressed similarly to Fisher, then two other men positioned further down the hall.

Fisher pushed a folded paper at his chest.

"This is a warrant to search your apartment for, and to seize, any and all computers and digital records."

HONOLULU

Three Weeks Later

GENTLE 78-DEGREE trade winds wafted through the wide-open sliders, serving up another to-die-for gorgeous day in paradise. Arnold Gold was replacing the fresh pot of Kona blend on the Mr. Coffee burner when James Brown and the Famous Flames began blasting *Three Hearts in a Tangle* from his iPhone—one of three custom ringtones he'd cut and uploaded to the device.

Caller ID displayed PALMER DAVIDSON.

It had been three months since the criminal defense lawyer and his ex-wife, Martina, visited him and his girlfriend Rachael Weinstein for hors d'oeurves and wine on his back deck during a brief trip to the island to work on Davidson's vacation condo.

"What up, Mr. Davidson?"

"How long have we known each other, son?"

He leaned against the kitchen counter; coffee forgotten.

"I don't know…what? Two years, give or take."

"And during that time, we have grown to be friends, have we not?"

"Yeah, guess so, why?"

"In that case, might it be appropriate to address me by my

given name?"

Arnold paused, having never considered it. Mr. Davidson was, well, Mr. Davidson. That's just the way things were.

"I guess, but truthfully, don't think I can."

"Really? Why is that?"

What more could he say?

"Well...because you're Mr. Davidson."

After a brief pause, Davidson continued.

"Do as you wish, but the reason I am calling is we have a job for you if you are available."

We?

Davidson ran a one-man law practice and, far as he knew, typically worked solo.

"Mr. Davidson, I'm always available for you. What sort of problem we talking about?"

"We represent a client who is presently the focus of an aggressive federal investigation for crimes we steadfastly believe he is innocent of committing. We would like you to assist us with his defense."

Hmm, interesting pitch. Plus, there's that plural pronoun again. This alone was intriguing. And hey, new business was new business, right?

"You bet. What alleged crime's your client suspected of?"

Since first enlisting the lawyer's services a couple years ago—during the investigation of his best friend's murder—Arnold had learned to liberally sprinkle "allegedly" into any question or assertion containing the slightest whiff of accusation. Besides, it sounded so, what...cautious? Circumspect? Erudite?

"For hacking two company computer networks for the purpose of disseminating misleading information to manipulate their stock prices for personal profit."

Wow! What a hook. For a shitload of reasons, but mostly on account of his own fascination with the market.

"No shit? He actually did that?" he asked, absentmindedly finger-combing his curly black hair.

"No, of course not," this said with a completely dismissive tone. "But *some* hacker did, and he is presently being singled out as the perpetrator."

"Interesting." Pause. "Huh…just for grins, how many shares we talking about?"

"Ten thousand."

Arnold whistled, his mind running some fanciful numbers, ten thousand being such an easy multiplier.

"Huh. So, I got to ask, how many points did they gain?"

"Their stocks *plummeted*. One dropped seventeen points to close under a dollar."

"Plummeted?" Did he hear that right? "You mean, like, *dropped?*"

"Yes, dropped."

Wow.

Now *that* wrinkle drove the hook even deeper. Especially considering the shares involved.

"Oh, man, if you're lucky enough to hit it just right, that'd be upwards of hundred and seventy thousand, right?"

But nailing the freaking top and bottom was, like, dream on dude. But then, do this on two stocks and…

"Approximately, depending upon transaction fees and acquisition prices."

"And this dude's, what, your average Joe? I mean like, he's no day trader, nothing like that?"

"That is correct. Like you, he does IT work. Something to do with security, I believe."

Well, Gold and Associates wasn't all that much into security, but he wasn't about to quibble. Arnold shook his head in amazement.

"Man, that's a massive tank in price. How'd he do that?"

"Both companies were small-cap, which made them

extremely vulnerable to selling pressure, so once shares began to drop and programmed selling kicked in, the bottom fell out."

Arnold whistled again.

"Your use of past tense…that intentional?"

"I am afraid the complete story must await a future time, son. At the moment, we must know if we can count on your help or not. I do not enjoy pressuring you, son, but circumstances do require an immediate answer."

There's that "we" again.

"You should know I'm always available to help you, Mr. Davidson, but I need more of an idea what you want from me. If it's just talk, why not go ahead and discuss it? Or if you prefer face to face, schedule a Zoom?"

"We *strongly prefer* that you to meet the accused *in person*. There are nuances you can only glean from direct personal interaction. We will, of course, reimburse your travel plus per diem."

Mr. Davidson had a cleverly deceptive way of channeling a choice into no choice. Regardless, no way Arnold could refuse the man. On the other hand, another, unrelated factor was strongly influencing the equation: Rachael. He flashed on her hair-singeing tirade when returning from his last Seattle case which had necessitated staying there an extra week.

Essentially, the timing couldn't be worse: she'd just moved in with him. *On a trial basis*, as she'd termed it. Trial for what? Far as he was concerned, soon as he got up the nerve, he would propose; something that had been his dream since puberty.

"There's no other option?" he asked, in spite of Mr. Davidson's clarity.

"There are always other options, son. If you cannot help us, we will, of course, offer the job to someone who can."

Ah, Jesus…now what?

Stall, that's what.

"So, I got to ask, who's *we?*"

"Yes, I apologize for failing to clarify that. Noah Cain and I are teamed up on this. This was initially his client, but because of the hacking angle, he requested my help and is now asking for your involvement as well."

Oh, man. That's huge.

Cain was the senior and founding partner of the prestigious Cain, Tidwell, Stowell, a boutique law firm specializing in white-collar criminal defense. Early last summer the partners had flown him to Seattle in a private jet to neutralize a time-sensitive ransomware attack that had paralyzed their office. Not only did Arnold neutralize the malware, but in the process uncovered a junior partner embezzling from the firm.

During that time, Arnold had developed a deep-seated respect for Noah Cain's integrity. The lawyer had since become a rich referral source at a time when Arnold's fledgling company was struggling for business. So yeah, he felt a strong obligation toward both men. On the other hand, he knew damn well Rachael would be livid if he jetted off again.

Then again, the scant details Mr. Davidson dangled at him seriously piqued his curiosity. And besides, it would be very cool to spend a few days in his newly rebuilt Seattle home.

Hmm, what were the odds Rachael could possibly score a few vacation days and go too?

Man, like, seriously doubtful. Especially given the nursing shortage since the pandemic...

Mr. Davidson's unrelenting heavy silence did nothing but jack up the increasing pressure inside his skull, making it feel on the cusp of exploding.

Crunch time.

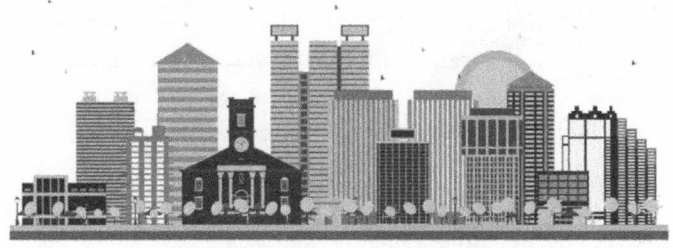

HONOLULU

CHAPTER 2

"LOOK, I'M MORE than willing to help, but how about this; before you go to the time and expense of flying me over, how about a quick Zoom so I can tell you if I'm the right one for the job?"

"No, son. Noah and I feel it is in *everyone's* best interest for you to meet the defendant *in person*. Furthermore, at least initially, your work will necessitate your presence. Have I made our position clear?"

Crystalline.

Blowing an audible breath, Arnold palm-wiped his face. There it was, your classic clusterfuck. Opposing forces emotionally quartering him; a strong commitment to the lawyers pulling forcibly against Rachael's anticipated reaction. Besides, the freaking timing seriously sucked, what with her growing irritation over his ever-increasing workload.

"To be perfectly honest, Mr. Davidson, this's, like, an exceptionally bad time for me to leave. I'm worried about Rachael's reaction."

"May I ask what the issue is?"

Arnold would resent anyone but Mr. Davidson prying into his personal affairs, but this man was family. Okay, adopted family, but a surrogate father, nonetheless. *Ah, man...* another blow through pursed lips.

"She's still royally miffed over the extra time I spent on the last case, so leaving town now, especially for an unspecified period, would blow some serious oxygen on the embers."

Davidson responded with two words expressing unequivocal disappointment.

"I see."

Time for the pitch.

"Look, how about this: I finally have a Seattle associate."

Associate was a bit of a stretch. Pieceworker was more like it.

"How about if he does the face-to-face, reports back to me, and we go from there? Then, if you still need me, hey, no problem, I'll be there. How's that sound to you?"

Until two months ago, Gold and Associates had been a one-banana show with Arnold covering both the Seattle and Honolulu "offices." Although he'd always intended to hire at least one associate in each city to cover exactly this sort of situation, he'd been, well, heel-dragging. Then, a month ago, he had hired Primal Fear, a renowned hacker, to cover Seattle.

Problem solved. At least for that location.

The benefit of additional help instantly became forehead thumpingly obvious; his backlog fell to manageable levels, but, as a result, more work began landing in his in-box, increasing the pressure to fill the Honolulu slot. Problem was, freeing up time to search for an associate while maintaining workflow was proving problematic.

Silence.

Uh-oh. Time to backpedal.

"I mean, we work closely. Besides, when you think about it, it'd actually save time. I mean, best-case scenario it'd take me like, what, twenty-four hours to get there, right? You, of

all people, know the earliest flights out of here don't touch
down at SeaTac until around ten, so even if I snagged a flight
today—which is, like, extremely doubtful—I couldn't
possibly be in your office until morning, right? My associate
could be there in a few hours. See?"

And Rachael wouldn't have to know a thing.

Davidson's silence became deafening.

Eventually, the lawyer said, "Point taken." Another
pause. "Noah will be *extremely* disappointed." Tick-tick-tick.
"However, I, of all people, am quite cognizant of how such
issues are capable of becoming relationship irritants, as Martina
and I can attest."

"Okay, so's that a yes?"

At least it didn't sound like a resounding thumbs down.

"You leave us no choice, son."

Oh, shit.

Guilt rippled his heart. Here he was, letting down the
men he so admired.

But what other option was there?

Having Primal Fear do an in-person data-gathering
interview was the best—well, the only—reasonable
compromise. After all, it would provide an immediate
assessment. And besides, if his business continued to grow, his
clients would eventually need to adapt to dealing with an
associate. True. But still…just didn't feel right…not for Mr.
Davidson and Mr. Cain, his most valued clients.

True that, but the only other option…

"Look, Mr. Davidson, I'm *really* sorry but this is the best
I can do on such short notice. If things weren't so damn
sensitive with Rach…" Still, it simply felt *wrong*. "Tell you
what, I'll call him now to make sure he can meet today. Uh, I
assume you want to meet ASAP, right?"

"That is correct."

"Okay, then, call you right back. Hopefully I can get the

ball rolling and take care of this for you ASAP."

"I will wait to hear back from you before I speak with Noah. He will be extremely disappointed, but if this is the best you can do…"

Ah, Jesus.

Another wave of guilt rippled his heart.

Oh, man, hope I can track him down.

Fear was at times, well, elusive.

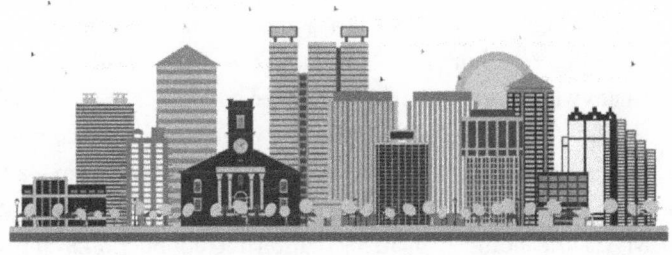

HONOLULU

CHAPTER 3

ARNOLD FINALLY LOCATED Primal Fear—or at least his account—in a Dark Net chat room. But the account showed he'd been inactive for the past five minutes, which, for Fear, was atypical. Fear loved dominating exchanges and being the all-knowing guru of all things digital. Arnold figured he probably just stepped away for a few minutes, so posted a message asking him to reply ASAP, then sat back to wait.

Fear responded immediately.

Shocker: *What up?*
Arnold: *Go Cyber32*, referring to a private chat room.
Fear: *Why?*
Arnold: *Need to talk.*
Fear: *Okay, in a few.*

Arnold was now in his "real" Honolulu office, the guest bedroom he'd specially tricked out to accommodate SAM 2.0, his elaborate Artificial Intelligence neural network. SAM consisted of twenty fully loaded Dell workstations networked to function synchronously as one supercomputer for tackling difficult problems and managing his stock-trading algorithm.

Typically he accessed SAM via Wi-Fi from his laptop or Surface while kicking back on a deck chaise with a mug of Kona coffee or a hot chocolate but could just as easily access it from anywhere in the world with internet.

His present "Seattle office"—which he'd inaugurated during the ransomware gig for Mr. Cain's law firm—was nothing more than a laptop on the kitchen table connected to SAM via the home's giga-speed internet connection. One of Arnold's many pipe dreams was to replicate SAM in the specially designed basement computer room of the new house. Although SAM was backed up twice daily to both on-site external hard disks as well as three different cloud-storage platforms, the network was now so crucial to Arnold that building a duplicate system in a geographically separate location was a prudent safeguard.

Hmm... wonder what Fear's real name is?

Or, for that matter, the infamous hacker's sex. For some reason, he'd automatically assumed he was a dude. Probably on account of the name. But what if Fear was actually Prsicilla Higginbottom, a gangly, bubbly, seventeen-year-old acne-riddled fluffy blonde?

Naw.

Very unlikely simply on account of the hours he (or dudette, as the case might be) spent tapped into cyberspace. Yet the fact remained; he had no clue who was on the other end of the magic cyberspace link. Especially in view of how fervently hackers protect their identities. Verged on paranoia. Then again, his pool of potential employees was, well, limited.

Fear's name began blinking in the private chat room indicating he was now signed in.

Then came: *S'up?*

Arnold: *Go Audio.*

That was their established communication mode for discussing non-routine work. Arnold routinely posted work assignments on a spreadsheet in a shared Dropbox account. Once Fear completed a job, Arnold would deposit the fee in his Bitcoin wallet. A nice, efficient system. Except for Arnold's gnawing concern that Fear really didn't need the money but was using the jobs for other nefarious purposes. Fear was, after all, a hardcore card-carrying Black Hat. So, handing over passwords to clients' network was, well...the thought made him more than a little queasy.

On the other hand, the reality was undeniable; his relentlessly growing workload only increased his reliance on Fear's assistance. All of which underscored his acute need to hire a valid and trustworthy fulltime Seattle associate to replace him.

But when would he ever find the time?

In addition, Arnold knew all too well that he didn't possess the hands-on, detail-oriented management skills his business required if it were to sustain further growth. Hell, he was barely keeping it together as-is. Rather than a day-to-day grind-it-out manager, he was a terrific concept guy.

He also knew it was inevitably the damn little niggling details that always circled back to bite you in the ass. Which— as long as he was on this particular rant—reminded him that he'd yet to install QuickBooks and its payroll and accounting modules. And speaking of critical To-Do List items, what about the gigantic headache of how to pay social security tax on a dude who goes to freaking extremes to keep his identity hidden? Just don't declare it? Hell no. Too risky. Especially if he continued to deduct it as an operating expense.

Jesus, dude, you can't continue to Scarlett O'Hara these issues forever.

A Darth Vader-like electronically distorted voice said, "Yo, s'up, man?"

"Have a new job for you, but this one's different and extremely important."

"Cool. Lay it on me."

That damn voice distortion was gratingly annoying, but what can you do? These hackers.

"A couple things. For starters, I need you to do a face-to-face sit-down with—"

"Have you lost your fucking mind?"

Arnold recoiled.

"No. The client insists on it."

The distortion couldn't mask his shouts.

"No fucking way, man. Absolutely *no* fucking way."

Arnold rolled his eyes and shook his head. What did he expect? Especially from a dude as shady as Fear. But work was work, and if he really wanted the money.

Yeah, but he doesn't. Tells you something, doesn't it?

Ah, man...

"Look, I wouldn't ask if this wasn't, like, super-super important, dude. Besides, there's no reason to use your real name, right? Hell, use any name comes to mind. Far as they know, you're just another geek punching in for the paycheck. Like, what's the big deal?"

"Think I give a fresh flying turd what they *think*? It's fundamental, dude: I will *not* allow *anyone* to see my face. Nonnegotiable. Besides, if this's such a big deal, why don't *you* go show your face?"

Arnold shook his head, anger escalating.

"Because I'm in Honolulu and the client's in Seattle."

"So? Fly there and do the meet."

There?

Arnold's antennae were now oscillating. His anger inched up a notch.

"If for one second you think I'm showing up *in person*, you're meth-smoking crazy, man. As stated, it's nonnegotiable. Take it or leave it."

Fists clenched, back rigid, Arnold opened his mouth only

Deadly Odds 5.0

to find himself verbally bankrupt.

Fear added, "Besides, I don't live anywhere close."

Arnold recoiled in shock.

"*What?*"

"Hell, I don't even live in that state, man. What's so hard to get?"

"You lied about that?"

Fear scoffed.

"What kinda fool you take me for? Fine for you to broadcast that shit to the world, assuming Gold's your real name. Hey, it's your company, man. But for the rest of us? Considering our line of work? *Please* don't tell me you're seriously *that* naïve?"

Arnold was teetering on a choice rejoinder when a bolt of fear skewered his heart. Dude wielded a ginormous advantage: he knew Arnold's name. Which enabled him to dig up critical personal information, like his properties. Maybe even Rachael's identity. In contrast, what did he know about Fear? Freaking zilch. Not only that, but the dude carried a hugely nasty rep as one seriously malevolent vindictive asshole. Which now, given the painfully focused acuity of retrospect, made hiring him a dumbshit decision of gigantic dimensions. Piss off *that* dude and God only knew what might come zinging back.

Well, the good news is you just learned an important lesson. Sure as hell won't be repeating that mistake soon.

If ever.

"Okay, okay, I get it," Arnold finally said as deferentially as possible through clenched teeth. "It's on me. I get it and I'll take care of it."

Fear cut the link before Arnold could add anything. He slumped in his tricked-out gaming chair, eyes open yet his mind was off in a distant galaxy of hardscrabble reality, grappling for a miraculous flash of inspiration, some path forward that held a prayer of maintaining a delicate harmony

17

amongst the three most important people in his admittedly confined life: Rachael, Chance, and Mr. Davidson.

Okay, sure, he respected and admired Mr. Cain.

But there was more involved than respect; he felt a deep sense of obligation to accept the job. Especially after Mr. Cain had applied his considerable influence within the close-knit Seattle legal community to help Arnold develop his company's growing cachet as *the* boutique IT solution for small law firms.

So yes, he owed both men.

But, Jesus, flying to Seattle…talk about leading with your chin. But—and let's be perfectly truthful here—there was no freaking way could he refuse them.

With a resigned sigh, he pushed out of the chair to drift reluctantly though the house to the back deck.

HONOLULU

CHAPTER 4

LUCKILY—*WELL,* MAYBE not so luckily—instead of being at work, Rachael was comfortably ensconced in a chaise, a cup of black coffee on the small end table to her right, reading *The New York Times* on her Microsoft Surface, Chance, his beloved Belgian Malinois, stretched out on the deck beside her, snoozing, black snout tucked between forepaws.

"Uh, sweetie," Arnold said apologetically, dropping onto the parallel chaise, letting his preamble hang with about as much subtlety as a Day-Glo orange tuxedo.

She glanced up from the screen.

"Oh, finished with your call? Who was it?"

He paused, scrambling for a slick way to broach the subject.

"Ah...Mr. Davidson..."

Tick-tick-tick.

She arched an eyebrow.

"And?"

Arnold sucked an incisor a moment.

Out with it.

"I need to fly to Seattle."

Head cocked slightly, she studied his face a beat.

"Because?"

A jar of butterflies was suddenly released in his gut.

"See, that's the thing. Mr. Davidson and Mr. Cain have a complex issue that desperately—*desperately? Hey, it works*—needs my help."

There. He lanced the abscess.

He waited, hearing only the rustle of nearby palm fronds dancing in the gentle trade winds while her gears mentally processed this news.

"Okaaaaay, but isn't this the reason you hired an associate?"

Oooh, shit, here we go.

"Exactly. And I *thought* that had all been taken care of, but see, that's the rub…when I asked him to meet with them, he refused."

She weighed this for a moment.

"He refused?" her face a display of bewilderment. "Why?"

"Two reasons: he insists on remaining anonymous and, as it turns out, doesn't live there."

She lasered him.

"Where *does* he live?"

Arnold felt his face flaming.

"I don't know," with a dismissive shrug as if this were nothing but a simple oversight.

She shook her head, seemingly confused, flashing him a lavish dose of suspicion.

"What's the big deal about being seen?"

"Because he's a *hacker,* Rach." As if this should be self-evident. "Makes him, like, super paranoid. I'd probably be the same if I was in his position." Then, to pre-empt a rebuttal, Arnold added, "The reason I hired him was his incredible skills. Just figured it was a bonus that he's in Seattle, but…."

No sense finishing the sentence; he was royally hosed and

knew it.

He simply shook his head, deeply regretting his glaring stupidity.

Should've checked. But you didn't. Why? Because you're too freaking lazy or you didn't really think it mattered?

Because when it comes to management, I suck.

It's that simple.

Sitting here, listening to his pathetic internal dialogue only underscored how seriously flawed his reasoning had been.

She seemed to be amused watching him roast.

"Let me get this straight: you originally claimed to hire him *because* he lives in Seattle. Now you're saying it was actually because of his *hacking skills?*"

He didn't like the direction this was heading, but wasn't in any position to argue, so he simply nodded lamely.

"True. I mean, why should I have thought he's lying?"

Another dismissive shrug.

She paused for a sip of coffee, either carefully selecting her next words or simply watching him squirm. Likely both, from her look of disapproval.

"Because, as you just pointed out, he's a *crook*. Hey, guess what? You *still* don't know where he lives. Or am I missing something?"

He glanced away.

Point made.

But he sensed there was more going on here than just the Fear thing. For some reason he couldn't pinpoint, his work had turned into an inflammatory hot-button issue for her.

Why?

He'd done exactly what she had asked of him; he'd nailed down a legitimate job. Just happened to be self-employed, is all.

"In other words, he's useless," she finally said.

Arnold shook his head.

"No, not true at all. He *is* useful. Dude does tons of work. After all, the business keeps growing. Turns out, he just doesn't fill the Seattle Associate role, is all…"

She continued shaking her head, giving him that sarcastic laugh she did so effectively, showing absolutely zero sympathy or inclination to cut him a millimeter of slack. He waited for her to wind down.

"The question is, Arnold, are you *ever* going to hire someone for that role?"

Arnold?

She only addressed him by his given name when super pissed.

"I'm working on it."

"Really? And just how hard are you working on it? How long before you finally find coverage for *both* places?" Her eyes burned into him. "Why do you refuse to take even the most fundamental steps to cover the two cities in which you claim to have offices?"

Aw, shit, here we go.

She sat up, tossing her legs over the side of the chaise, facing him directly.

"Know what you are, Arnold? You're a goddamn poster child for procrastination and indecision when it comes to running a business. To tell you the truth, I'm sick of staying here holding the fort while you run off to do the work someone else could and should be doing."

Arnold raised both hands in surrender.

"Look, you're right, okay? We're *not* adequately covered in both places right now. But at the moment that's not my most pressing problem. Right now Mr. Cain and Mr. Davidson—my two most important and influential clients—need my help. No, I *don't* have anyone there to take care of it, so…"

He paused for effect.

"I'm left with either telling them *no* or doing the job myself. And you know damn well there's no way I can tell Mr. Davidson no. Not after all we've been through." He took a breath. "I'll do everything in my power to wrap this thing up as soon as possible. Besides, being there improves the odds I'll find someone I *know* lives there, so we won't have to go through this again, okay?"

He intended the last point as a statement, but it just sort of slithered out as a question.

Rachael flashed her signature squint.

"Know what? Those lyrics are just way too familiar. Remember the last time you worked for Mr. Cain? The job that was supposed to take two or three days but ended up taking a *week* longer because you felt compelled to wrap up a few loose ends? Or did you forget that already?"

Oh, crap, this again?

"You make it sound like I *wanted* to stay. That's not true and you know it. Okay, sure, I did stay on account of feeling the need to pay my respects to the Koch and Thompson families, but Rach, it was the right thing to do. After all, their sons had been murdered. It was the least I could do under the circumstances. Besides, I still feel guilty about what happened. If I hadn't been poking around…"

It was obvious she wasn't buying.

"In other words, you *chose* to be *there* instead of here with Chance and me."

Oh, for Christ's sake. Enough.

"That's bullshit." He decided to abort his next remark so settled on, "I'm sorry you choose to take it that way, but I had to do what I thought was right. I have no regrets."

Boy, did that sound as sanctimonious as hell.

He immediately regretted his choice of words, but…

Rachael shook her head in obvious disgust.

"What?" he asked, defensively.

"It's not that you aren't well intentioned, Arnold. It's that you don't grasp the fundamental issue here."

He was genuinely curious.

"Apparently. So, what exactly is the fundamental issue?"

She let out an exasperated sigh.

"Establishing a business in two cities sounds cool in concept, but in reality, it sucks. Why? Because you don't have either location covered and yet seem to be dragging your feet about it. What makes this so incredibly irritating for me is just how much your grandiose delusion impacts *us*."

She was finally opening up and he wanted to know what her issue was.

"How so?"

"Because when you flit off for these jobs, you dump the entire responsibility of caring for Chance and this house on me."

What?

Even the slow-motion instant replay made no sense.

"The hell you talking about? I've taken exactly *one* trip. Last summer. And I boarded Chance at the clinic. And as for this house, what responsibility do I *dump* on you?" He took a deep calming breath. "You weren't even moved in yet, so, I don't buy that. I get this feeling something else's bugging you about my work and you're either not telling me or maybe you don't even know what it is. What I *do* know is you're becoming increasingly irritated at me since I returned from the ransomware gig. Or am I totally wrong?"

Rachael glanced away, muttering, "You have no idea how I feel when you leave me here alone. I feel responsible for this place, and I don't like it. And, as much as I love Chance, I simply will not be your dog sitter. If you have to go, take him or board him, but don't expect me to look after him." She shook her head in obvious frustration before returning her eyes to him. "It's not like I don't love him. I *do*. But with my twelve-hour shifts there's no way I can take care of him, and all the good doggie daycare centers have hours that don't accommodate my schedule." Her hard eyes were drilling him now. "It's your call, Arnold."

"All right already. I get it. You don't want to take care of him." He threw up his hands, said, "Fine," then glanced at his beloved pooch lounging on the deck, big brown eyes staring up at him questioningly, obviously aware of the disharmonious lightning bolts zapping back and forth.

Ah, man...

He knelt, giving him reassuring choobers.

"Chance is a good boy, yes he is."

A moment later he was back up, facing her.

"Look, Rach, I don't want to go, but I *have* to. You know I'm building a business. For *us*. This's *our* future. There has to be some sort of compromise we can reach. You couldn't, ah, like, request a leave of absence and come with us, could you?"

His suggestion was met with freezing silence.

Uh-oh...

She glared, unquestionably pissed, making him feel as if he'd just stepped in a mound of steaming dogshit.

After a beat, she said coolly, "Why should *I* stop work so *you* can work? Why don't *you* tell Mr. Davidson and Mr. Cain you can't just hop a jet at a moment's notice and fly halfway across the Pacific to *chat* about a case that could just as easily be discussed on Zoom? How *dare* you have the cojones to ask me to dump a huge scheduling imposition on my friends? Especially knowing how shorthanded the pandemic left us. How many times have we talked about this? I refuse to stick my friends with a scheduling nightmare. It'd be, what? A two-day notice? No, that's *not* going to happen."

Arnold backed away with his hands raised.

"Okay, I get it, I do. I obviously didn't think that through before asking. But the thing is, building a business requires sacrifices along the way, right?"

Her body language dismissed his last remark as irrelevant.

"If you go, what do you plan to do about Chance? I'm dead serious about not dog-sitting." She folded her arms defiantly, her face serious as malignant melanoma.

"Well?"

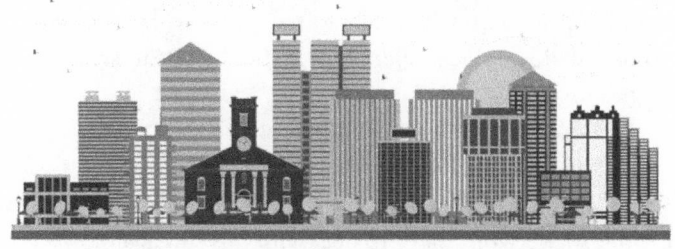

HONOLULU

CHAPTER 5

ARNOLD SAT IN his plush gaming chair, weighing his buddy's fate. Boarding him was, well, distasteful. It wasn't that the clinic didn't take excellent care of him. It was knowing just how much they would miss each other. As for bringing him, he hated to crate him in a cargo bay for six hours. Especially after so many horror stories of pets lost in transit, or accidently placed on a wrong flight, or worse yet, dying *en route* on account of some weird malfunction with the cargo-bay temperature or oxygen supply. Plus, he'd seen a few baggage handlers recklessly toss dog crates to one another.

Okay, sure, odds were that nothing bad would happen, but, man, if anything ever did...

Board him?

Naw. Rachael was right about one thing; he had no clue how long this gig might take and certainly didn't want Chance to feel abandoned if it ended up requiring more than a few days. And really, did a six-hour flight present *all that* much risk?

Then again, how much risk was acceptable?

The more he stewed, the more bringing him seemed to be his only option. Slowly, his reticence to crate him melted.

He reached down, gave him—sprawled out beside the chair, peering up at him with such soft expressive brown eyes—a prolonged dose of choobers, the behind-the-ear scratches all doggies love.

"Want to go to Seattle with me, boy?"

Thump-thump-thump.

"Can you help me find a super-skilled associate, one I can rely on, so we won't have to deal with this shit again?"

Thump-thump-thump.

Man, if only Rachael was this agreeable.

Growing more comfortable with the decision (though still distraught and confused over Rachael's pushback), he logged onto the Hawaiian Airlines website and *whoa*, snagged a Sunday flight.

Eyes closed, he dissolved into the padded chair to wrack his brain for an enticement that might just pique Rachael's buy-in to his vision for Gold and Associates. Their discussion had left him worried and unsettled. But she was certainly smack-on about his management skills (or lack thereof).

In his defense, from her perspective as an RN in a high-demand market, finding a qualified candidate should be chip-shot easy, right? She wasn't factoring in that the majority of qualified candidates for this kind of work were hackers who weren't exactly spotlighting their resumes on LinkedIn.

Besides, he *was* working on it. Maybe not as hard as she preferred, but hey, she wasn't taking into consideration the attention drain caused by his unrelenting daily workload of covering the IT needs of several small law firms.

What was so damn confusing and unsettling, was her recent antagonism toward his business.

Where was that coming from?

And what exactly was her issue? He loved that she preferred for them to be together instead of thousands of miles apart. After all, he loved her deeply. Always had. There had never been another woman in his life. Well, okay, sure, last summer he'd briefly been tempted to fool around with Kara. Once. But only once. And besides, he never did, so did that even count?

He'd been ecstatic when Rachael agreed to move in, for it inched them closer to marriage. But this new vibe...*man*, what a total downer. What the hell was driving it? If forced to bet, he'd put his chips on her childhood, when her dad's frequent business trips had fomented family turmoil. (Like the huge screaming matches he'd witnessed.)

"I'll be in your office Monday. What time works best for you?"

"Thank you, son. I will advise Noah Cain. Unless you hear to the contrary, nine o'clock will suffice."

* * *

Singh drummed the cap of a Bic ballpoint against his teeth while rereading the email string between Davidson and Cain. Who the hell was Arnold Gold? What did those two shysters think Gold could contribute to Lopez's defense—especially in view of the overwhelming evidence against the bastard?

Fascinating questions.

A Google search for Arnold Gold yielded nothing but a Gold and Associates website; apparently, a boutique IT service for small clients, in particular law firms. Nothing earth-shaking nor illuminating there. Similar companies were a dime a dozen around this high-tech city. What the hell did they want him for?

Even more intriguing was, why Gold specifically? What could he provide that another employee in the firm couldn't?

More on point, did Gold pose a threat to the success of his plan? (Unlikely as that might be.) The skillset of someone in Gold's business barely exceeded that of a junior-high-school geek. After all, any prepubescent adolescent with an IQ greater than fifty was capable of mousing their way through a software install or update, or defrag a hard disc.

No, there had to be more to Gold than the email string disclosed.

The more Singh mulled it over, the more intriguing the questions became. Especially since his Google and Bing searches yielded nothing but a website. Gold was obviously hiding something, which made his involvement with the defense team now assume far greater importance and intrigue than a moment ago.

What he now needed was an accurate assessment of Gold's skill level. Singh continued tapping the Bic and took another glance at his website.

Ah, yes, the answer might be right there on the screen.

If Gold was a serious player, he would have coded the site himself rather than farm it out to another coder or rely on one of those out-of-the-box solutions peddled on the Web. A quick inspection of the code would provide him a good measure. Not only that, but there was a reasonable chance the code itself might yield a link back to Gold's computer network.

Then, by penetrating that network, he could obtain a more accurate read on the potential threat. The more he considered this strategy, the more it appealed. Plus, if he could weasel into Gold's network, he would have a direct route to sabotage his work and, in the process torpedo Lopez's defense if necessary. Yes, this was definitely his preferred tactic. The *coups de grace*–once the jury found Lopez guilty—would be to totally destroy the Jew's network. Singh liked the concept.

He smiled.

Okay, Mr. Arnold Gold, savior of the Lopez's defense team, let's see if you're worth a shit.

CHAPTER 6—Seattle—Sunday 11:01 PM

ARNOLD OPENED THE front door of his recently built Green Lake home, allowing Chance to trot into the great room first. Before his Uber had pulled into the Sea-Tac airport loading area, Arnold had freed him from the travel crate and leashed him.

Thankfully the driver hadn't been a tight ass who refused to allow a pooch to ride uncrated in back seat. As a show of appreciation, Arnold had slipped him an additional five-dollar bill on top of the 20 percent tip he routinely added to the app. Cash was always appreciated.

Just before the tractor had begun pushing the huge Boeing 767 from the Honolulu departure gate, Arnold used his iPhone to bump up the Wi-Fi-accessible thermostat in his Green Lake home from the sixty degrees maintained while in Honolulu to a comfortable seventy-two. This being his first visit in a colder month, he was eager to discover if the house would be pleasantly warm by the time he arrived. An unusually strong tailwind allowed the jet's large wheels to kiss the Sea-Tac tarmac thirty-seven minutes ahead of schedule; a nice bonus. Flying first-class with only a backpack and Chance's travel crate (which handlers typically unload first) had allowed him to bypass any baggage-claim bedlam and proceed straight to the designated Uber zone.

Arnold ducked inside the great room, glad to be out of the driving rain and garment-penetrating wind so typical of shitty Seattle Novembers. Two years of kicking it in Hawaii had blotted out just how freaking annoying and depressing this dreary weather could be.

Oh, well, he wasn't planning to stay away from the Honolulu "office"—aka chaise lounge—and palm trees longer than necessary.

Standing in the great room shivering, hair dripping, clammy damp sweatshirt clinging to his torso drove home just how seasonally inappropriate his meager upstairs wardrobe was. Scoring a few cold-weather clothes would be just one more task to wedge into his (hopefully) limited stay. Thank God for Wi-Fi accessible thermostats; at least the interior was blessedly warm.

After dumping his backpack on the kitchen counter and draping his soggy sweatshirt over a chair, he set the crate in the corner, then dropped to his knees, got nose to nose with Chance, and gave him a serious dose of affection. Thank God Chance survived the flight.

"Chance is a good boy. Yes he is. A *really* good boy. You did really good, boy."

Tail going like crazy, Chance returned a series of wet doggie kisses before dropping to the floor and rolling onto his back, exposing his tummy in a doggie's ultimate sign of absolute trust. Arnold responded with a series of rabber-de-jabber tummy rubs, thankful for bringing him. Sure, having him here meant extra work, but hey, it would be totally worth it.

Chance sprang to his feet, pressed his nose to the French doors:

Okay, dad, enough of this, time to take a leak.

Arnold opened the door for him to run into the back yard.

He slipped on a dry t-shirt from his pack, popped the cork on a bottle of BV Rutherford Cab, poured a glass. A moment later, Chance's nose was back against the pane, eyes emitting silent doggy telepathy. Having accompanied Arnold and Rachael here during their September visit, he was familiar with the house and its associated routines.

Arnold let him in, locked the doors, and began to unpack. Chance curled into a ball in his bolstered doggie bed at the foot of Arnold's king-size bed. With Rachael in Honolulu, there was a good chance he would find him curled up beside him periodically during the night.

He set the wine glass on the bedside table, connected his iPhone to the charger, told Alexa (also on the bedside table) to wake him at seven A.M., tossed his Kindle on the bed, then turned on the water for a long hot shower to warm up before turning in.

Much as he loved this opportunity to enjoy his new home, he needed to wrap up this job ASAP so he could return and start repairing whatever was going on with Rachael. Not knowing what was bugging her was like one of those irritating little thorns that work their way into a sock during a hike: it needed to be dealt with.

Monday 8:55 AM

The moment Arnold entered the reception lobby of Cain, Tidwell, Stowell—Grandé latte in hand from the Starbucks downstairs—he paused to take in the all-too-familiar surroundings. Gray carpet, gray walls, even the gray-haired secretary in the gray suit at the reception desk; the visual ensemble triggering an oddly off-putting déjà vu that, for some weird reason, dampened his eagerness to meet with the two men he so admired.

Last summer he'd spent ten days in and out of these offices tackling a ransomware case that ultimately resulted in two cold-blooded murders and the arrest of a junior partner, Bundy Phillips, on embezzlement charges. That longer than anticipated business trip now seemed to be the nidus from which Rachael's present "issue with his work" was crystalizing.

"Good morning, Mr. Gold."

Although he blamed Primal Fear for needing to be here this morning, it was his own damn fault for not having vetted the asshole. Rachael was right about that part.

"Mr. Gold?"

He raised his Starbucks cup in greeting.

"Oh…hi, Marci."

"They're expecting you in the conference room."

Really? Am I late?

A glance at his watch. Nope, two minutes early.

How can I be late?

"Thanks."

He beelined for the glass-walled conference room at the end of the short hall.

And nearly collided with Kara, the cute red-haired paralegal, who came barreling around the corner, hugging a wad of manila folders to her chest. They started the awkward side-to-side two-step that inevitably results from such near misses, realized they were juking in rhythm, stopped and laughed.

"Do tell. Arnold Gold, the ransomware savior. Just can't stay away from me, can you," she said with her trademark sarcasm and beaming smile.

Cute as ever, what with her luxurious red hair, dimples and freckles. Inappropriate as ever, too. Which, for him, strangely boosted her pit-of-the-gut sexual allure. He felt his face going into space-heater mode, which in turn, ratcheted up his embarrassment.

"Uh, uh, uh. Lookin' *good*, girl," he said, "but I am late for a meeting." He tossed a nod toward the conference room, then, staying in rhythm, added, "So, bye," and took off, relieved to escape further embarrassment.

He cast a sideway glance at the disgraced junior partner's old office. A woman of Phillips' approximate age was leaning forward, frowning at the monitor, finger poised above the keyboard. Phillips' replacement? He opened the conference room door.

Not surprisingly, Mr. Cain occupied the head of the table with Mr. Davidson to his right, and a somewhat disheveled Hispanic dude with well-healed acne scars marring his otherwise handsome thirtyish face, to his left. An untouched yellow legal pad with black-capped Bic was positioned precisely in front of each lawyer. Both attorneys wore crisp white shirts with sleeves rolled above their wrists, rep ties, their suit coats draped over the chair backs. Lopez wore a vintage Russell Wilson Seahawks jersey.

"Sorry I'm late," Arnold said to Cain, setting his latte on the table next to Mr. Davidson and pulling out the chair.

On clear days, the far floor-to-ceiling windows showcased a stunning panorama of the harbor and Olympic mountains across the harbor and Puget Sound, but today, low, dense monotonous overcast obliterated the magnificent view, turning the frigid saltwater a light gray. He dropped his backpack onto the empty chair to his left and sat.

Cain shook his head.

"To the contrary, you're punctual as usual, son. We needed to address a few housekeeping items before the meeting, so convened thirty minutes early. Allow me to introduce Carlos Lopez." Then to Lopez: "Carlos, Arnold Gold." Back to Arnold: "Thank you for flying over. I hope this hasn't been too much of an imposition."

As Arnold nodded a greeting to Lopez, he clicked on a hint of familiarity in the man's dark brown eyes as if they had just connected at some level. Perhaps those eyes betrayed the quintessential social awkwardness of an introverted geek. That's me two years ago. If not for a Las Vegas escort and Mr. Davidson...

"No imposition at all," Arnold lied. Mr. Davidson had undoubtedly tipped him about Rachael's issue. "I noticed someone in Mr. Phillips' office," Arnold said, partly out of curiosity, partly to shift focus from Rachael.

"Yes. Bundy Phillips' replacement." Cain cleared his throat, signaling the end of perfunctory chatter. "Just so you know, a two-day retainer was wired to your Bitcoin account earlier this morning. I was operating under the assumption your prior rate still applies. If that's in error, please email me the revised rate and I'll correct the sum *tout suite.*"

"No, it's the same, so thank you."

Smooth. Remember that.

Totally awesome how adroitly the seasoned lawyer had preemptively dealt with such a potentially sticky but essential subject. As front man for Gold and Associates, he should definitely devote some serious attention to buffing his social skills to the lawyers' exemplary luster. If there were role models to emulate, these were the ones.

Cain glanced from Arnold to Davidson, to Lopez, gave a slight nod—as if attendance was now taken—said, "Now that we're assembled, I'll begin with a description of the crimes."

* * *

Lips pursed, Singh ruminated over the Gold and Associates website. The information was, to be charitable, sparse. Why such a glaring lack of content? Was it an intentional ploy or blatant incompetence? Good question. Relevant one at that. Alarm bells began to clang in his brain, giving him pause, prompting him to weigh the issue in greater depth.

More notable than the lack of substance was its underlying code: concise, tight, functional. A minimalistic homage to functionality. The hyper-svelte economic design sparked an initial twinge of serious concern that went like this: the shysters hired Gold to assist the Lopez defense team rather than provide routine services. Logical conclusion? Gold had been hired to conduct a forensic examination of the digital evidence. Meaning, among other things, he would be an expert witness at trial. Okay, made sense. But what evidence was there to find? Nothing. He was certain of that.

Or was he?

No, he'd been meticulous. All evidence pointed unequivocally at Lopez—including the IP address.

Nonetheless, the first whisper of doubt just slipped in through a mental back door, now making Gold a clear and present threat. The only issue now was, just how much of a threat?

On several occasions, Singh's father had sagely advised, "Boy, insecurity is noisy, confidence is silent."

For whatever reason those words embedded in his brain rang as relevant here. After all, the shysters had specifically and glowingly singled out Gold as their go-to consultant.

In spite of its precise trim functionality, the website code did yield one tiny, intriguing point; a security vulnerability that might easily have been glossed over by a less experienced eye. He studied it closely.

Interesting.

But at the moment there were other, more pressing matters to deal with. He jotted a note on a yellow Post-it to revisit this vulnerability once he'd researched Gold in more depth, then stuck it to the bottom edge of the center monitor.

Careful. Don't underestimate him and wait too long.

His initial internet search on Gold had yielded nothing, so

where should he look now? He began tapping the Bic against his teeth again.

The law firm?

He'd read the complete email string, so there was nothing more to glean from it. Yes, but Gold had previously been employed by them, meaning there would be a record of his Social Security number and other personal information in their network, probably in an HR folder.

Also, Gold apparently owned a house here, so there were property records too. Between these two data points, he should be able to construct a complete dossier on him. He paused, quite pleased with himself.

Yes, Gold might be a threat, but only if he could identify his adversary.

And Singh would make certain that never happened.

CHAPTER 7

NOAH CAIN DIRECTED his explanation to Arnold.

"Carlos is under investigation for alleged stock manipulation. More specifically, he's accused of hacking two different company computer networks for the specific purpose of releasing devastating false reports to major business news outlets. Parenthetically, it's because of this hacking angle that I asked Palmer to join the defense team." He smiled briefly at Lopez before returning to Arnold. "In both cases, the victims—Camano Biopharma and Curchfield Technologies— were Seattle startups and the incidents occurred mere weeks following their IPOs."

Camano Biopharma...

The name triggered a vaguely familiar echo in a far recess of his memory.

I know that name. Why?

He raised his hand, "Sorry to interrupt, but could you repeat the first name, please?"

"Camano Biopharma." Cain paused and arched his eyebrows. "Why?"

"Nothing," waving off the question. "Rings a bell's all. Sorry, please continue."

"As long as we're focused on them, we may as well start there. Camano was a clinical-stage pharmaceutical company. The use of past tense here is intentional because the end result is that the company was forced to file for Chapter 11 relief."

"Excuse me," Arnold said, embarrassed at interrupting again so soon. "But what's *clinical stage* mean?" using finger quotes.

He had a vague idea, but when dealing with attorneys, he'd grown accustomed to being crystalline.

"A company in the process of developing a commercial product, so is conducting the prerequisite clinical trials for FDA approval." A brief pause. "At the time the incident occurred, not only was the company knee-deep in one such trial, but the board of directors was in the final stage of selling the company to a large, well-established pharmaceutical firm. The aforementioned news release claimed that their experimental drug resulted in the deaths of three subjects and that the FDA had consequently suspended the trial indefinitely."

Cain quickly raised his hand, halting Arnold's next question.

"They were developing a nasal-spray vaccine against the two common diseases, Norovirus gastroenteritis and seasonal flu. Said news bulletin was quickly disseminated to all major business news outlets, Dow Jones, Barron's, et cetera. As one might predict, this triggered a massive stock sell-off that decimated its price and, not surprisingly, their suitor immediately walked away from the buyout, leaving the company insufficient operating funds to continue and forced them into bankruptcy."

All remained silent, waiting for Cain to continue.

"Said press release was subsequently proven false, but the damage to Camano was irrevocable and the company became one more tombstone in the Wall Street cemetery for start-ups.

"Six weeks later, a carbon-copy disaster befell another startup, Curchfield Technologies. This company was scheduled to announce the results of their pivotal study on a Friday after close of trading. However, at ten AM Eastern Standard Time that day their media relations department released a statement claiming the study fell shy of the FDA's agreed-upon target, thus rendering their device worthless. Again, the news triggered a massive sell-off, devastating the stock. This news release also was subsequently proven false."

"Look, sorry to keep interrupting," Arnold said, "but who'd publish something that critical without verifying the story?"

Cain's smile hinted at the question being embarrassingly naive.

Okay, so perhaps it was, but...

"Nothing about either bulletin drew suspicion. Both originated from the respective media relations departments and once one major news service released the story, the others followed suit."

Mr. Davidson added, "Review of these releases revealed extraordinarily sophisticated acts of deception. Together with the timing, one may only conclude the intent was to sabotage the stock prices."

"In both cases," Cain continued, "because subsequent complaints filed with the SEC allege that the misinformation was intended to manipulate the stock prices, the feds became involved. Within days of the first formal complaint filing, a joint SEC-FBI investigation was launched." Cain paused dramatically. "Carlos knew nothing of either case until your friend Special Agent Fisher appeared at his door with a warrant to seize his computers and all digital-related materials."

"Whoa," Arnold said, confused. "Isn't Fisher assigned to antiterrorism?"

A small smile crept over Davidson's face.

"I also questioned that. Apparently an increasingly frequent tactic of domestic right-wing extremist groups like QAnon and the Boogaloo Boys is to mine databases for sensitive personal information on targeted U.S. citizens, then post it on the Internet with the expressed intent of provoking acts of violence against them, not too dissimilar to the way the January 6th insurrection initiated."

"And this doxxing," Cain chimed in, "isn't confined to the United States. A few years ago, Rabitat al-Ansar, a pro-ISIS media group, released the names, email and home addresses, and phone numbers of four hundred targeted citizens—U.S. and foreign—under the hashtag #WeWillBurnUSAgain. They posted this on the QuickLeak website. The site identified the targeted individuals as 'traitors' who will 'pay for their treason' and vowed multiple terrorist attacks." Cain spread his hands. "These serve as a few examples of why such actions are now viewed as terrorism. Unfortunately, such activity is becoming more common."

"More recently," Mr. Davidson added, "there was a massive theft of personal information from Facebook that was released to the public."

"Carlos," Cain resumed, "surrendered his laptop to Fisher, but before he'd agree to be interviewed, he contacted our office for legal representation."

Arnold coughed a sarcastic laugh.

"Isn't it a bit suspicious, lawyering up so quickly?"

Cain recoiled; either truly taken aback or displaying a perfect example of a theatrical lawyerly flourish. Arnold wasn't sure which but found it amusing anyway.

"Not at all," Cain promptly answered. "The search and seizure simply underscored how very serious the issue was. Carlos—completely innocent and caught totally off guard— was understandably frightened, confused, and emotionally distressed over such blatant Gestapo tactics. Under such adversarial conditions we,"—he pointed from Mr. Davidson to himself, as if the *we* needed clarification—"consider his request extraordinarily levelheaded." A brief pause and accentuating head nod. "Once he secured our legal backing, he very willingly complied to an interview with Agent Fisher, duly appeared, and answered all questions to the best of his ability. Carlos is, after all, completely innocent."

So you say.

The conference room settled into a muted blend of traffic and construction noise wafting up twenty-six floors from the street. Fascinating story, a total hook. Especially given his keen interest in the market. But the confusing thing was, why was he here? Mr. Cain and Mr. Davidson were Lopez's Defense Dream Team.

And speaking of lawyers, Mr. Davidson was massaging his right shoulder, something he'd noticed him do periodically the past year or so...but unlike previous occasions this time his face was distressingly pale and grimacing.

"Um, Mr. Davidson, are you okay?"

CHAPTER 8

DAVIDSON SWALLOWED BEFORE saying, "I am fine. It is just this damn shoulder," verbally brushing away the question, then, with a nod to Cain, "Sorry for the interruption, Noah. Please continue."

Also concerned, Cain studied his colleague a moment.

"Palmer, are you sure?"

"I am. This damn shoulder has been pestering me for over a year now. It is of no concern."

Cain eyed him another concerned moment but didn't press it.

"Agent Fisher stated they were investigating a case of stock manipulation and went on to describe the particulars surrounding the two selloffs. He claimed the Bureau had compelling evidence—his terminology—incriminating Carlos in both cases."

"Like?" Arnold asked.

Smiling, Cain nodded.

"Not surprisingly, we asked the very same question." Pause. "Fisher claims to be in possession of records for a Charles Schwab day-trading account in Carlos' name that document short sales of both companies in the days leading up to their respective crashes. Furthermore, he claims said short positions were covered during the selloffs at a considerable profit." Cain paused again. "Agent Fisher then *graciously*"— the word dripping with sarcasm—"offered Carlos an opportunity to plead guilty to the charges without being indicted."

"Whoa." Arnold gave the time-out signal. "Please explain that to me?"

Cain nodded.

"Ah, yes, *that*. A guilty plea without indictment is an all-too-common Fed tactic, one they're quite fond of. Typically it's applied to cases they prefer to close as expediently as possible; situations for which they believe they possess irrefutable evidence of guilt. By convincing a suspect to accept a deal, they avoid the time and expense of a thorough investigation and trial. We defense attorneys are well aware that law enforcement may not be completely truthful about the evidence they claim to have and will often use this to bluff for a quick close of a case. Of course, we respectfully declined."

Made sense.

Plus, he'd just learned something. Arnold appreciated the explanation.

"Our own investigation revealed several key points. First, Carlos doesn't have, nor has he ever had, a day trading account with Schwab or *any* brokerage house, for that matter. His only brokerage account, past or present, is a Roth IRA with only one mutual fund. That, however, and perhaps unfortunately, *is* with Schwab."

Carlos finally broke his silence.

"The only other financial account I have is a Capitol One savings account. I dump every extra dollar I get my hands on into paying down my mortgage."

Mr. Davidson added, "His tax records verify this."

Cain continued, "We, of course, inspected the Schwab

account paperwork." A sly smile crept onto his face. "Several salient points quickly became apparent. Most importantly, the signature is *not* Carlos'. In addition, the account was established ten days prior to the first stock sabotage." Another emphatic pause. "Account records reveal that in each case the profits were transferred immediately to a Cayman Island bank. The Monday after the second incident, the Schwab account was closed, making it appear it was established for the express purpose of conducting the short sales."

Arnold glanced at Mr. Davidson again.

Holy shit.

His color and obvious discomfort seemed to be worsening.

Say something? Oh, man...better not, it'd only irritate him.

Besides, Davidson would say something if this wasn't his typical pain, right?

Several questions pinballed though his mind, making it difficult to track any one in particular, so he went for the most crucial.

"How'd the feds zero in on that account?"

Cain chuckled.

"Indeed. We asked, but Agent Fisher refused to answer under the guise that it's an ongoing investigation. However, from our involvement in similar cases, we realize the SEC always asks, "who benefits?" There are only two ways to benefit from this scenario: either to destroy a competitor or for monetary profit.

"Keep in mind that both companies were startups without real competitors, so we are left to suspect that the SEC ran a computer search for all significant short positions covered during or immediately after the selloffs. The aforementioned Schwab account was likely the only non-institutional investor holding a significant position in both companies." Cain wagged his eyebrows in classic Groucho Marx fashion. "Sadly, the Schwab account placed Carlos squarely in the investigation spotlight."

Lopez shook his head vigorously; the most animated Arnold had seen him so far.

"This is such bullshit. I've *never* shorted a stock. Ever. In fact, I don't really understand that shit."

"Easy," Arnold said, "you sell a stock, then buy it back when the price is below your purchase price."

Lopez glanced from Cain to Davidson then back again, his face reddening with anger.

"*Seriously*, dude?" Lopez flashed Cain an irritated, condemning look. "I know *that*. What I *don't* understand is how someone can sell something they don't own. Period. I mean, how the hell does someone get away with that shit?"

"Simple," Arnold answered, "they *borrow* the shares from the brokerage house."

"I know *that* too, *dude*." Lopez's glare hardened. "Why's that even allowed? For one sane moment, do you believe I could get away with selling something on eBay I don't own? Hell no. So why the hell does the government allow some asshole to sell stock they don't own? It's disgusting. It serves no purpose other than allowing someone to profit at someone else's expense."

"They," Arnold said, putting the word in finger quotes, "say it's a way for professional money managers to hedge portfolio risk."

He hiked his shoulders in a that's-just-the-way-it-is shrug.

Lopez emitted a disgusted snort.

"Right, so Wall Street parasites can cover their nut on weekend Hampton mansions. Big fucking help for society."

Time to move on. Arnold turned to Cain.

"What about the offshore account? Do the feds have any evidence it was actually Lopez's?"

CHAPTER 9

"WE DON'T KNOW," Cain replied. "At least, not yet. Agent Fisher assured us they subpoenaed those records but said they haven't the foggiest idea how long the bank will take to process or *if* they'll even honor the subpoena."

Arnold turned to Lopez.

"What do you do for a living?"

Lopez stared at his folded hands on the table, as if his answer would be incriminating.

Finally, he said, "I help pen-test for a cybersecurity firm."

Arnold's ears perked up.

"Really? Cool."

"To the contrary," Mr. Davidson quickly added, finally re-engaging in the conversation, his color having improved, to Arnold's huge relief. "From the feds' point of view, this clearly demonstrates the complex skillset required to execute said crimes and further buttresses their case against him."

"Perhaps," Arnold acknowledged, kicking himself for not immediately realizing the obvious downside. "Have you ever worked for either company?"

Lopez shook his head.

"Nope." A brief staccato sarcastic laugh. "That's the first

question they"—indicating Mr. Cain and Mr. Davidson—
"asked."

Arnold mulled this over for a beat.

"So, what do you think went down?"

Lopez tensed.

"Isn't it obvious? I've been framed."

So you say, but...

"Okay, but *why?*"

Lopez's expression became one of pissed-off frustration.

"Don't you think I would've mentioned that by now if I knew?"

Interesting, I believe him. Why? His sincerity?

It dawned on him: this was exactly why these two canny defense attorneys insisted the interview be in person. The dude exuded intangible yet palpable sincerity that could never come across on a Zoom call. But pushing his subjective impressions aside, it made zero sense for a super-intelligent dude—a pen-tester of all people—to pull off such an intricate caper yet leave a Greek chorus of fingers pointing at him. "Pen-testers" were hackers hired to actively sniff out a client's security for exploitable flaws; the equivalent of employing a jewel thief to tell you exactly how a jewel thief might break into your home.

So, yeah, he believed the guy.

Hands raised apologetically, Arnold asked as neutrally as possible, "There *any*thing you might've done—in your work or personal life—that might've pissed someone off to this extent? A dissatisfied client? Pissed off a friend? *Any*one?"

"Nope. And believe me, that's all I've thought about since this...this...shit grenade exploded on me." Lopez shook his head, seemingly more collected now. "It's driving me up a wall."

Figuring it was time to change subjects, Arnold turned to Cain.

"Sorry to be so dense, but why am I here? You've got all the technical aspects covered."

"Ah, the perfect segue to my next item." Cain nodded deliberately, as if sagely formulating his answer. "If we intend to build the strongest possible defense, we must identify the perpetrator who framed Carlos as well as their motive. Only a highly skilled hacker—such as yourself—stands any prospect of determining who that is. Certainly, we can't rely on the feds for this. They've already locked down what they believe to be an ironclad case. Hence, we need you to find him for us. I'm sure you can appreciate just how critical this is for Carlos."

Just like that, huh?

Arnold whistled and scanned the faces focused on him, Lopez flashing an anemic, slightly apologetic smile, something along the lines of *sorry dude,* as if he'd been benched after throwing two third-down interceptions in a row.

"We are at a standstill, son," Mr. Davidson quickly added. "Our working hypothesis is that in the conduct of his routine work, Mr. Lopez created an *issue* for a hacker. We are all keenly aware that characteristically most hackers are extremely thin-skinned and quick to perceive disrespect and slights from even the most unintended benign action. Whatever happened must have been of sufficient significance to provoke this reprisal. In all likelihood, the slight did not even register in Carlos' memory." Mr. Davidson paused. "It is critical to us that you identity this hacker before we are forced to prepare for a lengthy and *expensive* trial."

And, *boom*, there it was, the job from hell, the balls-in-the-vise double bind. Accept this tar baby and he'd be mired here for God only knows how long. Refuse and he'd be turning his back on Mr. Davidson and Mr. Cain. The upside: he *was* running a business, and this *did* represent a paying job from his two most important referral sources. He owed them. Essentially, how could he say no? He had no choice.

"Well?" Cain asked, pointedly.

Arnold studied his fingernails, envisioning the repercussions that would be waiting for him back home.

Jesus.

"What is it, son?" Mr. Davidson asked.

Arnold stared out the window at the non-existent view, momentarily at a loss for words.

Finally turning to his old friend, "Odds are, you're absolutely right, another hacker *is* responsible. Problem is, from the little I know about this, whoever he is, he's at, like, grand-master level...which makes it extraordinarily unlikely there's a shred of evidence to work with."

"We are all well aware of this, son," Mr. Davidson countered. "However, we would be derelict in our duty if we failed to put forth an honest effort at identifying him."

What could he say to that?

Nothing, not a damn thing.

But Rachael...wow. Didn't even want to think about that...

Mr. Davidson added, "Can we all agree that it takes a hacker to find a hacker?"

It was a rhetorical question; no one bothered to open their mouth.

"You are the only person," Mr. Davidson continued, "that Noah and I trust implicitly to provide the most honest concerted effort, so this leaves us no other choice."

He sat back in the chair, arms crossed. The room settled once again into muted city noise.

Stomach churning, Arnold blew a long breath, acutely aware of the three sets of eyes boring into him, awaiting a reply.

No way he wouldn't try. It's just that...

"I'll give it my best shot," he said, reluctantly, "but I have to warn you, don't get your hopes up." Then, to Lopez, "You realize this, right?"

"Believe me, I do," Lopez intoned forlornly. "For what it's worth, my mind's so messed up over this I'm sure I overlooked something when I gave it a shot. This needs a fresh set of eyes on it." A quick sarcastic snort. "Can't tap my friends for help. They're all…hackers, so who knows, could even be one of them. See?"

"Excellent. Then the issue's settled," Cain said with a definitive slap on the desktop. "I don't intend to put undue pressure on you, son, but have you any idea where you'll start?"

You're freaking kidding me, right?

Hell, it didn't look like it.

He blew through pursed lips while grinding through the little he'd assimilated about the case, searching for a toehold. *Start with concrete facts and work out from there* had always been a solid, time-honored strategy that'd served him well.

He asked Carlos, "How many computers you have?"

"Two," he said, decidedly deadpan. "One desktop, one laptop…both pretty old machines."

Arnold let out a derisive snort.

"The ones the FBI took?"

Carlos nodded.

"Uh-huh."

"Hold on," Cain interrupted. "What's going on?"

Davidson was also studying him quizzically.

Arnold glanced at Carlos, who, in turn, returned a you've-got-the-floor shrug. Arnold said, "Our client"—totally loving the sound of *our*—"is a pen-tester, right? So you got to believe he's got way more than those two clunkers."

"Yes, but they're the only ones the FBI found," Cain said.

"No doubt," Arnold said with a laugh. "I also keep a couple old ones lying around…just in case."

"In case of what?" Cain asked.

Arnold smiled, a bit surprised that Cain would ask, given that he had a rep for defending hackers.

"They're expendable. They're terrific decoys in case the place is burglarized or as happened here, raided. I'll bet he's got at least three *primary* machines the FBI doesn't even know exist."

Cain shot Lopez a questioning glance. Lopez shrugged.

"A fully loaded tablet," Arnold continued. "A top-of-the-line laptop, and at *least* one seriously tricked-out desktop. Then, of course, there're probably a couple world-class servers for storage and the occasional brute-force task like password-cracking."

Lopez remained poker-faced.

"Did the FBI return them?" Arnold asked.

Cain answered, "No. I requested that, but Fisher said they intend to hold them until the case is completely adjudicated and all possible appeals exhausted. I, in turn, argued they're essential for Carlos' gainful employment. Fisher remained steadfast."

Arnold laughed. Yeah, sounded about right. Back to Carlos.

"So basically, you're intact, right?"

When Carlos didn't answer, Arnold asked, "Okay to have a look through your primary network?"

"No problem. When?"

Wow, dude really does want to help.

Just one more reason to believe him.

"How's this afternoon work? Have a couple things to do this morning before I start in." Then, to Cain, "Which brings up another issue. Since Agent Fisher and I have a history, I feel obliged to tell him I'm involved with this."

"I see no problem with that," Mr. Davidson answered. "We intend for our investigation to be as transparent as possible. Especially if there is any chance of uncovering

Allen Wyler

exculpatory evidence. Up to a point, that is."

Uh-oh.

"What exactly does 'up to a point' mean?"

"Our intent is to rectify this unfortunate misunderstanding before it progresses. Having said this, we also want to exercise extreme caution to *not* disclose information that may fall under the rules of discovery should a formal trial date be set. For you, this means do *not* provide the FBI with *any* investigation-relevant information without first clearing it with Noah or myself. Is this clear?"

"Yeah, I get it. Don't say a word without running it past you. Okay, we done for now?"

* * *

Singh drove his Tesla 3 slowly down the winding road, which had been narrowed into a single lane by bumper-to-bumper vehicles lining the east curb. He stopped abreast of Gold's address long enough to snap four shots of the house. Instead of the Tudor shown on Google Maps, this one was an ultramodern two-story stucco-and-glass cube on a postage-stamp sized property bordered by a security wall that conjured up vaguely suggestive images of Bin Laden's compound.

He had no idea how often Google updated their street views, but this modernistic structure was obviously newer than pictured. Meaning it had a recent paper trail scattered around various municipal and county departments. In particular, there would be a building permit containing the architect and general contractor information, as well as other pertinent data. Though Gold maintained a zero social-media footprint and nothing more than his business website on the Internet, documents were always available to provide a wealth of information if you knew how to dig.

The property records would be a superb trailhead for the search.

CHAPTER 10

AS HE APPROACHED the revolving door to the sidewalk, Arnold could increasingly feel the marrow-penetrating Seattle November chill.

Shit.

As he rotated out the door onto the street, a gust of frigid wind sliced savagely through his thin cotton clothes as if he were bare-ass naked. Hugging his chest, he mentally ran a list of nearby clothing stores, remembered Fjallraven, started trotting north, up Second Avenue, blowing through a red light to the unmistakable irritation of a driver who laid on his horn. Hooked a left on Pine, almost collided with a customer exiting the store. He stopped just inside the door to briskly rub his upper arms in blessed warmth while orienting to the new layout since he was last here in August.

You've become a total pussy since moving to Honolulu, dude.

"May I help you with something?"

Arnold hadn't noticed the clerk approach; a tall, trim, anatomically perfectly proportioned Scandinavian-looking young man with dirty blond long surfer hair, startling intense blue eyes, in a praying mantis posture, what with his fingers pressed together and up against his chest.

"Yes, you may. Where are the men's sweaters and coats now?"

"Certainly, right this way. They're in this area," he said leading Arnold to a far corner. "Do you have something specific in mind or are you just browsing?"

"I want a down parka and a couple heavy wool sweaters…something more appropriate for this weather than what I have on." Then, for some reason, felt obligated to justify his summer weight clothes. "Flew in from Honolulu last night and wouldn't you know, the airlines managed to lose my luggage."

Hey, not so bad for straight off the cuff.

The clerk stroked his chin professorially.

"How very inconvenient. They'll have it for you soon, I hope."

"Hope so."

The clerk took one step back, then shot a head-to-toe.

"Medium, you are," he stated before promptly pirouetting 180 degrees to point decisively at a rack of parkas. "The mediums are from here to here," his hands designating a precise section. "I see by your rucksack you're already familiar with our products and their unsurpassed quality."

"Exactly. That's why I'm here instead of The North Face."

Oh, bullshit. You're here on account of The North Face and Arc'teryx are several blocks further.

Unabashed pragmatism. But, hey…

"Do you have a particular preference in color or style?"

Much to Rachael's dismay and consternation, he could give a rat's ass about style, favoring functionality over form. He was consistently amazed at how many people eschewed comfort for fashion.

"Yeah, I need something *warm*."

A couple years ago, as his original Green Lake Tudor had become a smoldering smoking pile of cinders, every article of his clothing—except the 501s, Adidas kicks, and Seahawks sweatshirt he was wearing—had gone up in flames. Although he'd returned to Seattle since the new house became livable, those visits were during warm weather months when stocking the house with cold weather duds didn't ping consciousness.

"Ahhhh, here's one I'm sure you'll absolutely *adore*. It's our Singi Down Jacket," the clerk said while unhooking a handsome dark olive number from the rack to hold open for Arnold to slip into.

Arnold shrugged into a luxuriating cocoon of warmth.

"It's a *massively* comfortable and durable jacket made with our G-1000 and padded with *ethically* produced goose down. The shoulders are padded with Supreme Microlof for extra weather resistance and wear. It's styled in a traditional long cut to keep your upper thighs dry. As you can see, it includes a storm hood with synthetic fur edging. Besides olive, it's available in black and dark blue, but I believe this's the only medium presently in stock. I'd be delighted to check the storeroom if you prefer another color but suspect we'll need to order it if that's the case," this said in a conspiratorial manner.

Arnold checked himself in the mirror.

Hey, looked fine, felt deliciously warm. What's not to like?

With an approving nod, he said, "I'll take it."

* * *

Half an hour later and infinitely more comfortable in his new dark gray wool turtleneck and dark olive down parka, Arnold lingered a few steps from the store's front door, debating whether to burn the additional time it would take to hike six or so blocks to the Army/Navy surplus store before heading home to start work.

The coat he dearly missed was the genuine U.S. Navy peacoat he had purchased the fall before the Tudor burned down. Honolulu's lovely tropical winters had totally submerged that memory, but boy-oh-boy, this shitty weather brought it back front and center.

A glance at his watch.

What the hell.

Wouldn't take all *that* long.

And hopefully the store still stocked them. Assuming, of course, the store even still existed given all the changes boiling through downtown Seattle since the pandemic hit.

* * *

"May I help you?" asked a mid-twenties skeletal female boasting a gallery of body-art in addition to an armory of piercings covering just about every accessible inch of anatomy that he could see.

He cringed at the thought of other potential sites.

She had severely vibrant pink hair moused and swept left that clashed with a blinding purple half swept to the right. She was a stark contrast to the slick Fjallraven sales dude. In spite of the chilly drafty store carrying the vague scent of mothballs, she appeared comfortable in a tie-dyed tank top and vintage pedal pushers. All the better to display her fashionable art.

Arnold glanced out over the sea of clothing in the general direction of where the pea coat rack had been two years ago.

Holy shit, amazingly the rack was still there.

"Thanks. I see what I'm looking for."

"Yo bro, leave the pack. Pick it up on your way out," she said beckoning with a finger.

Took a moment to click.

We ain't talking Nordstrom, dude.

"No problem." He shrugged off his rucksack, said, "Here

you go," passing it to her over the display case.

"It'll be down here," she said, unceremoniously dropping it on the concrete next to her feet with a solid *thunk*, immediately refocusing on the iPhone in hand.

The limited stock of thick wool coats was—unlike the hyper-organized Fjallraven parkas—a string of random sizes necessitating slipping into each one until finding a fit.

Lucked out, at that.

His other one had someone's name inked on the neck tag, but not this one. Out of habit, he eyed the price tag (not that that it mattered since he intended to buy it anyway). One fifty. He laughed out loud. The spiffy whoop-de-doo high-tech Fjallraven had set him back six bills, but cool as it was, this one just seemed way cooler. Plus, a screaming deal.

What's not to like?

He appraised himself in a full-length mirror duck taped to a nearby cement pillar.

Perfect.

The familiar heft, texture, and distant mothball-scented luxurious black wool felt...what? Like better times? Honestly?

Yeah, probably.

On account of he'd bought that first one when his parents were still alive, so in that respect those years *were* better. But those memories were fading into being strangely illusory, as if he was slowly losing grasp of their significance.

He pondered that a moment.

Were those days actually better or was his mind selectively editing out the not-so-good-times he knew coexisted? Time's relentless march not only smoothed the edges of those memories but stopped them from breaking surface as often, increasing their distance at the expense of vividness.

Jesus, how depressing; leaving him uncharacteristically sad and bitter at the growing loss of a precious chunk of personal history. If there were any upside to this, it was the less often the memories surfaced the less often he felt the pain associated with their deaths. Which would he prefer? He shook his head—*stop it*—and inspected the familiar image in the mirror.

Why am I buying this coat?

To cling to their memory? Or simply to replace a coat I loved?

Does it matter? You want it, so just freaking buy it. Enjoy it.

Arnold tenderly folded the jacket onto the counter. Without a word or skipped beat in the rhythm of gum chewing, the clerk robotically inspected the fabric, pockets, and price tag, then extended her hand for his credit card.

CHAPTER 11

"MR. FISHER, JUST wanted to call and say I'm in town working with Mr. Cain and Mr. Davidson on the Carlos Lopez thing and to ask if we can get together for dinner?"

Recently, he had worked a few cases that involved the FBI agent: most recently the Cain, Stowell, Tidwell ransomware fiasco. As a result, Arnold considered him a friend.

"Gold, you should know by now I can't discuss an active investigation."

"I do, but that's not why I'm calling. Just want to have dinner with you, is all, you know, touch base?"

"Long as you respect the subject-matter limits. What'd you have in mind?"

Easy answer, especially seeing how it'd been months since last there, which had put him in the throes of Flavio withdrawal.

"I'm thinking pizza, my place?"

"That place in your hood?" was Fisher's first hint of enthusiasm.

"There any better pizza?"

"Not that I know. If memory serves, you drink Anchor

Steam."

That Fisher.

Memory like an elephant.

* * *

"Hey, boy, want to go for a walk?" Arnold asked, closing the door to the coat closet after lovingly draping his new peacoat on a wood hanger, now bundled in his spiffy new Fjallraven and a thick wool turtleneck; his Nanook of the North look.

The other newly purchased sweater and the light-weight cotton sweatshirt from this morning were neatly folded on the stairs to haul up to the master closet later, the lightweight windbreaker now condemned to the coat closet to await Spring. How cool to be slowly stocking the place with enough clothes to not have to schlep items back and forth from the island. The idea was to eventually be able to hop a flight any time he wanted with nothing but a boarding pass and credit card.

Chance's paws began frantically skittering for traction, suddenly caught, rocketing him straight toward the front door, tail fanning like crazy. Once outside, they headed for the PCC market off Aurora to grab a few essentials to tide them over until he had a better fix on how long this gig might take before stocking up on too many perishables.

Arnold grabbed a tuna salad sandwich for lunch, a dozen pouches a Newman's Own Dog Meals, a fresh half gallon of milk for hot chocolates, and a few other necessities. Earlier this morning, he'd ordered for a 30-pound bag of kibble from Chewy but had no clue how long delivery would take, so the Newman's would tide him over. Figured he would pick up breakfasts at Starbucks during Chance's morning walks. A daily rhythm was already settling in for however long the stay.

While munching the tuna sandwich, with a can of diet Pepsi on the table next to his Surface, he glanced at Chance curled up nose-to-tail on the back porch. It was his favorite spot. From the get-go, he'd shown a preference for the porch, in spite of the chilly weather.

After washing down the last of the sandwich, he balled the wrapper into the paper towel and tossed the wad (*swish—two points*) into the compost bin. Time to call Lopez. But first, he needed to call Rachael. A mild dread wafted through his gut. What kind of a mood was she in? What would be her reaction to the quagmire he had agreed to? Well, for sure she wouldn't be doing cartwheels over it.

"Hey, sweetie, what up?"

"How'd your meeting with the lawyers go?" she said, in an even, measured tone.

It was very un-Rachael-like. His antennae began tingling.

"Well, it's a very unique and weird situation," he said, hoping to hook enough interest to perhaps soften the news of the gig being open ended at the moment, which, after all, was the crucial issue, right? After a pithy summation of the problem, he added, "It makes me understand why Mr. Davidson demanded I speak with Lopez in person. It's obvious he's been framed. And know what? I now see why Mr. Davidson goes to bat for defendants. I never really *understood* that until now."

Spoken like a true convert.

His attempt to inspire some enthusiasm while simultaneously buttressing his need to be in Seattle was met with stony silence.

Arnold's gut knotted.

"Uhhhh…something wrong?"

"I don't know yet. I'm trying to figure that out. You didn't mention the most important point: how long do you think this will take?"

Uh-oh, there it was.

His brain began scrambling for just one scintilla of

positive spin, some way to put at least a touch of lipstick on this pig. Nada.

Jesus, just freaking man up, dude.

"I don't know. I haven't had any chance to get my hands around this yet. I *just* finished with the lawyers. I should know more by, oh, tomorrow morning maybe?"

"I don't get it, Arnold. You've met all the parties involved. What more do you need to do there?"

Oh, Jesus, here we go…

"Don't forget, I have some other important items to take care of too, like hiring our Seattle associate," intentionally slipping in the plural possessive pronoun. "I haven't even been able to start on that. I mean, that's huge, right?"

She spoke with a note of disgust.

"In other words, you have no idea how long you'll need to stay."

Ah, man.

"Well, guess that's one way to put it. But sweetie, I'll be working this hard as possible. I *will* have a clearer idea by morning."

He waited for her to say something but heard only heavy, condemnation-steeped silence.

Jesus. Her escalating irritation over his work grated at his patience. He sucked a deep calming breath. The upside—he reminded himself—was that she wanted him *there*, with her. That's good, right? Right. So, by reverse logic, being irritated by his absence was a good thing, right?

Maybe. Maybe not.

What she didn't seem to grasp was that these occasional separations were long-term investments toward a financially solid future together. Why did she have such difficulty grasping this?

"Look, Rach, we're talking just a couple days out of our entire life together. You have to realize I'm building a business

for *both* of us. If we want to have offices in both cities, I need
to invest time building the infrastructure. Consider it as an
investment in *our* future, okay? The better help I recruit now,
the more time we'll be able to spend together in the future.
Believe me."

"I get all that, Arnold. What *you* don't seem to grasp is
how uncomfortable it makes me to stay in *your* house alone. I
feel responsible for everything. I never felt this way when I had
my own space. For some reason, it's totally different now that
I live here. Why can't you understand this?"

Arnold? Not sweetie or Arnie?

"Well, that's easily solved soon as I'm back," he said
without thinking.

"That's hard to believe. How?"

"Easy. Marry me and then it'll be *our* home, right?"

Holy shit. You just proposed, dude. A wave of relief
rippled through him for finally uncorking the question. But on
the freaking phone? How totally uncool.

"No."

One freaking word. Decisive, to the point. Dripping
icicles.

His skull began vibrating like a ringing bell.

His mind blanked, then slowly began to reboot,
"Wh...why not? I thought..." A chilling notion slammed
home. "Or have your feelings changed?"

"You don't get it, do you? I *do* love you, sweetie. *That's*
not the problem. I just don't want to be—no change that, I
refuse to be the wife of an absentee husband. Why's it so hard
for you to realize that part of loving someone includes
resenting the time they're away from you?"

"*What?*" Even the instant replay made no sense. "Do you,
for one minute, think I'm happy about being away from you?
No. I hate it. But right now, I'm scrambling so I can be a good
provider for *us* by building this business. That's what good

providers do."

"Okay, fine. Point made. I guess what I don't understand is why this sudden fascination of yours. It's so not you. Being goal-directed isn't part of the Arnold Gold I know. Where does this sudden passion come from? You've never mentioned this before last summer."

"Wait, what? You resent me for being an adult and having goals?" He spent a moment reorganizing his thoughts. "You're lucky. When you were, what, thirteen, you knew exactly what you wanted to do and were laser-focused. I've always admired and envied that and was thrilled for you when you were accepted to nursing school. Me? I was the total opposite. I had zero career ambition until I removed that virus from Mr. Davidson's network. Remember? Okay, sure, I've always been into computers and AI," he stated as fact. "Which is why I ended up building SAM. But then when you demanded I stop gambling—"

"*Demanded?* Stop right there, Arnold Gold. Don't you *dare* try to pin this on me."

Whoa.

He held up both hands in surrender in spite of her not being able to see him.

"Okay, okay…poor choice of words perhaps, but sweetie, this isn't a prepared statement, so please let me finish my train of thought."

Yeah? And where was I?

"Okay, you *stipulated* you'd move to Honolulu only if I gave up gambling. Is that fair to say?"

It damned well better be because he remembered the conversation clearly.

He suspected that no answer implied agreement.

"So I began wracking my brain, asking myself how could I possibly earn a living? Sure, I work the market, but I needed a real job. I decided that whatever it is, it should meet a few basic requirements. Be my own boss, flexible hours, the ability to work remotely, and involve computers." He paused to let those points sink in. "So, after some objective soul-searching, starting an IT business doing things like I did for Mr. Davidson made perfect sense. What I never saw coming was once I started getting customers, the more exciting it's become. And now I'm really into it. Aside from falling in love with you, it's the next best thing to happen to me. I love it and want you to be happy and proud of me for building it."

"You haven't heard a word I've said. I *get* all that and I *do* support you. But I still resent it when you leave like this. Can't you realize you can love a person and still hate some things about them? The moment you claimed to have offices in both cities you knew these problems were bound to come up. How long have you been saying you'll hire an associate in both places to cover those times you're not there? Seems to me you've purposely avoided doing that. Why? Is it that you can't delegate responsibility?"

The accusation irritated him. After all, he'd hired Fear...sort of.

"Oh, come on, Rach. Seriously? What are you saying? That I'm here to get away from you? The person I hired turned out to be a liar."

"No. What I'm saying is you're not doing what you said you would do. Instead, you're procrastinating. And it's pissing me off," she said with alarming conviction.

Wow. He was momentarily struck dumb by what felt like her escalating ire. But he had to try to take this to the mat.

"Look, *we* live in both cities, Rach, Seattle and Honolulu. Why not have offices in each place?"

She blew a rasping wrong answer buzzer sound.

"*Wrong. You* live in both cities. *I* live in Honolulu where *I* work and where *I* rented an apartment. That's not the point. I'm sick and tired of you claiming two offices but not doing what's needed to make them function. It's taking a toll on us."

Shaking his head, he tried to wrap his mind around how mind-blowingly at odds they were. He'd hired Fear to do piece work and cover Seattle. Why did she refuse to acknowledge that?

Yeah, and how'd that turn out?

"Why name your business Gold and *Associates* when you didn't even have one goddamn associate?"

Felt like he was being sucked into the gravitational field of a black hole and that if he didn't free himself, he would end up compressed into an infinitely small mass.

"C'mon, Rach, you know why I chose that name. I *will* have associates in both places, so we can move between them when we want."

"No, Arnold, they're *your* homes. What's more, *we* never discussed it. That was entirely *your* decision. Besides, how am I supposed to live in both places and hold down my job here?"

Ah, man...

"Don't forget, sweetie, you've made choices too."

"And what's that supposed to mean?"

"Reality check, Rach." He was fighting to keep his voice even. "My work has caused me to come here exactly *twice*. So if you want to talk inconvenience, don't forget the impact your freaking twelve-hour shifts have on us week after freaking week. Point is, you're not the only victim here."

Oh, Jesus. What did I just say?

Cringing, he prepared for the blowback.

Icy silence. Tick-tick-tick.

"Rach?"

"Thanks for clearing a few things up, Arnold. Have a nice day."

"Rach—"

But the line was dead.

CHAPTER 12

ARNOLD REALIZED CHANCE was whimpering, his nose prodding his elbow. Doggies know. Their exquisitely sensitive noses process the spectrum of scents radiated by human emotions, allowing them amazing insight into their partner's mental state.

Then again, it probably didn't take a rocket scientist to sense his present state of mind. Regardless, he started in on a generous dose of choobers while rehashing the disastrous nosedive the conversation had taken. For sure he could have (and should have) managed it more, well, adroitly, more diplomatically.

On the other hand...

"It's all good, boy," he muttered without conviction.

He and Rachael saw things so...differently. This left his gut simmering in sickening queasiness. Yeah, he got the part about the associate—and she was right—but something else was eating her. What? He had no sense of what that might be other than it wasn't good.

He blew a long slow breath, glanced at Chance again. His buddy. A being who loved and accepted him for who he was.

"Chance is a good boy."

Chance flopped onto the floor and rolled onto his back, asking for rabber-de-jabber tummy rubs. Arnold knelt beside him and started in, repeating "good boy" like a mantra.

*Unless...*he could come up with some bright idea to pique her interest in Gold and Associates. That sounded good, but what the hell would that be? He'd have to ponder that. But in the very least, nailing down an honest-to-God Seattle associate seemed to be one tangible step toward resolving a major issue. With a whine, Chance curled his head toward Arnold and gave him a doggie kiss. Doggies know.

"Sorry boy." He resumed the tummy rubs. "At least I have you."

Dogs don't jam you into high-intensity emotional quagmires. They simply love you and accept life as it plays out, living only in the moment. Making Chance his true soulmate.

Seriously dude? You actually thought "soulmate"? Oh, please, just freaking gag me.

All right, already. Get on with it.

It was time to call Lopez and arrange to search through his network for evidence.

CHAPTER 13

"I'M REALLY JAMMED at the moment," Lopez said, with a distinct note of frustration. "We're up to our assholes in alligators so it's all hands on deck, which is just another reason this other shit's...oh, never mind. Look, how's this sound; I'll upload a temporary encrypted password to my network and send you the key."

A perfect solution. Efficient. Sensible. Arnold liked it.

"Great. That saves time."

"What email address do you want me to use?"

"I'm sending it now. If it's not in your inbox in two minutes, ping me."

By the time Arnold had nuked a hot chocolate and sat back down, the link was waiting for him.

A two-hour investigation convinced him that Lopez hadn't overlooked the trap door their unidentified hacker had presumably implanted in the Curchfield network. The asshole had undoubtedly removed all evidence the moment the press release hit the wires. No big surprise there. But Arnold knew he would've been remiss if he neglected to check. Dumb-ass mistakes spawned by simple overconfidence never ceased to amaze him.

Next, he focused on scrounging up every byte of information out there on the Curchfield Tech fake press release, then he carefully compared the forgery against three valid releases. Had to admit, the bogus one looked flawless, making it easy to understand how nary a news service had raised an eyebrow.

Mr. Cain was right; Hacker must have done some world-class due diligence. The dude's attention to detail reminded him of some phishing scams so sophisticated that they were indistinguishable from actual notices sent by the big guns like Microsoft, Google, or Apple.

He created a new case file—his routine first step when initiating a new investigation—and titled it, *Carlos Lopez Case*. He inserted a reminder to review the press release again at a later date just in case he'd missed anything. In the meantime, he would let this information percolate subconsciously. For his first substantive entry, he summarized the discussion with Lopez and his lawyers.

He paused to check SAM's firewall, a task he did periodically throughout the day. Although SAM was programmed to alert him should a probe occur, an extremely talented hacker might just be clever enough to disable the alert, so Arnold went out of his way to check the firewall integrity.

His stomach growled. Hmm…5:30.

Already?

Time for Chance's afternoon walk.

Should've gotten more done.

True, but his progress was glacial on account of every time he focused, his mind boomeranged straight back to the Rachael thing. At this rate…

Get it together, dude. The quicker you wrap this up, the quicker you get back.

He put in an on-line order for a large pepperoni and

sausage with extra cheese, asked them to throw in extra packets of peppers and parmesan cheese, then bundled up in a sweater and jacket, leashed Chance, and used the front door instead of slipping out the back to cut through the alley.

No rain. Just crisp humid November chill. This longer route would allow Chance to enjoy more nose time for reading doggie bulletin boards on shrubs and grass. Despite the day's progress, a haunting suspicion gnawed that he'd overlooked a vitally important step.

What?

The harder he struggled to snag it, the more teasingly it danced just beyond the periphery of his reach, festering like an inflamed molar you can't stop tonguing. Worse yet, he realized, he was beginning to blame Rachael for the mental cyclone messing with his concentration. Which, he knew, wasn't healthy for the relationship.

Jesus, what am I forgetting? It's important.

CHAPTER 14—Monday, 6:47 PM

TO ARNOLD'S DELIGHT, John Chang—an FBI geek he'd resonated with on prior cases—stood on the porch shoulder to shoulder with Special Agent Fisher.

"Oh, wow, you came too. Cool," Arnold said enthusiastically. "Good thing I picked up a large."

"C'mon, bro, I don't eat *that* much," Chang said with a laugh, tailgating Fisher into the great room.

Arnold shut the front door, cutting off a particularly harsh blast of biting wind. By the time he turned from the door, Fisher was in the kitchen, dropping a six-pack of Anchor Steam on the stainless-steel counter, Chance greeting him with enthusiastic doggie kisses and tail wags. Arnold trailed Chang into the kitchen as Fisher tossed his coat over a kitchen chair. Arnold kicked himself for not offering to hang them in the closet like a good host.

Oh, well, they'll undoubtedly survive.

After giving Chance a Bully Stick, Arnold opened the French door so he could proudly strut the treat out to the back deck to enjoy.

"Go ahead, dig in," Arnold said, setting the large pizza box on the table along with a roll of paper towels from the counter dispenser. He already had a stack of paper plates waiting. Mr. Entertainment.

"I'm starved. Who wants a beer?" Fisher asked, uncapping a bottle.

Without waiting for a reply, he handed it to Arnold.

"Need you ask?" Chang quipped, before taking a bite of pizza.

"Don't forget the packets of parmesan and pepper." Arnold pointed out the two piles on the table.

Without another word, the three dug into the spicy, cheesy, pizza, all of them apparently ravenous.

After washing down his first bite with a generous swig of beer, Arnold kicked off the conversation.

"As I mentioned, Mr. Cain and Mr. Davidson hired me to help on the Lopez defense by double-checking everything to see if I can figure out who the hacker is."

Fisher and Chang exchanged a glance. Fisher then nonchalantly took another bite of pizza while Chang busied himself with a pull of beer.

A previously choreographed response? Probably. Smacked of it.

Silence. Totally atypical for them, especially considering their history of working so closely before, most recently on the ransomware thing which wrapped up just months ago.

What gives?

Fisher was studying him now, tonguing a molar.

After a few beats, he said, "You're working for them, huh?"

Arnold recoiled. Something in his tone. Subtle, but clearly accusatory.

"What?"

"It's a simple question, Gold. Go ahead, answer it."

Boy, clearly loaded words. Totally unexpected, too. He raised a just-a-second finger to stall under the pretense of

another sip of beer. At face value, Fisher's question seemed
benign, but his inflection packed it with accusation and
condemnation. Why?

Well, duh.

Until now, he'd always suited up for Team Righteous.
But not this time. This time, he was in a Team Lucifer jersey.

*I'm beginning to get a feel for the animosity between
defense attorneys and law enforcement.*

Although he'd always subliminally been aware of the
dynamic, it'd never impacted him until now.

*Okay, but isn't this dichotomy true for just about any
adversarial stance? Each side believes they're right? Just like
Rachael and me.*

He slowly set his beer beside his plate, cautioning himself
to be as objective and dispassionate as possible.

"I'm sorry, but what are you implying? That this corrupts
me? That I'm playing for the wrong team? What?"

Both FBI agents continued nonchalantly munching pizza,
as if the question had not been asked.

The heavy awkward silence got to Arnold, forcing him to
add, "Look, my company provides services to clients, which
means I work for anyone who ponies up the coin. They hired
me to provide a service, okay? Nothing more, nothing less.
Or"—he locked eyes with Fisher—"are you insinuating
something more than is actually there?"

Neither Fisher nor Chang seemed to acknowledge the
question. Which struck Arnold as a major slight, and again
completely out of character. But what did he expect under the
circumstances? Beerhall, stein-clinking camaraderie? No, not
that exactly, but certainly not this...antagonistic vibe.

Their silence compelled him to add, "Hey look, all of us
want the same thing, don't we? To find out the truth?"

Fisher slowly set the chunk of crust he was holding on the
white paper plate, tore off a paper towel.

"What's your lawyer friends' take on the case?"

Arnold sucked a chunk of anchovy from between his teeth before answering.

"Let me see if I have this straight. *You* can't discuss an active case with me yet have no problem trying to wheedle information out of me. How's this supposed to work?" He raised his hand. "Hold on, that sounded...slanted." He paused to regroup. "Look, let's reboot this conversation. Only reason I mentioned the case is to let you know I'm working it. There's no other agenda."

Fisher raised his hands in mock surrender.

"Lighten up, Gold. Did I ask for classified information? No. I'm asking for your general impression of the case."

"Okay, but why? I mean you guys have been investigating this for weeks. I just got involved this morning, so basically don't know jack."

"I ask because you've heard their side of it and I'd love to know what that is."

"Yeah? In other words, I show you my cards, but you don't show me yours. How's that fair?" There was a brief pause, then, "Okay, fine. You win. There's no reason *not* to tell you. Here's all I know. Two local startups had their stock torpedoed by bogus press releases. Hence, the Bureau and SEC opened an investigation that uncovered a day trading account—*allegedly* Lopez's—that covered a significant short position in both stocks. So, obviously this made him your prime suspect. There, that's it."

While listening to Arnold, Fisher nonchalantly pulled another slice of pizza from the box and examined it with a strange, detached air. Meanwhile, Chang seemed content to sit back, eat, listen, sip beer, and stay clear of the conversation.

Goddammit. What the hell game were they playing?

He finally said, "Look, we all know that Lopez's name on that account proves nothing. Anyone with false ID and a Social

Security number can bop into a branch office and open an
account. Just complete a few forms, hand over a check that
doesn't bounce, and bingo, you're good, right?"

Fisher nodded, as if Arnold had just confirmed a
suspicion.

"See? You're already biased."

"*Bullshit,*" Arnold said, surprised at the strength of his
irritation. "You asked what I know. I just told you. How does
that make me biased? Besides, if I'm wrong, why not set the
record straight and enlighten me. Why're you so sure Lopez is
the one responsible?"

Fisher turned to Chang, "John?"

"Part of my workup on the Curchfield case included an
analysis of the network logs. I found nothing unusual," Chang
said with a shrug. "My conclusion was the hacker likely
embedded a trapdoor, quite possibly a RAT. After more
digging, I found the hacker's IP. And guess what? It matches
Lopez's laptop, the one we have in evidence."

Arnold snorted sarcastically.

"You seriously believe someone with that dude's chops is
so dumb as to leave a discoverable IP?" He shook his head.
"Get real. I'm not buying it."

Fisher spread his hands.

"I've been at this long enough to see some very smart
criminals commit some extraordinary acts of stupidity.
Typically, that's exactly why they're caught. If you're saying
he shouldn't be a prime suspect because of a fuckup, then it's
time for us to switch to a less controversial topic like politics,
religion, or infinity."

*Good point. What exactly am I saying? Why am I so
defensive?*

He locked eyes with Fisher.

"Look, here's the deal. Mr. Cain and Mr. Davidson hired
me to take a deep dive into this to see if I can find evidence

that someone *other* than Lopez is responsible. I'm not taking sides, okay? I'm completely impartial and simply doing my job."

Fisher nodded.

"Understood."

"We," Arnold said, pointing to himself and then to Chance enjoying his Bully Stick on the back deck, "only just arrived late last night and I spent the day getting things in order so I can actually start work soon as you leave. The only thing I've done so far is check out the press release. Okay?"

Fisher nodded.

"So, let me ask you this," Arnold said, trying to avoid a question directly related to the investigation, "do you have any evidence indicating Lopez has a history of black-hat work?"

Fisher deferred to Chang.

"Not that we know of. But," Chang said with a sarcastic laugh, "you damn well know that's not the sort of job they list in their resume. Hackers are hackers. He's a hacker." With an it-is-what-it-is shrug, he continued, "I've never known one who hasn't bent the law at one time or another." His eyes bore into Arnold. "Present company included."

"Touché. Hey, look, both capers are so damn sophisticated, they must've taken a truckload of time and effort. Doesn't make a hell of a lot of sense to put in that much effort into planning a caper like that and leave your IP address as a freaking business card. I mean, like, *seriously*? Makes way more sense if someone intent on framing him put it there. And I have to say, it sure as hell looks like they've succeeded."

Chang shrugged, neither agreeing nor disagreeing.

"Hey, bro, you asked, we answered. That's it." During the ensuing pause, a thin smile appeared to tug at his lips. "But since it sounds like you don't think Lopez's a suspect, let me ask this; if you're the douchebag who went to such meticulous lengths to frame him, what would you think if we turned around and gave him a pass?"

Holy shit.

Arnold wanted to slam his palm against his forehead.

I'm mashugana.

"You're saying he's *not* your prime suspect?"

CHAPTER 15

CHANG GLANCED AT Fisher with an exaggerated expression of innocence.

"Did I say anything even remotely close to that?"

Brow furrowed, Fisher shook his head.

Agent Serious.

"Not that I heard." Then, to Arnold: "We appreciate the heads-up, Gold." He casually took a pull of beer, swallowed, smacked his lips. "Over the past years, we've worked up a few cases together. In the process we've learned to count on each other's word."

Arnold waited for the punchline.

"However, this case is a bit different. You're working for a potential adversary." He quickly held up an index finger. "Mind you, I said *potential*." Pause. "Think *very* carefully before answering this next question." Pause. "Can I trust you to keep tonight's conversation strictly confidential? Specifically, to not repeat a word to Cain and Davidson?"

Good question. Not easily answered given his strong allegiance to both lawyers. But...

"When something's told to me in confidence, I treat it as such. I'm surprised you have to ask."

"You should know by now it's better to ask than assume."

Fisher glanced at Chang, likely an another agreed-upon signal established during the drive here.

Chang said, "Truth is, we're thrilled at having another set of eyes on this quagmire, especially since we're knee-deep in another case. As you so aptly point out, there're things about this that don't ring true. So, yes, we have questions. We'd love it if you'd share relevant findings obtained in the course of your investigation. Specifically, any information pertaining to the hacker's identity."

A surge of excitement zapped Arnold.

"Are you saying you believe Lopez is innocent?"

Chang shook his head.

"We didn't say that. Presently we don't have sufficient evidence for a strong opinion one way or the other. We certainly can't *exclude* him as a suspect. However, we agree the present case against him has *issues*. We also agree there's a very distinct possibly he's been framed. *Possibly.*"

A breeze of vindication blew through Arnold but simultaneously raised questions and concerns.

"Do you have another suspect?"

Fisher returned a quick admonishing headshake.

"You know better than to ask that, Gold."

"Then, let me rephrase it: can you give me anything at all that might help point me in a direction to start digging?"

Fisher glanced at Chang, who nodded.

Fisher said, "We think it's unlikely our unsub was a disgruntled employee at either company. We initially ran a list of employees terminated prior to, or immediately after, the IPOs. Nothing turned up." Fisher paused for this to sink in. "If our hacker set Lopez up to take the hit it's clear he harbors a fierce hatred toward him. Put another way, we believe Lopez was the primary target of revenge rather than those specific companies. This means they *must be* connected at some point.

This is just one more reason to suspect that Lopez *and* this case are being scrutinized to see what shakes out."

Of course.

"In other words, he's bait, right?"

Fisher glanced away for a beat.

"Don't know if I'd put it in exactly those words…"

Arnold kicked himself for not considering this. Then again, why should he? But something else was out there in the air. What? Took a moment to sink in.

"You want me to be a CI on this?"

Fisher raised his eyebrows.

"You're still on record…"

Arnold thought about this a moment, saw no real downside, and if it helped…

"You know I have to run *this* by Mr. Cain and Mr. Davidson, right?"

Fisher nodded.

Arnold turned to Chang.

"I assume this implies reciprocity and you'll share intel too."

Chang cocked his head slightly.

"Unless, of course, our intel might potentially compromise this or any allied investigation."

It was a boilerplate disclaimer. Quick translation: not really.

This gave the Bureau enormous wiggle room to welch on the agreement if it benefited them. On the other hand, Arnold saw no problem handing over information that might potentially exculpate Lopez.

He asked Chang, "Do you have any evidence Lopez works with other hackers?"

Chang pursed his lips in thought.

"Other than the ones he works with?" He chuckled. "I'm under no delusion they're choirboys, bro. A few are probably still into that shit in their off time." Then, with a shrug, "Hell, maybe even on company time. But that company's legit."

* * *

Pizza polished off and on well into their second beer, Arnold figured the waters were sufficiently calm to probe again.

"What can you tell me about the Camano case?"

Fisher asked, "What do you already know?"

"Nothing other than it ended up tits-up." Arnold swiped condensation off the neck of the bottle. "Essentially. They'd just gone public when the hit occurred and ended up declaring bankruptcy."

He turned to Chang.

"Find anything relevant to the case?"

Chang spent a moment in thought.

"Not really. Why?"

"On account of I might know the head of IT when the hack went down. I plan to check that out later. Any problem with that?" he asked, glancing from one to the other, expecting no pushback.

Fisher shook his head.

"Not if you don't do anything to interfere with our investigation and you share findings."

"No problem. But just to be sure, I plan on running everything past Mr. Cain and Mr. Davidson first."

Fisher nodded.

"Change of topic," Chang said cheerily, "how's business?"

Wow, for a few blessed minutes the Rachael thing had taken a vacation from consciousness, but Chang's question brought it screaming back.

"Too good, actually. I'm snowed under." Ah, a perfect segue to his other priority. "Hey, long as you brought it up, I'm in the market for an associate here. You run into anyone with good credentials who's looking for work and lives here, let me know, okay?"

"Absolutely, bro."

"And Rachael?" Fisher asked, wiping his fingers with a paper towel.

Ah, man...

"We're good," he answered too abruptly, then scrambled to change subjects. He turned to Chang, "Hey, let me ask you, how'd you nail this gig with the Bureau?"

Chang flashed questioning eyes.

"Whadaya mean?"

"I mean, like, you recruited out of school or what?"

Chang's face changed to a bemused smile.

"Course not. I applied like everyone does."

A surprise to Arnold.

"For the geek squad?"

With a laugh, Chang shook his head.

"Naw, bro, doesn't work that way. You have to apply just like everyone," with a nod toward Fisher."

Interesting.

"Seriously? You mean to be a Special Agent?"

"Exactly. And then make it through the same basic training."

"At Quantico? So, you're, like, Special Agent Chang or are you a geek?"

Another laugh.

"Both. I'm a Special Agent who happens to be assigned to the Cyber Program. The day I was assigned, I applied for CART training. That's the Computer Analysis Response Team. We're the ones who manage the digital devices for any case that pops up. I'm presently on the cyber squad."

Fisher stood, pizza and beer now completely consumed.

"Hate to eat and run, but it's been a long day." Then, to Arnold, "You'll keep us updated?"

Meeting over.

"I will."

Chang was up now too, but clearly not finished with a point despite Fisher's push to leave.

"You'll contact your friend at Camano?"

"Yep."

Chang slipped on his coat.

"Good luck with that." He said, flashing a wry smile. "Let me know what you find."

There was something in Chang's tone...

"What aren't you telling me?"

Stretching, Chang yawned.

"We have their servers as evidence."

Arnold gave a so-what shrug.

Chang cocked his head, his smug smile vanished.

"What're *you* holding back?"

Arnold just smiled and walked through the great room to open the front door for them.

CHAPTER 16

WITH FISHER AND Chang gone, Arnold spent a few minutes giving Chance some scribberger-jibbergers before rolling him over for a dose of rabber-de-jabber tummy rubs.

He started his investigation by running a Google search on Camano Biopharma, then repeated the process using the Bing and Yahoo search engines. After discarding duplicates, he began sorting through hyperlinks in search of relevant information (which he'd recognize when he saw it).

After tossing a truckload of stock evaluations and irrelevant statistics, he hit paydirt: a list of employees at the time of the sabotage. It was a testament to the durability of info posted on the Internet. What happens on the Web stays on the Web. In perpetuity.

This gave him the name he was searching for, Prisha Patel. He'd interacted with her during three on-line cybersecurity forums, during which she'd impressed him as extremely knowledgeable. Some additional searching gave him a personal email address.

He sent her a message, then waited to see if it would immediately bounce back as invalid. After two minutes without an automated NO LONGER VALID report, he figured the address was okay, but was it active? He knew of three chat rooms she'd hung out in, so he checked there. No luck.

Oh, well, might as well start cleaning up the dinner mess.

He was cramming the empty grease-stained pizza box into the compost bin when his iPhone dinged that he had an email. *Rachael?* He glanced at the banner on the screen.

Holy shit. Prisha.

He responded on his Surface with an invite to meet in a secure online chat room. She accepted. A moment later they linked by audio only. (Arnold always kept the built-in web cam disabled unless a compelling reason dictated otherwise. Which was, like, never.)

She greeted him with, "Hey, dude, s'up?"

Shit. Should've prepared a pitch.

Hadn't thought to do that, but figured, what the hell, just plow ahead with, "Thanks for answering my email. I wasn't sure if you'd remember me."

"Sure I do. You're the Gold and Associates dude."

"I'm impressed you remembered." Either that, or she'd thought to Google it. "Okay, so here's the deal…I'm working a job and would love to run a couple things by you, if you're down for it."

An unambiguous note of suspicion seeped into her voice.

"Such as?"

"It has to do with the clusterfuck that destroyed your old company, Camano."

"Yeah? What about it?"

Arnold grabbed a ballpoint pen and nudged a legal pad closer to make a few notes.

"What's your take on what happened?"

She remained silent a good ten seconds.

"You're picking a very tender scab, dude. You understand that, don't you? I mean, why exactly are you interested?"

"As I said, it's a long story."

"So what? We're watching a seriously sucky Netflix show, so go ahead, lay it on me."

"Okay. It's simple. I'm doing a job for two lawyers who're looking into two hacks. Yours and a carbon copy of it. I'd like to know your thoughts on what you believe happened?"

Another pause.

"Lawyers? I dunno, man…what exactly you doing for them? Why're they involved?"

"Ah, shit…look, if you're worried about legal blowback, don't be."

"Then why're you getting all hesitant and shit about explaining it?"

Aww, Jesus…

"Like I said, it's complex…okay, look," he scrambled for a concise summary, "they're defending a dude we think has been framed for them. We suspect both hacks were done by one, like, supernova hacker. Okay?"

"My ears are open. Go on."

"That's it. There's nothing more to say other than they hired me to look into it for him, so thought I'd ask for your thoughts on what went down."

"And you think it's me?"

"*No*, of course not. You missed the point. I just need some answers, is all. I'm trying to find a place to start searching and need a lead to follow. So far, I've got a grand total of diddly squat. I can tell you unequivocally that no one *remotely* suspects you're involved, so forget that."

Several seconds ticked past.

"Straight up?" she finally asked. "That's all there is to it?"

"That's it."

After a curt sarcastic laugh, she said, "What went down should be painfully obvious to anyone with more than one synapse. Some asshole got his rocks off sending out that press release. End of story."

Her tone was now decidedly bitter.

"Look, you're justified at being super sensitive about it. I'd be too. But here's the thing, what happened to you is *exactly* what went down at the other company."

"Yeah? What's their name?"

"Curchfield Technology," he said, even spelling it for her.

"Yeah, yeah...heard some chatter about that."

"Which makes me ask, do you know for sure a hacker did it instead of some pissed-off employee?"

Although Fisher had assured him of this, he wanted to run it by her too. Just for completeness.

She scoffed.

"Yeah, at about a ninety-five-percent level."

"Wow, that high, huh. So, what're you saying? You found footprints?"

"You kidding? No, nothing, absolutely nothing. That alone's huge. Besides, when this shit blew up, we were all holding stock or options. Not only that, it went down in the lock-up period."

"What the hell's that?"

"A defined period after an IPO when insiders—usually employees and investors—can't sell their stock. In other words, we all ended up holding nothing but a pile of steaming dogshit. *That's* the reason I can't see any of *us* doing it. Follow?"

"Yeah, I buy that. So, what happened to you guys?"

"What do you mean? You know damn well what happened. The company folded."

"Then let me rephrase that. When Camano filed for bankruptcy, what happened to *you* guys, the employees?"

"We got massively stiffed, is what. The company couldn't make payroll, so everyone but the CFO was laid off *without* a cent owned them. After that, every tangible asset including all the shitty secondhand furniture and office equipment was sold for pennies on the dollar and that was that. Every scrap of IP we ever generated went for fire sale prices to divvy up among the initial investors but not one of us peons got a penny. And, like the Looney Tunes ending, *That's all, Folks,*" she said with a surprisingly good imitation of the cartoon voice.

Her words sparked an idea.

"Sorry you got screwed," he said, and waited a respectful moment. "So what happened to the old computers?"

He took her hesitation to mean she was weighing an answer.

"The workstations were sold along with everything else," she finally said.

He sensed she was omitting something. He could feel it. Thought about her wording a beat.

"Okaaay…but what about the *servers?*"

A telling pause ticked past.

"Feds took 'em as evidence. Why?"

She was still holding out, but he wasn't about to push her.

"Damn! I was hoping to search them."

Dead air.

Arnold waited, convinced she was weighing another decision.

Several seconds later, she asked, "I need for you to prove you're being totally straight-up with me."

Arnold held out the phone, studied it a beat, put it back to his ear.

"Now *that's* interesting. Which begs the question, why would I be deceptive about this?"

"Seriously? You're working for lawyers, man, and those slimeballs're always up to some dangerously devious shit. Always. It's just how they roll."

"Not these two, girl. These dudes are *defense* lawyers and they're defending one of *us*. That's how I know."

Was that a scoff?

"Yeah? What's their names?"

Man, talk about paranoid.

"The lead attorney's Noah Cain, founder and senior partner of Cain Tidwell, Stowell."

"Hold on."

He heard clickity click in the background and assumed she was Googling him.

"No shit, you're crazy right, dude. That's the firm snatched Cap1tol's ass out the alligator's jaws."

Arnold nodded.

Cap1tol, the infamous hacker.

"Right you are. The other one's Palmer Davidson. He's defended me. Satisfied now?"

"Yeah, I get it."

Hmmm, an idea sparked…

"Were you in Seattle then?"

Suspicion returned.

"Sure, why?"

Nice!

The budding idea grew.

"Still live here?"

"Look, dude, is there a point to this game of Twenty Questions?"

"Bear with me, okay? You have another gig going?"

"Sorta."

But the word lacked conviction.

Encouraging.

"What's *sorta* mean?"

"Well, like you, I do spot IT work, so there're always ebbs and flows, why?"

"Because I was wondering if you'd have time to squeeze in an additional job now and then when I need help?"

She laughed dismissively.

"Not without knowing more."

"Works both ways, girl. You still haven't said if you're still here."

"Okay, I'll bite. Yeah, we're in Ballard."

A Seattle neighborhood.

Hmmm. Test drive her with a no-brainer update? For damn sure vet her more thoroughly than Fear. And if things go well...

"Look, here's the deal. I'm really jammed at the moment, so if you've got the capacity, I have an update I'd love you to do. I pay in Bitcoin."

He mentioned the rate he paid Fear.

"No prob, Glad to do it. How do I get the details?"

"I'll pop you an email the moment we finish up."

"Cool." Pause. "Dude?"

"Yeah?"

"Do you still want to look at those servers?"

Whoa.

"You *serious?* That's why I pinged you. Why?"

CHAPTER 17

"BESIDES SUFFERING A mild case of OCD when it comes to security, I'm four-plus paranoid about protecting my network. In particular, I make damn sure *everything's* backed up across redundant systems. Camano's tight-ass finance committee refused to allocate funds for off-site backups, so I simply took it upon myself to do it anyway. I mean, if I could get away with it, hell, why not?"

Holy shit.

Arnold rolled her words around his brain a moment. And loved it. Here was a stellar example of initiative, responsibility, cunning, forethought, and several other choice qualities he'd love to have in an employee. His interest meter pegged.

Hey dude, don't rush it.

"The thing those pencil-pushers didn't seem capable of grasping was the productivity lost if just *one* server took a dive. The work-around I came up with was to duplicate each server. For some reason those knuckleheads had no problem approving another server here or there, so over the period of a year I replicated the entire network *off-site.* Yeah, sure, the feds walked out with our servers while I sat in my office and said nada about any duplicates…you know, just in case we somehow pulled off a phoenix-out-of-the-ashes sorta stunt, but that, of course, didn't happen."

Double holy shit.

"You saying you still have them?"

She sounded shocked that he'd ask.

"Of course."

Wow. Couldn't believe it.

"Are they at your place?"

She snorted.

"You kidding? With the rents around here? No. As it is, we're cheek-to-jowl in a one-bedroom. No, those puppies are gathering dust in a self-storage place over in Interbay. Thought maybe I could use them one day but seriously doubt it now, way things are going."

Now for the killer question.

"Does one of them contain the press release?"

"Sure. I had the network programmed for an iterative backup each day at 11:59 PM. Things blew up the following week, so everything's exactly as it was the day the pin got pulled on that shit grenade. I never touched the duplicate servers, so they're like a time machine."

Her tone segued from suspicion to curiosity.

"Why do you ask?"

This conversation had just become The Greatest in the short history of Gold and Associates. Excitement began scintillating up and down his body.

"Is it possible to get a look at them?"

That would be a feat tantamount to a detective inspecting an untouched pristine year-old crime scene.

"Not a problem. Need help?"

Did he just detect a note of eagerness?

Hmmm…

"Long as it doesn't take you away from your work. Uh,

just how busy *are* you?"

She snorted derisively. True-confession time.

"Full disclosure? I'm not busy enough. Camano was my last steady gig. Meaning I'm delighted to do as much work as you throw my way."

"Great! But I'm just getting started so don't know what the hell I'm looking for yet."

"Understood. When do you want 'em?"

Arnold checked his watch. Oh, Jesus, he was already late, and he didn't want to inconvenience her.

"How does the morning work? Like first thing?"

"No prob on this end."

"Great. Give me the address and a time and I'll be there."

She recited the name, address, time, and told him to look for her in a silver Toyota in the parking lot as close as possible to the front door.

With the call finished, he worked through his next steps, made a few notes. Time for Chance's final walk of the day. Besides, he needed sleep. If possible. The problem was being so totally amped about getting his hands on those servers that he needed to unwind first.

But, he reminded himself, if something seems way too good to be true…

CHAPTER 18—Tuesday Morning

AS THE UBER bumped over the seam dividing street concrete from mud-stained parking lot asphalt, Arnold eyes locked onto Prisha's silver Toyota. It was the only vehicle near the front door of a boringly bland five-story battleship-gray box at the end of a string of concatenated cubes painted various hues of gray; perhaps reflecting the architect's dilemma over how to unobtrusively blend a large dull building into the aesthetic of a nearby apartment complex.

"This is fine," Arnold told the driver. "Thanks."

Arnold pushed out of the back seat, ran through wind-driven drizzle, and hopped into the front passenger seat of the waiting car. In the driver's seat sat an attractive dark-skinned female showcasing a wide engaging smile of perfect ultra-white teeth and piercing brown eyes.

"Prisha?" he asked, having never seen her face.

The woman recoiled.

"Who?"

Oh, shit.

Arnold grabbed the door handle.

"Sorry."

Laughing, she tugged his coat sleeve.

"Whoa, just messing with you, Arnold."

He slumped in the seat, hand on his chest.

"Jesus freaking Christ, I thought you were serious. You scared the crap out of me."

Another laugh, then, with a quick nod toward the storage building.

"Run for it?"

They streaked along a short stretch of sidewalk through what had just become a flat-out puddle-splattering rain, pushed through a glass door into a stark square lobby of drab gray sheetrock and roughly polished bare concrete. Prisha thumbed an elevator call button.

"Saw an Uber drop you. Are you one of those urbanites who don't believe in car ownership?"

He opened his mouth to mention the Mini in his Honolulu garage but figured it might precipitate further explanation, so he decided to lie. His friends—well, *acquaintances* was a more accurate descriptor—knew zip about him. Likewise, they were nothing to Arnold but an assortment of online assumed names—Primal Fear, for example—who placed a heavy premium on never disclosing a scrap of personal information of any sort to anyone under any circumstance.

"Naw, it's just that I'm in town for this job, so staying at a friend's…"

He instantly knew that somehow, someway, this lie would inevitably circle back to bite him in the ass.

They entered the elevator cage. She punched 3.

"Cool. Where's home, then?"

"Honolulu."

He felt his face light up in embarrassment for admitting to someone trapped in such a shitty November climate that his winters were spent there. On the other hand, Seattle *was* paradise the rest of the year.

She simply said, "Nice."

He tailed her down a hallway of fluorescent lights, drab primer-coated sheet rock, rubberized tiles, to a door secured with a single padlock, the interior hinting of dry wall, caulking, paint, and decaying sawdust.

"Here we go."

She unlocked the door, reached in, flicked on a two-bulb fluorescent ceiling fixture.

"Voila."

Filling the back half of the narrow rectangular space were a cluster of cardboard U-Haul boxes, a floor stand fan, and miscellaneous boxes stacked haphazardly around them. Prisha pulled apart the folded end of the closest box. Arnold saw Dell and Intel stickers affixed to a black metal case unscratched or dented. Obviously well cared for.

"Are they all in this good shape?" he asked.

"They are." Then blurted, "I'm happy to sell them to you, you want."

Was that a note of hope in her words? He turned to her. Yep, dead serious.

Probably needs the money.

"Sure, how much?"

"A hundred per?" She had no hesitation in her voice.

Yeah, she needs the cash.

Another idea sprouted in his brain.

"And the backup hard drives? You willing to part with those too?"

Her face brightened. She nodded.

"Hell, yeah. They're not doing me any good sitting here collecting dust. I'll let them go for fifty each."

He extended his hand, and they shook, cementing the sale.

"To sweeten the deal I'll even drive you back. How's that sound?"

"Definitely a plan. *Plus,* I know a bank on the way where I can score your cash."

She smiled broadly.

"Works for me."

They slapped high-fives.

* * *

"Where're we headed?" she asked, engine idling, as they waited for the light to turn green light so she could turn onto 15th Avenue West from the storage lot.

"Just aim for Green Lake. I'll give you more specific directions when we're closer to the street. The place's a real thrash to find if you don't have good GPS."

He'd noticed that hers either wasn't working or was not turned on.

She turned left, headed northbound on 15th Avenue toward the Ballard Bridge, the interior of the car settling into repetitive wiper slaps melding with the slosh of wet tires on a rain-soaked arterial, the heater struggling to disperse dimly tepid, humid air smelling loosely of damp wool.

After four blocks of silence, she asked, "How's business?"

"Can't complain."

He left it vague, hoping her question supported her interest in additional work, but he didn't want to push it until he had a clearer read on her.

The conversation settled back into the slosh of the tires and wipers as Arnold worked through a strategy. Collaborating on a project or two should give him sufficient opportunities to evaluate her more completely than their prior online encounters had. But for now, he was focused primarily on her honesty; a crucial point he'd neglected to nail down with Fear.

"Happy with your present work?" he asked as three lanes of traffic began funneling into two bridge lanes.

"Not really."

After sucking through her front teeth, she added, "Work's okay. Just not enough of it. Especially with all the shit that's hit us recently. Last year a repeat DUI offender T-boned my husband's Subaru. We're talking, like, a major-league impact. He's been partially disabled since, which makes me the sole breadwinner, so, to be honest, we're struggling financially, which makes living here difficult."

Ah, man...

"The other guy wasn't insured?"

A disgusted headshake.

"Nope. Said he couldn't afford it. Not only that, but the asshole's license had been jerked after his prior."

Another disgusted headshake.

"Ah, man, talk about a seriously sucky situation..."

Again, the conversation died, but was now flavored with the growing ease that two people develop when bonding at some level.

* * *

The rain had abated by the time she curbed the Toyota in front of his house.

"Lemme give you a hand with those," Prisha said, jumping out of the driver's side.

"Thanks. We can just set them on the porch, and I'll take them inside once they're all unloaded."

Hugging a U-Haul box, she paused to scope out the house.

"Nice place. Sure you don't want help getting them out of this shit?"

"Naw. My friend's a little weird about people being inside when he's gone," he said as the security system scanned his retina.

He then typed the security code into the keypad. He'd incorporated a killer security system for the new house during the planning phase of construction.

"No problem. I'll grab another box while you get these out of this dampness."

* * *

As she turned to leave after the last box was unloaded, Arnold remembered a critical item.

"Hey, before you take off, I assume I need a password and login info?"

After a laugh, she said, "Oh, man, thanks for reminding me. Absolutely. I'll text it from the car."

She was turning to leave once again when Arnold added, "And I'll send the info on the job I need done."

Continuing toward the car, she called over her shoulder, "Thanks, I appreciate the work."

"Hey…"

She stopped and turned.

"What?"

He opened his mouth, changed his mind, waved her off again. Better not take the shortcut that had tripped him up with Fear.

"Nothing. Thanks again."

Yeah, she was increasingly looking like a great candidate.

CHAPTER 19

ALL THE SERVER cases were in pristine shape, without a sign of physical abuse.

With his back propped against the kitchen sink, he considered their fate. A major item on his To-Do List for this place was to duplicate SAM here, just in case, God forbid, Honolulu SAM had to be shut down, even temporarily. A mirror network in a different geographic location would allow for uninterrupted workflow.

These second-hand screaming-deal machines—although older—would be great for kick-starting that project. On future visits, he could easily add and reconfigure newer machines until an identical neural network was operational.

And, as an added bonus, starting the project would be one more justification to peddle to Rachael (although she'd undoubtedly see it for exactly what it was: a situational afterthought). But it was also an excellent use for Prisha's old machines.

Problem solved.

He began to haul the boxes downstairs to the special room he'd designed to replace SAM 1.0's birthplace. The original one, along with all the contained equipment had been a total melt-job in the explosion and subsequent fire that had leveled the family Tudor.

Just like that original room, this one had proprietary temperature and humidity control and an independent electrical supply backed up by a 20KW self-activating generator in the unlikely event of a power failure.

Overkill?

No kidding.

But he would hate to lose one byte of work. Immediately after buying the Honolulu place, he'd made similar modifications to that guest room to accommodate SAM 2.0, the replacement neural network that replaced 1.0.

The striking resemblance to the prior room uncorked a flood of warm sepia-toned memories of countless hours cobbling together SAM from trial-and-error scratch. It now seemed like a lifetime ago. Perhaps it was. After all, he'd endured a significant evolution—technically and personally— since plugging that first PC power cord into the 110-volt outlet.

All right already, back to work.

What next? Organize a plan, that's what.

* * *

Leaning against the counter, the microwave warming a mug of chocolate milk, Arnold wrestled with offering Prisha the Seattle Associate position. No doubt she needed the work. And would probably jump at the offer. And her technical competence was impressive. She lived here in town. Why hesitate? Why not just offer it to her and scratch that item off the list? And in the process, perhaps gain a few brownie points with Rachael.

Well, because you didn't do your due diligence with Fear, dude. That's why.

Shit.

Management issues already and he hadn't even hired his first associate. How much more complicated would this become with, say, five employees? Exponentially increasing headaches? Restless nights? This was just one more glaring example of why Gold and Associated needed a dedicated business manager.

His iPhone pinged; an email. He checked the screen. Kara? Seriously? Before he could look at the message, his custom ringtone started blasting. He did a double take.

Martina?

Why would Mr. Davidson's ex-wife be calling?

"Hey, Martina. What up?"

"Oh, God, Arnold. Medic One is rushing Palmer to the hospital."

Arnold's stomach hit the floor.

" *What?* What happened?"

"I'm not really sure, but I suspect it's a heart attack?"

Jesus.

"Which hospital?"

"The one up on First Hill, the old Catholic one...I'm blanking on its name..."

Yeah, so was he.

"Okay, I know it. You there now?"

"No, not yet. My Uber's about to pull up to the ER now."

"I'm on my way."

* * *

C'mon, c'mon...

Arnold muzzled an almost overwhelming urge to scream. Had some nefarious city traffic engineer purposely lengthened the James and Boren traffic light for some weirdo personal pleasure? His driver had correctly jumped on I-5 southbound to the James Street off-ramp, but since exiting the ramp every damn light turned into a bottleneck, allowing only two or three cars through with each green light, taking for-fucking-ever. His double-me-over gut-ache was now back, slicing through him like an acetylene torch. He had his right hand pressing against his abdomen in spite of it rendering absolutely no relief.

Shit, grab a pack of Tums or something, dude.

Oh, God, please don't let him die.

C'mon, c'mon...

If Mr. Davidson died, it would be like losing a parent all over again. Since becoming Arnold's lawyer in the aftermath of Howie's murder, the man had slowly assumed the role of father-figure and mentor. Well, maybe the father-figure part was a little overdramatic, but he'd definitely become a major influence in his life. Family, for sure. Okay, adopted family, but family, nonetheless.

Oh God, please don't let him die.

C'mon, c'mon...

* * *

After an excruciatingly endless wait in line to speak to the single clerk manning the information desk—a grossly obese, bleached-blond, African American with glistening gold incisors, shocking pink lipstick, and an in-your-face aura of bored indifference—Arnold finally was able to locate the Cardiac Care waiting area.

Martina was perched fence-post rigid on a worn reddish-orange fabric chair, her typically well-put-together face mascara-streaked, injected red eyes focused somewhere distant. The transformation was disorienting, like viewing a dead friend's face; you know it's them, but then again it isn't. Although clearly tense, she came across as atypically vulnerable and fragile; a side otherwise hidden, and this frightened him.

Was she destined for the ER too?

He squatted on his haunches directly facing her, gently taking her hands in his.

"Martina," he said softly.

It seemed to take a moment for her to register that he was there, but then she immediately reached out to bear-hug him, her body heaving with muffled sobs.

Jesus, did he die before I could get here?

A moment later, she was squeezing his biceps at arm's length with what felt like a death grip, eyes boring into him, sobs tapering into a silence.

He asked, "What is it?"

"A heart attack, a serious one."

"But he's alive, right?" he asked with every ounce of hope he could muster.

"Yes, thank God."

She spaced again for a beat, as if silently giving thanks.

He hugged her, indebted for giving him hope that his mentor stood a chance of surviving this crisis.

"He'll come out of this okay," he said with surprising conviction that wasn't really not there. "Some of the best doctors in the city practice here." Proclaiming this as much to shore up his own spirit as hers. He dropped into the chair to her right, leaned forward, elbows on knees. "Tell me exactly what they said."

After a vacant robotic nod, she jerked a tissue from her purse, dabbed the corners of her eyes, glanced at the mascara-streaked paper, wadded it into a tight ball, tossed it back in her purse as if annoyed at such a public display of emotion.

"*Oh, caro*," she moaned, with a sorrowful headshake. "I must look a fright."

She gave a short, embarrassed laugh.

He opened his mouth to deny it, realized how disingenuous it would be, so settled for, "That's the least of our worries right now."

Finally reigning in her emotions, she dabbed her eyes again with a fresh tissue, inspected it, again shaking her head with obvious disgust. Arnold waited, silently praying for God to spare Mr. Davidson's life.

She drifted off, eyes growing vaguely distant, but then seemed to snap back.

"The doctor—I think she was a doctor, but I guess she could've been a nurse...she had on blue scrubs and a white coat, but I didn't think to check her name tag—told me they would take him straight to the cath lab for an angiogram and if need be, a stent..."

She slipped back into nail-biting silence.

While waiting for her to continue, he began reviewing various pleasant memories of him, then realized she was silent because that was all she had to tell him. This left him at a loss for what to say or do, so they remained side by side, simmering in respective anxieties as seconds glacially incremented to minutes, waiting for an update on what was transpiring beyond two heavy swinging doors ten feet down the hall. Sturdy doors, each one with an eye-level rectangular red sign engraved with bold white letters: AUTHORIZED PERSONNEL ONLY. Perhaps she too was praying for God to spare the man she clearly loved but, for whatever reasons, had divorced.

Are Rachael and I headed for a similar relationship stalemate?

A paroxysm of guilt rippled through him for thinking of his own situation while Mr. Davidson's fate lay in the hands of an unknown physician somewhere on the other side of those intimidating doors.

I should be doing something for him instead of sitting here doing nothing.

What?

Well, anything but sit here, staring at a beige wall as

seconds evaporate. Do something for him.

There was nothing to do here but wring his hands.

Why not put the effort into the work he wanted done?

But there was also Martina to consider. She clearly needed emotional support. Leaving him torn. Support her or do something to help Mr. Davidson.

He began to pace, struggling to prioritize conflicting emotions. Stay with Martina to await an update? That seemed like the right thing to do. But how long would that take? No way to know. And what about Chance? How long since he'd been outdoors? Hours? He *should* stay, but...

Ah, man...

He dropped to his haunches again, gently took her hands.

"I need a favor."

She remained distant, off somewhere before his voice registered, then turned to him.

"What?"

"Did the doctor say how long this might take?"

Brow furrowed, she shook her head.

"I...don't know...I didn't ask."

She withdrew her hands, knuckle-wiped the corner of an eye, inhaled deeply, then swiped her nose with the back of the hand, seemed to realize what she'd just done, and with a frown wiped her hand on her skirt, disgusted at herself.

He sat down next to her.

"Look, I'm in a bind. Chance's at home. I need to take care of him, but don't want to abandon you. There anyone who can come sit with you until I can come back? Family, friends?"

She shook her head, dabbed the corners of her eyes again with a sodden tissue, glanced around perhaps for a trash can. Seeing none, she angrily stuffed the soggy mass back into her purse.

"My relatives are in Italy, and we don't have children.

Our friends have their own obligations..."

Aw, shit.

Now he felt worse for what he was about to do but needed to check on Chance.

"Look, I'm really sorry but I need to walk and feed him. I'll come back soon as that's taken care of, okay?"

She studied his eyes intently.

"You *really* care about Palmer, don't you," she stated as unambiguous fact. Then quickly added, "Don't worry. In spite of how much of a mess I must seem, I'm fine. It's just...this hit so unexpectedly..." A bitter laugh. "That sounds all wrong; you never expect something like this..."

"No, you never do," he agreed, still torn.

"I've pleaded with him to see his doctor about that damn shoulder but..." she trailed off, slowly shaking her head.

"But it's his *right* shoulder," Arnold said, "I thought—"

"So did I," she said, cutting him off. "About a month ago I Googled angina. Guess what? It manifests in any number of bizarre symptoms all over the chest. It doesn't have to be in the left shoulder area as so commonly thought..."

She drifted again, her vacant stare returning.

"Martina, this isn't your fault. This isn't anybody's fault. It is what it is, and we have to be here to help him get through this."

Jesus, Little Lord Trite!

He hated such hackneyed clichés, but, hey, there it was.

She patted his hand in a *thank-you* or *it's-all-right* sort of way.

"Go. Take care of your boy and please, don't come back. That would only be a waste of your time that I'm sure you can put to more productive use. After all, you will be helping Palmer if you work on this case for him. I'll call the moment I have news. Go. Please. Take care of Chance *and* Palmer."

He squeezed her hand.

"You sure? Seriously, I can be back in forty-five minutes to an hour."

She smiled.

"I *am* serious, Arnold. You'll be more help to us if you focus your energy on Palmer's case. I know that's what *he'd* want."

An idea popped to mind.

"How about this: once you have an update and they're done in there"—he jutted his chin at the doors—"come by my place for dinner, okay?"

She returned a quick pursed-lip headshake.

"That's sweet of you to offer, but I have no idea how long this might take. It could be fifteen minutes or could be three hours."

A resigned sigh.

"Doesn't matter, long as you'll eat reheated pizza. I'll have one ready for whenever that happens to be. Midnight, one AM, whenever. You *still* need to eat, remember."

"I really doubt I'll be hungry." She gave his hand a motherly pat. "I'll call when I have news."

CHAPTER 20

AFTER TEXTING RACHAEL Arnold slumped into the seat to stare blankly at apartments blurring past. Felt guilty as hell for leaving but would feel just as guilty if he'd stayed: your classic no-win situation.

James Brown jolted him back to reality. He glanced the phone in hand. Rachael. Swiped Accept.

"Hey, Rach."

"Where are you?"

It was an excellent question. He glanced out the window.

"I'm on Aurora, heading home to take care of Chance."

"How serious is it? Will he be okay?"

More good questions.

"We don't know anything yet."

"We?"

"Yeah, Martina and me. She called me soon as Medic One took him. I went straight there."

He explained what little he knew about Davidson's condition.

"I can only imagine how upsetting this must be for you. *I'm* upset and I'm not nearly as close to him as you are. Do you have an idea how long it'll be before you know anything more?"

He blew a resigned heavy sigh.

"Not at all. Martina said she'd call the moment she has an update."

"Text me soon as you hear. Hey, I'm really sorry, but I'm at work so need to go. I just thought we could get more said if I called instead of texting. Fingers crossed."

Although he was relieved to hear her voice, the unmistakably frost coating her words left him unsettled and worried. It felt like some nebulous threatening emotion was steeping inside her. Then again, he assured himself, she *was* at work, so this wasn't an appropriate moment to ask the "what's wrong" question.

Still...

"Yeah, will do. Love you."

But she was already gone.

* * *

Arnold decided to take the long route instead of ducking out the back to cut through the alley, which would give Chance more nose time and exercise, but at the expense of time that otherwise could be spent on work, especially since every delay was rippling through to his Honolulu return. Regardless, Chance's welfare shouldn't be sacrificed on account of this issue with Rachael.

Rachael, Jesus...

Her ill-defined ominous tone totally uncorked the bottle that had been containing a waxing and waning free-floating anxiety, which, in turned cranked up his gut pain. Something was definitely bugging her; and it was more complex than this trip. Not understanding her issue stoked his anxiety even further—round and round in a self-regenerating miserable vicious cycle. He wanted to scream.

After dumping his parka in the closet, he tossed the box of Flavio's on the counter and called Martina.

"Any news yet?"

"I was just taking out my phone to call you. Yes. The cardiologist said she stented two severely clogged arteries, so *that* part's over and he's being moved to Coronary Care. I can't see him yet, but she said I could very soon, so if I cut you off, that's the reason."

"*Whew.*" Arnold fist-pumped air. "That's good news, right?"

"Yes and no."

She explained that from the time the paramedics applied the heart monitor to him, he'd periodically had a serious arrhythmia that required an IV injection to control. Was it serious? She hedged. From ignorance, or was she trying to protect him from worrying? Another anxiety bomb exploded in his gut.

"Look, give me"—he checked his watch, factoring in traffic—"fifteen, twenty minutes, and I'll be back."

"No, no, *please* don't, Arnold. Knowing that the stents are in and he's in CCU, I'm in a much better place emotionally. I prefer it if you'd stay put and focus on being productive. I'm certain this is what Palmer would want."

His first impulse was to ignore he words and go anyway. On the other hand, she had just scored a couple major points; the root problem *was* taken care of, so the *most* critical danger was over. And, knowing Mr. Davidson, she was undoubtedly right about what he would want.

Besides, what could he accomplish wringing his hands in the waiting room other than provide Martina emotional support? Sure sounded as if she was in a better emotional state and going against her wishes might just piss her off. Especially considering what an extremely guarded, private person she was. She'd been mortified by her earlier emotional display. He believed she sincerely preferred that he stay and focus on work.

Still...

"You sure?" he asked tentatively, still undecided.

"Yes, Arnold. I'm quite certain. I'll call the moment I've talked to him."

Well, that was clear.

"Okay, but look, please drop by for dinner regardless of the time, okay? Have you eaten *anything* today?"

Jesus, you're sounding like Mom.

"Not yet, but I will. I'm worried that if I leave this area, they'll be too busy to look for me and I'll miss an update."

"Okay, got it. So how about this: talk to him, make sure you're comfortable with his condition, *then* come by. The pizza's already here waiting for you and it's way more than I can eat."

"Thanks. I'll let you know."

Which he translated to, *don't expect me.*

"Look, I'm serious; you need to eat. Promise me you'll eat *something* tonight. And if you change your mind, the pizza's good either cold or rewarmed. Okay?"

"Thanks, Arnold."

Once again, making it clear to not expect her.

Arnold was shocked to realize it was now early evening. Where the hell had the day gone? Then again, why the shock? It had been busy, what with all the shit happening. Phone in hand, butt against the counter, he pondered what to do next? Eat? Naw. Not really hungry.

Probably exactly how Martina feels.

In the basement room, he surveyed the array of cardboard boxes.

Where to start?

Decided to power up each machine until he located the web server. He opened the nearest box and stopped.

Jesus, what a freaking idiot.

Not one damn keyboard, mouse, power cable, or monitor in the whole freaking house. The only fully intact computers here were an old laptop and his Surface. Aw, man, he could kick himself.

Okay, think…

After Siri coughed up the phone number for the nearest Best Buy—the one out by the Northgate mall—he listened to a curt recording stating that they closed at seven PM. It was precisely 7:01.

Shit.

Now what?

He shook his head in disgust. What a massive lapse of foresight. Jesus, if he didn't get *something* accomplished tonight…blowing an entire evening simply wouldn't cut it.

* * *

"Look, I'm *really* sorry to bother you, but is there any chance you have an extra power cable, monitor, and keyboard lying around I could borrow? I don't have any of that stuff here, and—"

"Wow, am I glad you called. I thought about that as I was, like, a block from home and wondered. Yeah, sure, all that stuff's over in the storage locker. Why, you need them tonight?"

A blast of relief whistled through him.

"Matter of fact, yes. And it's like super-important that I get them tonight. Is there any possibility I could meet you there, I mean, like soon?" He felt like a total dick for asking, but his only other option was to sit on his hands until Best Buy opened in the morning, and blowing an entire evening was—especially given the circumstances—unacceptable.

His iPhone pinged. A text. Uh-oh, the only person that texted him was Rachael.

"Not a problem, dude," Prisha said. "It's my bad anyway. They're supposed to be part of the deal. I had a total mind fart when we were there and forgot to grab them. Tell you what, it'd be faster if I run over, grab them, and drop them by."

Arnold would've hugged her through the phone if he could've.

"Thank you, thank you, thank you."

"No problem. Hey, I know what it's like to have a job hanging over your head."

Score another point in her favor.

"Look, let me pay for the inconvenience."

At least that would help placate his guilt for ruining her evening. Besides, she could use the money.

"Like hell you will. I'm stuck here having to watch this shitty Netflix series Vihaan loves, so this is my perfect excuse to bug outta here."

Okay, but there had to be some way to reimburse her for the inconvenience.

"Have you guys eaten?"

"Nope. In fact, we were debating what to order when you called. Could've been a Grubhub night, but now, since I'm going out…"

"Fine, it's settled then. I have a ton of pizza here. It'll need to be warmed up, but hey, it's here ready to eat when you guys arrive."

After hanging up, he checked the text. Spam. *Spam?* How weird…he never got spam, not with the filters he had. Oh, well…

He started drumming the phone against his palm, thinking; if Prisha, her husband, and Martina all showed up, he'd be short of food. Just to be on the safe side, he should probably run over and snag another pizza. By ordering it now, it would be in the oven by the time he blew through Flavio's front door. He sat down to his Surface.

And immediately noticed an email in his inbox from Kara.

Kara?

Seriously? Alarm bells began to clang from deep in his brain. Felt way wrong. He and Kara *never* exchanged emails. Their only communications had been during the law-firm-ransomware gig. Even then, they'd either exchanged texts or spoken face to face. *Never* via email. Meaning, if it walked like a duck and quacked like a duck, it was undoubtedly bullshit.

Okay, sure, he was, like, emotionally rattled over this Rachael thing, whatever it was, but he wasn't *so* rattled to fall for a punk-ass phishing scam. For sure, he would check it out, but only after going DefCon 5 and only then after scanning the living shit out of it for malware.

Hold on, dude, this is the Seattle house.

It's not equipped to deal with this problem. And if he were serious about building a duplicate SAM here, it would require having an "air gapped" work area: a digital equivalent of a biohazard laboratory. Hmm...wait for Prisha to drop off the peripherals? No, that would waste more time. Ahh, that old laptop tucked away upstairs in the bedroom closet.

Perfect.

After updating the malware software, he disabled its Wi-Fi capability, totally isolating it from his home network. Then—to be absolutely belt and suspenders cautious—he powered down the router, eliminating the house Wi-Fi. You can never be too careful about these things.

Although satisfied the laptop was air-gapped, he double-checked each step. Yep, good to go. Now, his worst-case scenario would be having to reformat the hard drive.

Sure enough, the suspect email contained a RAT—a Remote Access Trojan—which was a chunk of code that when embedded in your computer allowed the sender to access your machine. A jolt of adrenaline was pounding through his arteries, jacking his heart rate, tingling his fingers and toes.

You're under attack, dude.

After a momentary panic, he inhaled deeply and began to walk through what, if anything, needed to be done to harden his present security. Because SAM was pivotal to his financial health, he'd become obsessive about its firewalls. After mentally checking a few items, he grew satisfied with his present safeguards but began worrying about a new vulnerability: this house.

Especially now that he was initializing a duplicate network.

He powered down and unplugged the laptop, trudged upstairs, turned back on the modem, reestablishing his Wi-Fi. Then, using his Microsoft Surface, he tightened the bolts on SAM's firewalls.

Okay, did I forget anything?

Didn't think so. Went through it again.

Yeah, we're good.

Then he was pacing tight circles, finger-combing his curly hair, thinking hard. Who sent it? More importantly, why? This wasn't random, that's for sure. Not coming from the law firm. And under Kara's email. No, he was definitely being targeted. But why? Who had he pissed off? No idea.

Okay, so why Kara's email account?

Hmm…good question. Now *that* was no coincidence. Although he bet she hadn't sent it, that could be easily verified with a phone call. He was about to dial her when his phone rang.

CHAPTER 21

"HOW'S HE DOING?" Arnold asked.

"The doctors were annoyingly vague about that," Martina said. "They claim to not have a good estimate of how much damage his heart sustained."

The optimistic edge to her voice now replaced with indisputable pessimism.

Oh, shit, this doesn't sound good.

"But he's hanging in there, right?"

Please God...

"Yes. So far..."

Was that a hint of fear in her voice?

"But?"

She hesitated.

"The CCU doctor says the arrhythmia's more frequent and is extremely problematic...in her very words."

Arnold fought to swallow a ballooning lump in his throat.

"Oh, Martina..." he croaked, but his words evaporated before they could be uttered. He wanted to say something positive, but given her pessimistic tone, figured she wouldn't buy it, so opted for, "How are *you* doing?"

She dissolved into a series of gut-wrenching sobs

intermixed with wet, gurgling, snot-clogged gasps. He visualized her swiping at her face with a sopping Kleenex.

"Sorry, Arnold, I…"

Oh, shit, Prisha will be showing up any minute now.

He tried to estimate the drive time from the storage unit but had no idea where in Ballard she'd been or what time she'd left. He glanced at his watch, realized how irrelevant that was.

"Look, I'm expecting a delivery any minute and as soon as it arrives, I'll come back up there."

"No, Arnold. *Please don't.* I don't want *anyone* near me. I *am* serious about this. Do *not* come."

Emphatic, leaving no room for debate.

He frantically scoured his brain for a fallback position, a way to effectively support her remotely.

"Okay, I get it. But you have to look out for *yourself* so you can be there for him when he gets better. Understand what I'm saying?"

When she didn't respond, he added, "You need a break from the constant stress. That includes eating at least *something.* Please take a break from that waiting room for a few minutes *Then* go back and stay all night if you need to. Have you eaten *anything?*"

Jesus, enough with the Jewish mother schtick.

"No. And honestly, even if I were hungry—which I'm not—I don't think I could keep anything down. The thought of food…"

Yeah, got that.

His appetite was, like, adios, amigo.

"Martina, please at least drink some water, okay?"

Alright already. Jesus.

"I'll pick up something from a vending machine later."

Arnold caught himself glancing at the door, wishing the freaking bell would chime. The sooner Prisha dropped off that stuff, the sooner he could jet back up there. Despite Martina's emphatic denial, she did need support. Yeah, he totally got that she didn't want anyone seeing her in such a disheveled state, but hey, they're family, right?

"I'll be there soon as I can. This isn't up for debate."

"No. *Don't.*" Pause. "I'm not sure how I can make myself any more clear, Arnold. Stay *there.* I appreciate the thought, but *I do not want* to be around *anyone.* And that includes you. Just knowing you're only a phone call away is more help than you can imagine. Believe me."

Oh, man... was this her pride or her way of coping? Did it matter?

She couldn't be more crystalline. He nodded, decided on a compromise.

"Please promise to call me the moment you have more news? No matter the time."

"Of *course.*"

* * *

He paced again, hoping the physical activity might dampen the unrelenting waves of anxiety rampaging through his gut.

Think. Do *something. What was I about to do when she called...*

Ah, of course, Kara's email.

He read his notes and kicked the puzzle around his mind a few minutes. Point: it made zero sense for Kara to send the phishing scam. So, who the hell did?

Someone with a grudge, obviously. Who? Fear? Naw, that dude had no cause. Not yet at least. And how would he even know about her?

...know about her...

The point kept vibrating in his brain until some facts dropped into alignment like a string of oranges on a slot machine: the sender had to know Kara knew Arnold. The only way for that to work is if he had access to the firm's email server. Ergo…he picked up his cell phone.

"Hey, a quick question for you," he said.

Instead of zinging him with one of her typically flip retorts, Kara paused, perhaps picking up on the urgency in his voice, especially at this time of evening.

"Sure, what?"

"Have you ever had any interaction with a dude who goes by Primal Fear? Either at work or online."

Although she only dabbled on the fringes of amateur hacking, she did hang on some Dark Net chats.

"I don't think so. Why?"

Tell her? What would it hurt?

"I just received a phishing attack from you via the firm's office email. Did you send it?"

No hesitation, certainly not equivocal.

"From *my* account? Hell no. Are you *serious?*"

"Dead serious. I'm betting it's from our hacker."

Arnold waited for a reply, which took close to five seconds.

"How would Hacker even know we knew each other?"

"Did you and Mr. Cain mention me in any emails?"

"Of course. He sent a memo to the entire firm that you're on the Lopez defense."

Shit, it was so freaking obvious.

He whistled.

"In that case, he's in your network," he muttered as other pieces of the puzzle began snapping together. There was a brief pause, then: "I know that network was totally clean two months ago, right? You guys haven't picked up any new hacker clients since then, have you?"

"Just Lopez."

The doorbell rang. Prisha.

"Shit, someone's at the door. Call you right back."

"Don't bother. I'll call *you* soon as I find that fucker."

CHAPTER 22

PRISHA'S ARMS WERE wrapped around a cardboard box overflowing with power cords, cables, a keyboard, and mouse.

"Here." After setting the box at his feet, she turned back toward the car, calling over her shoulder, "I'll grab the monitors outta the trunk."

Leaving the door ajar for her, he lugged the box into the kitchen, set it on the floor next to the basement stairs. A moment later she placed two monitors next to the box and began eyeballing the interior.

"Wow, nice place."

"Thanks." He pulled out his wallet and nodded at the pile of cords and two monitors. "Here, here's for gas."

"Naw, man," she said, waving off the offer. "All part of the deal. I just kick myself for forgetting them when we were packing up the other shit. Wasn't thinking, I guess."

"Well then, here's for the home delivery." He pushed the bills toward her again.

She shook her head.

"Naw, not necessary. Fact is, I'm happy to do it." She paused, still eyeing the interior. "Truth is, I was looking for an excuse to get outta there for a few minutes," and gave a woeful headshake. "I know how totally shitty this must sound, but it's nice to just get away from him now and then, being cooped up together all day, day after day…"

"Your husband?"

"Yeah. Sorry. Know how bad that's gotta sound, but ever since his injury there're times he just wears thin. It wouldn't be so difficult if I worked in an office instead of our one-bedroom, but I don't, so it is what it is."

The subject was making Arnold uneasy, not sure what, if anything, to say.

"Hey, I've got some really good pizza here. At least let me feed you."

She shook her head.

"Naw, thanks, but I really need to bounce. I know dinner'll be waiting for me. He said he's planning to Grubhub-surprise me." She nodded toward the pile of equipment next to the basement door. "Hope this helps."

* * *

With Prisha gone, he called Martina.

"Anything?"

Her voice carried less-megavolt amperage and sounded more emotionally grounded—or was his perpetual optimism coloring his view?

"Only that he's stable but isn't out of the woods yet by any stretch. That damn arrythmia's the overriding concern now."

"And you? How're you holding up?"

She inhaled audibly.

"Truthfully? I'm emotionally bankrupt and utterly exhausted."

"Yeah, I bet. I'm doing about the same." Pause. "Have you eaten yet?"

"No, not yet," she answered with sufficient ambiguity to suggest it *might* be pending, but to not count on it.

"Me neither. Remember, there's a ton of pizza here waiting for you. It's cold, but hey, that's why God invented ovens, right? Offer's good any time from now until…forever," he said, trying for upbeat, but knowing it came out flat.

Another heavy resigned sigh.

"That's sweet of you, but I'll stay put for an hour or so, then go straight home to bed. I doubt I can sleep but a Xanax will certainly uncoil my nerves a little."

Yeah, he probably wouldn't be able to sleep either.

"Look, I'll be working all night, so feel free to call anytime for any reason. Consider me your personal emotional-support hot line. Seriously. I mean it."

"I know you do, Arnold. Thank you. I mean that in all sincerity."

* * *

"How do you want to play this?" Kara asked when she called back.

Her question caught him pathetically unprepared.

"Did you mention this to anyone else?"

Her hesitation answered the question.

Yeah, she had. Probably Mr. Cain.

She sounded apologetic.

"I did. This is a serious enough breach of security that I felt it necessary to notify Mr. Cain. I couldn't see any other option."

Arnold didn't blame her. As her boss and managing partner, Cain needed to be informed of a major security breach.

"I get it." He paused, still mentally flipping through options. "Done anything with it yet?"

Kara scoffed.

"You must be kidding. The moment I found it, I backed the hell off. This shit's totally outside my wheelhouse, dude. Last thing I need is to inadvertently tip the shithead who's using it. Why? What're you thinking?"

"Good move. Those can definitely turn into landmines if you're not careful." He paused, still scratching for a strategy and plan, but with everything bouncing off the walls of his brain, he couldn't focus worth a damn. "Truth be told, I haven't had time to think this through, but my knee-jerk reaction's to come up with a way to leverage it to our advantage. You cool with that?"

"*I* am, but seriously doubt Cain will be. He immediately went insanely apeshit when I told him and wants us to meet him in the office, like, first thing tomorrow morning. You better believe he'll want it removed before the office opens. I'm almost shocked he didn't demand it be removed tonight. Oh, and you better count on him requesting a full damage assessment."

Shit.

"I'll see what I can come up with."

* * *

Slumped in the chair, Arnold scoured his brain for a clever way to weaponize the RAT for an advantage, perhaps as a way to help identify Hacker or to leak selective disinformation. But, he couldn't focus clearly, and a half-assed poorly thought-out plan carried serious risk of serious blowback, especially when going up against this character.

The only good news was knowing about it answered a few key questions; like how the hell Hacker knew Arnold was working for the defense. Also, how Hacker sent the RAT from Kara's email. But the scary bad news was that Asshole now knew every detail of the work on the Lopez defense.

Kara was undoubtedly correct that Mr. Cain would

demand its immediate removal. In other words, it was a huge waste of time to even worry about how to weaponize the thing.

But the moment Hacker failed to access the malware and failed, he'd damn well know it'd been discovered. Logical conclusion? Arnold Gold removed it. Meaning, if Arnold was worried about Hacker now, he should double down on that concern from here on out.

He sat back to ponder how best to move forward. How severe was the risk to him? A key question: how much critical intel did Asshole possess about him? He knew his name and by now, undoubtedly knew about his house. But just how far would he take this?

Huh.

It all depended on his motivation and there was no way to judge that. The only good news was that so far SAM's firewalls hadn't been probed. Yeah, but how long before that phase kicked in? Given enough scratching through records...

Under the normal circumstances, locking horns with your ho-hum, run-of-the-mill hacker wouldn't give him indigestion.

But this asshole?

This was freaking different.

CHAPTER 23

ARNOLD DEBATED CALLING Rachael to update
her on Mr. Davidson's condition. She was probably snuggled
up in bed reading before lights out. Was she scheduled to work
in the morning? If so, was she sleeping now? He decided to
text so she could read it whenever.

He leaned back.

Okay, where was I?

Oh, right, sorting out which machine was Camano's web
server. Jesus, with everything going on, his mind seemed to
have turned into a thought kaleidoscope.

After lugging all the myriad equipment to the computer
room, he began organizing it by setting the five servers side by
side, then lining up the external back-up drives along the
opposite wall. For now, he would use only one monitor and
move it from machine to machine.

He started a new list in the iPhone Note app to keep track
of additional items he would need to build his SAM clone, then
ordered a small desk from Amazon for next day delivery.
Next, he ordered two five-foot high steel racks for housing the
servers. Might possibly need a third depending on the number
of additional hard discs added. Once those components were

up and running, he planned to stock additional hardware as needed. At least now the cornerstone was set, officially kicking off a pipedream project.

Thirty minutes later, the first Camano server was running on the network, making it internet accessible from any Wi-Fi connection to the internet he was using; the local Starbucks, Honolulu, or Abu Dhabi. Okay, sure, it was only the one server in a long-term project, but it symbolized a significant tangible start, a chest-warming start. The next task was to batten down every conceivable security hatch this small network expansion opened.

Finally convinced his network was Fort Knox-secure—at least as secure as possible yet remain operable—Arnold jotted down and reviewed each of his next steps. They appeared logical and sound but...was he missing something? Didn't think so, yet a niggling suspicion warned he was possibly overlooking something obvious, for the obvious ones were always the easiest to miss.

Couldn't see it, yet knew there must one out there, lurking, waiting to bite him in the ass.

Another wave of gut pain struck.

He paused to take a sober look at himself. His gut was hurting, his nerves were fried, and his anxiety was maxed.

Stop work until he'd had a chance to reboot his brain with some serious Zs?

Yeah, that was the smart move. He sent himself an email to review tonight's work in the morning. It was now officially time to pop the cork on a bottle of wine to let it breathe while he took Chance on an evening stroll.

"Want to go for a walk?"

Chance exploded into a blur of paws scrambling for traction on the polished concrete, finally caught it, and kicked into four-paw drive, rocketing toward the front door.

Laughing, Arnold hurried to catch up.

* * *

The rain had eased up, but the annoying wind chill continued discovering new paths through any opportunity. They headed for the Green Lake Park, Chance off-leash, savoring his late-evening nose time, investigating shrubs as only dogs can. Arnold slid into a morose funk over all the shit pummeling him.

Approaching East Green Lake Drive North, Arnold told Chance, "Stay," and paused to glance both ways, saw only a glistening bare street and streetlights strobed by wind-driven dancing branches. "Okay, boy."

Chance bolted into the street, beelining for the scent-laden park. Arnold trudged after him, hands deep in his parka, his mind a morass of counterproductive gloom. Suddenly, out of squid ink shadows, a blur grabbed his attention, triggering an alarm bell.

"Chance! Stop!"

Chance stopped, began to look back just as a mass slammed his right flank with a sickening *thump*, hurling him into an unyielding tree trunk. Chance let out a gut-wrenching yelp before sliding limply onto glistening grass.

Horror-stricken, Arnold bolted to him and dropped to his knees. Yelping, Chance was struggling frantically to right himself. To Arnold's horror, he saw white bone poking through a bleeding wound on his right hip.

Wanting to minimize further damage to the fracture, Arnold said, "Easy, boy, I've got you," and reached out to keep him from struggling to get upright. Chance yelped, reared up, bit Arnold's hand. Arnold jerked it away, immediately realized his mistake, gently replaced it on Chance's head, cooing softly, "Good boy, take it easy, I've got you."

"Hey, man, sorry, couldn't stop in time."

Arnold whipped around toward the voice: a kid in a black

coat, hood up, astride a Red Jump rental bike. His first impulse was to strangle the fucker, but he was too concerned about Chance, so returned to him. The injured pooch was now on his left side whimpering plaintively, Arnold gently pressing a reassuring hand to his head trying to calm him much as possible.

"Got a phone on you?"

Asshole.

"I swear I didn't see him, man, until it was too late, but yeah, I do. Why?"

"Do me a favor. Find the nearest emergency vet." Then added, "An *open one,*" just in case the dude needed clarity.

"I'm on it, man."

"Asshole," Arnold muttered before leaning into Chance's face, softly cooing calming assurances.

Chance's muscles unknotted a bit, but his soft gut-wrenching whimpers continued, shredding Arnold's heart.

"Yo, the Emerald City Clinic is over on Stone Way. That's gotta be the closest."

"They open? For sure? This time of night?"

"Website says twenty-four hours a day."

"Call them to make sure, then tell them I'm bringing in a severely injured dog." Then added, just in case the driver was hesitant. "Tell him he'll be wrapped in my coat."

"You got it."

Arnold continued consoling Chance.

"You're okay, Daddy's here."

Then he eased back. Chance seemed to find sufficient assurance from his words to stop struggling but continued whimpering in pain. Convinced that Chance would stay put, Arnold fished his cell from his pocket, punched up the Uber app, plugged in the emergency clinic as his destination. Thank God drivers were always circling this area. With the car on the way, he turned to the bike rider, but the dude was gone.

CHAPTER 24—Wednesday 1:35 AM

INTENSE WAVES OF restless anxiety rampaged through his chest—making him feel on the verge of aerosolizing and being blown through the waiting room by the humid, fur-scented warm air pouring from the wall vent.

Somewhere during the trip to the Emerald City Clinic, a lump of molten lava had formed in the center of his gut, making him want to scream. But he knew there was nothing he could do to soothe it; an unfortunate lesson he'd learned while narrowly dodging Naseem's lethal pursuit of him.

Once that sucker got started...

Jesus, he had to do *something* other than stand in the middle of the waiting room feeling totally useless. Call Rachael? No, it was 11:35 Honolulu time and typically, she would be asleep. Wake her? Hated to, but, after all, this was a flaming emergency.

No, don't call. Text. She routinely muted her phone before dousing the light. She could pick it up in the morning. Yes? No?

C'mon, dude, decide. Freaking do something.

Yeah, text.

He thumbed a concise description of Chance's injuries

and that he was presently awaiting a status report, then remained standing there, glancing anxiously this way and that, wanting to move or scream or just do *something,* all the while knowing there wasn't a damn thing he *could* do but continue to emotionally ricochet off the walls.

His phone dinged a text: *Hope he's okay.*

No three dots under the dialog box, meaning she'd immediately ditched the app. He typed *Thanks* anyway.

No dots appeared, yet he continued to stare at the screen, hoping...

Nada. He gave up two minutes later. Not a good sign. Not good at all. He continued standing uselessly in the overheated stuffy waiting room, staring blankly, fidgeting, miserable with his gut churning anxiety.

His phone dinged.

Rachael? No, dude, this one's a security alert. SAM! Shit-shit-shit.

The gut burn turned red-hot molten. Hacker. Digging around the backend of his website, scrutinizing the instruction set, searching for a way to weasel into his network.

Arnold nodded to himself: Hacker's opening move: Pawn to Queen 4.

Okay, okay, if he's starting there, SAM's still all right.

As if that was reassuring. Jesus, he was driving himself freaking crazy.

Pacing, now completely bouncing off the walls, Arnold repeatedly tried to assure himself—for the time being, at least—that SAM was safe. He mentally reviewed the website code, wondering if he'd overlooked a potentially exploitable weakness. Not that he could think of. But this did jog a memory; he'd programmed in one trap for precisely this possibility. Question was, would Hacker bite? Or if he realized it was a trap, was there any possible way to use it against him? Huh. No, not possible. Really?

You absolutely one-hundred-percent sure of this, dude?

Jesus. A chill scintillated along his spine in spite of the overheated room.

A thirtyish-year-old woman in blue scrubs blew through the AUTHORIZED PERSONNEL ONLY door into the waiting room. Not attractive yet not unattractive, what with the Auschwitz-survivor sunken cheeks of a seriously all-in vegan. Not a stitch of makeup. Her dark brown hair in a no-nonsense cut. Exuding a hyper-intense aura of extreme competence. He immediately locked onto the competence part.

"Chance Gold's dad?" she asked even though Arnold was the only one in the room besides her.

News. Finally.

"Yes!"

"Hi, I'm Molly Kramer, the vet tonight," she said, extending a bony, freckled hand.

A no-nonsense, clinically detached, handshake followed, which Arnold interpreted as being more focused on the urgency of the situation than any need to schmooze the patient's owner. That too scored points with him.

Seconds after carrying the panting Chance into the waiting room, the technician that collected him had vanished through the same door Dr. Kramer had just pushed through. Then the receptionist had handed him a clipboard with numerous forms to complete and sign before they would sedate Chance for an evaluation. They had then run his Visa to lock down estimated impending expenses.

Throughout all this bureaucracy he'd never given a single thought to whom he just surrendered his best friend or what their qualifications might be, his singular overriding concern laser focused on getting Chance cared for as expeditiously as possible. Not once, he now realized in gut-wrenching horror, had he questioned the quality of care this clinic provided.

Should he have been more inquisitive? Was he too trusting? Hoped not.

Guess we'll find out.

But those intense hazel eyes were so instantly reassuring that his mind exploded with at least ten questions about Chance's future, then they all suddenly coalesced into, "Will he be okay?"

Molly Kramer flashed an impatient smile.

"At the moment, your boy's under anesthesia, so he is comfortable. He has, as I'm sure you're well aware, a compound leg fracture. The wound needs a thorough cleaning and the broken bones pinned together. Then a cast must be applied to hold everything in place. The surgery must be done as soon as possible—tonight—to decrease the risk of serious infection." She glanced at the round-face wall clock. "Are you willing to sign a consent for the surgery?"

"Yes, anything. Just fix him, please," he said with an emphatic nod. "Whatever you have to do, just do it. Please."

"In that case, you need to sign this," she said, proffering a clipboard.

With the clipboard flat on the reception counter, he scrawled at each line inked with a red X, not bothering to read a word.

"You'll start immediately?"

Molly Kramer nodded to the doorway she had blown through just moments ago.

"The moment I get back, we'll begin to prep him."

"I'll be right here. I'm not going anywhere, so please let me know how it went the moment you're done, okay?"

She placed a reassuring hand on his shoulder and locked eyes with him.

"Like any good pet owner, you're understandably concerned and extremely upset, but this process will take time. And then when surgery's done, he'll need time to awaken from anesthesia. How long that will take varies widely. My advice is—and I'm *extremely* serious about this—go home and *try* to unwind. I assume your contact number's on the intake form, but please check with the receptionist to make sure of that before leaving. I'll personally call the moment I have a good assessment of how he's doing."

Arnold shook his head.

"No, I can't wait at home." He started fidgeting, unable to be still. "I'll just"—he gave another glance around the small room—"hang over there in the corner out of the way and not bother anyone."

She shook her head again.

"Arnold, listen to me. I'd really prefer it if you wait at home." This time it was said clearly as a command rather than a preference. Those serious hazel eyes bored straight into his. "Believe me, there's *nothing* you can do here. Do you understand?"

It took a moment to process her request. Probably the last thing the staff needed was an anxious pet owner rebounding off the waiting room walls in the throes of emotional meltdown.

After a beat, he nodded.

"*You'll* call? I mean *you* personally? The moment surgery's done?"

"I will."

Must be those intense hazel eyes, but he trusted her word implicitly.

"Okay, but just so you know, he's my everything...the most precious being in my life. Corny as that sounds, it's the God's honest truth."

A quick nod.

"That's obvious, Mr. Gold."

"I mean, if anything happened to him..."

She replaced the gentle comforting hand on his shoulder.

"I can't give you a guarantee because unexpected things can and do happen during any surgery. But please understand that this is a routine case. I've done my share of these over the years, and most were worse than his, so I don't foresee a problem. All I can tell you is, don't worry as much as you obviously are. Go home, *try* to rest, and I'll call. But don't expect the call until late morning."

CHAPTER 25

ARNOLD STOOD ON the chipped cement portico to the one-story cream-colored stucco rectangle, a tiny square awning the only possible shelter from the rain when the wind wasn't gusting as it was now, chilling his ears and nose.

In front of him stretched a shadowy, glistening deserted street in the heart of a sleeping city, with occasional road noise filtering in from the distance. Though he zipped the parka to his chin and flipped up the hood, chilling gusts continued to snake along his spine.

Call Uber? Walk the three miles home?

His first inclination was to trudge north along Stone Way toward home, hoping the exercise would short-circuit at least some of the high voltage sparking across his synapses, destroying all ability to concentrate. An Uber would save time, which would allow him to possibly accomplish *something* to at least maintain a semblance of momentum.

Jesus, do something. Don't just stand here wallowing in destructive counterproductive self-indulgence.

Problem was, his rational self seemed incapable of reconciling his emotional self, leaving him with a split decision.

Aw, fuck it.

He punched the Uber app.

* * *

Armed with a glass of wine, butt against the edge of the
stainless-steel counter, Arnold sniffed the cabernet's bouquet
out of habit rather than conscious intent, his mind mired in an
endless loop of Chance, Hacker, work, Rachael, Mr.
Davidson, round and round like a dog chasing its tail.

Call her?

Way too late now; she would be sleeping. But she'd
asked for an update, right? He texted a pithy summary of the
situation.

Now what?

Too mentally fractured to trust doing even the most
menial task, he opted to at least *try* to sleep.

His phone rang as he set foot on the second floor.

"I was so worried about Chance I didn't mute my phone.
How's he doing?"

Arnold headed back down to the kitchen to add another
splash to his glass in hopes her call might last a few minutes,
perhaps give *them* a chance to finally get into a substantive
discussion. After updating her on Chance and Mr. Davidson,
he peered into the darkness of the back yard, dreading the
subject he needed to broach. He swallowed.

"Look, Rach, there's obviously no way I can fly back until
Chance is able to fly and Mr. Davidson's out of imminent
danger, so is there any way—any possible way at all—for you
to, like, come here?"

Several seconds of conspicuously dead air inched by.

"Let's hope they both recover."

As he replayed her words, a fresh gust of anxiety whistled
through his chest. Her tone and intonation were…like…he
opened his mouth to speak, thought better of it, so waited.

"I need to try to get some sleep now, Arnold. I suggest you try to do the same."

"You working tomorrow?"

One word. Concise. Frosty as a Sno-Cone.

"No."

WTF?

"Good night, Arnold."

Arnold stared at the dead phone for five seconds before dropping into a kitchen chair. He picked up his wine glass, mind swirling in confusion. Was Rachael right to be angry with him over how he ran Gold and Associates?

The brutal truth—as long as we're being brutally honest here—was that he ran his business like a day care instead of a *real* business. And was he handling Chance in the same lazy fashion? Why did he bring Chance instead of boarding him? Why walk him *off leash* at that particular time of night in totally shitty weather and visibility? Why hadn't he bought him a reflective vest? Why can any dipshit with a phone rent a battery-powered bike?

Why-why-why....

He downed the wine in one gulp, glanced at the bottle— a cab Mr. Davidson had introduced him to—and drifted back to that evening in Mr. Davidson's kitchen. He'd just flown to Seattle after narrowly escaping Naseem. Jesus, that particular disaster seemed so far away. A year? Longer? Mr. Davidson...he poured another splash, corked the almost empty bottle, wedged his butt against the counter, sniffed again, this time fully appreciating the cab's complex essences.

Mr. Davidson...

Finally, too physically and emotionally exhausted to not sleep, he upended the wine, rinsed and inverted the glass on the drainboard, and headed upstairs.

CHAPTER 26—6:30 Wednesday Morning

HIS RINGTONE JARRED him awake. He rolled onto his left side, disconnected the phone from the charger.

Good news? Oh, man, could sure use some.

No caller ID. This tied his gut into a square knot.

"Arnold?" a female voice asked.

"Yeah?"

A split second later he registered Kara's voice.

"I was so worried I couldn't sleep. Fucker must know everything we've done…"

He was upright now, legs over the edge of the bed, palm wiping his face, struggling for some semblance of mental traction, having been, like, seriously dead-to-the-world asleep. He squinted at nothing in particular, still trying to get his shit together.

"You there?" Kara asked.

"Yeah, yeah, just thinking is all…"

Undoubtedly, she was right. He blinked, ran his tongue over dry teeth (he mouth-breathed while sleeping).

"Okay, tell you what—"

The phone beeped. Another call. This one from the Emerald City Emergency clinic.

"Oh, shit, look, got to take another call. Call you right back at this number?"

"That works, but—"

Arnold switched to the vet call.

"Hello."

"Mr. Gold?"

He immediately recognized Dr. Kramer's voice.

"Yes?"

Eyelids scrunched together, awaiting the verdict, silently praying.

"Your boy's out of surgery but isn't completely awake yet. Everything went as planned. We cleaned the wound, pinned the fracture, and closed the skin without a problem. If there's no complication, he should be ready to come home sometime tomorrow. This depends, of course, on how well he's eating and responding."

"You're saying he's going to be okay?"

"Nothing's guaranteed Mr. Gold, but unless he develops an infection days from now, or develops another unanticipated complication, yes, he should do very well. Having said that, you need to also realize—and I can't emphasize this strongly enough—that bones take *much* longer to mend than does skin. Please just keep that in mind."

"*Thank* you, doctor. I can't tell you how much I appreciate what you've done for us."

"That's why we're here, Mr. Gold. Have a good day."

All business. Probably past the end of her shift.

He sat for a moment, thankful for the good news. Definitely in need of another hour or two of sleep but knew he was too amped now for any chance of that happening. And besides, he needed to call Kara back.

* * *

Showered, shaved, bundled in a wool sweaters and parka,

Arnold plodded—phone to ear—through chilly misty drizzle along East Green Lake Way toward the welcoming humid warmth of Starbucks.

"For now, don't do a thing but copy it to a sterile flash drive, okay?" he told Kara. "Although I know you know this, I'll say it anyway; make damn sure to sanitize the hell out of your computer afterwards, okay? You want to be super cautious to not infect your machine."

"I figured that's what you'd say, so I already took care of it, Stud."

Stud?

"I'm just about to go into Starbucks to score breakfast before I call a ride. Meet you at the office in...forty minutes, give or take?"

"See you then."

* * *

"How's he doing?" he asked Martina from the back seat of the Kia, rolling southbound on Aurora toward downtown, the earlier drizzle having transitioned into nothing more than a menacing, heavily saturated, dark pewter low enough to obliterate the towers atop Queen Anne Hill.

"Holding his own, I guess is the only way to describe it."

Say what?

"Ah...is that good?"

"I have no idea. I guess it depends on whether you're a glass-half-full person."

"Okay, next question." Hoping for something more encouraging, he said, "How're *you* holding up?"

Martina snorted sarcastically.

"I could say something glib, but truthfully, I have no idea. I can find no words to describe the countless emotions bubbling inside...just that I'll be greatly relieved when this situation finally sorts itself."

She paused, as if debating her next words. Her voice was laden with weariness.

"Not knowing one second to the next if he'll live or die is... *taxing.* That's the only word I can summon to describe it, yet it's woefully inadequate."

Arnold knew that particular emotion too damn well and wished desperately for comforting words.

But he knew that sometimes even the most well-intentioned ones can produce the opposite effect, so settled for, "How about I buy you dinner tonight."

She hesitated briefly.

"Know what?" with a sparkle to her voice. "What a *perfect* change of pace. I accept. What's your pleasure, sir?"

His off-the-cuff proposal caught him flat footed but then flashed on a restaurant they all enjoyed.

"How's Uptown China sound?"

"Wonderful..." She paused. "What's wrong?"

"Nothing," he answered too tersely.

"Oh *please.* Don't do that, Arnold. I know you better than that."

He opened his mouth, reconsidered, so settled for, "I will explain later when we have a glass of wine, food, and more time."

* * *

"How do you propose we deal with it?" Noah Cain asked Arnold, after assuming his down-to-business pose: leaning forward, elbows atop the desk, fingers interlaced, right index knuckle tapping his chin thoughtfully. Kara occupied the chair to Arnold's left, looking tired from lack of sleep.

"My gut says to leverage it to an advantage by feeding him disinformation and in the process, try to use the opportunity to capture his identity."

There. At least he *had* voiced an opinion. For what it's

worth.

Cain considered this.

"And the pros and cons of this strategy?"

Easy enough.

"The pro is the possibility of getting us Hacker's identity. The con is it's going to chew up some serious planning and carries no guarantee of being successful."

Uh, dude, you're talking yourself out of any chance...

Again, Cain nodded sagely, as if seriously considering his suggestion.

"In the meantime this *hacker*," the word laden with unambiguous distaste, which Arnold found amusing coming from a lawyer who'd defended several, "has full access to our confidential documents."

Arnold shrugged.

"That's one way to look at it."

Leaning back in the chair contemplatively, Cain massaged his chin.

"The problem with your suggestion is that our law firm would knowingly allow a breach of confidential information to continue unabated. Now that I am aware of the breach, I can see no reasonable justification to allow it to continue. In other words, the malware must be removed *tout suite.*" Then, turning to Kara, "Thank you for bringing this to my attention so promptly."

She responded with a silent nod.

Cain turned to Arnold, "How soon can you remove it?"

"It'll take about ten minutes."

He stood, assuming the attorney wanted him to start work immediately.

Cain pushed up from behind his desk.

"Good work, both of you, for finding it."

In the hall outside of Cain's office, Arnold said to Kara, "You copied it, right?"

Damn well hoped so.

He'd been in such a rush since being rousted from a dead sleep, that he'd forgotten to pocket a clean flash drive.

"I did but didn't remember to bring it. It's at home." Her face brightened. "Hey, I'll be happy to drop it by your place tonight?"

Hmmm...

What's with the hesitation? On account of their history? Which when viewed with objectivate clarity, amounted to precisely zilch. Or...did he actually regret his prior inaction? Interesting question. Difficult answer. Regardless, he needed that copy.

Okay, but as long as nothing comes of it, what's the issue?

Well, what about Rachael? How would she take it?

How would she know?

He fought to keep from grinning.

"If it's not too much hassle."

* * *

Ramesh Singh decided it was time to check for new email exchanges between Davidson and Cain concerning Gold's progress with his investigation. He entered the command to access the firm's email server. Nothing happened. A typo? He seldom made them, but...he retyped the command paying rapt attention to every character.

Again, no response.

Sonofabitch!

The Jew. Had to be. After all, Gold had worked on the system last summer. Maybe those shysters retained him as a part-time SysAdmin. Hadn't thought of that before now. Come to think of it, he hadn't received a response to the phishing attack either. Did Gold realize he'd been targeted? That had to be it. He slammed his palm on the desk.

Fucking Jew.

Eyes closed, Singh began a series of deep measured inhales, timing each breath to last three seconds, an exercise practiced during meditation and periods of extreme stress. He repeated these until he was convinced that he could evaluate the situation more empirically.

Obviously, Gold was proving to be more problematic than anticipated. Rather than a mere nuisance, the bastard was potentially threatening the success of his plan, and so he needed to be dealt with accordingly. The most expedient way to eliminate any immediate threat would be to annihilate his network. Although this would undoubtedly only delay him, by the time he was up and running again, the Lopez trial should be well under way.

A quick nod of self-approval.

The problem now was finding his network. If Gold had fallen for the phishing attack, he would already have the Trojan embedded there and ready to go. Which raised an interesting question: had Gold recognized and then neutralized the phishing email, or was it still in his inbox unopened? It was an intriguing question but totally irrelevant since it changed nothing. He needed a conduit into Gold's network.

Eyes still closed, he concentrated on possible ways to burrow through Gold's defenses. So far, his solitary lead was Gold's website. Although he'd done a cursory inspection, it remained only cursory. The time had come to revisit it, and this time disassemble the instruction set line by fucking line, searching for even the slightest clue to its origin.

* * *

Arnold constructed a temporary doggie bed on the kitchen floor by rolling up two spare bath towels for a bolster around an extra-large folded bath towel. He positioned it between the table and the French doors so Chance could guard the back yard while Arnold kept a close eye on him. He was looking forward to his best friend's return, the absence having driven home just how tightly they had bonded. With the makeshift bed assembled, he chose a medium-size, bolstered, orthopedic doggie bed on Amazon and ordered it for next day delivery. Perfect. What else did he need?

Huh.

Thought he'd covered everything but figured he probably was forgetting something.

Oh, well, time to move on.

He would deal with whatever it was when the need arose.

Using Prisha's login credentials, he started searching the Camano web server for the bogus press release. Despite trying to stay on task, his mind constantly rocketed off on tangents, one thought spawning another, in an endless loop...

C'mon, dude, get a grip.

He stood, paced three tight circles, returned to the chair. This one simple task seemed to be taking for-freaking-ever. Unless he lasered every amp of concentration into every individual move—moves that under normal circumstances were executed on autopilot—his mind would boomerang from Chance, to Rachael, to Mr. Davidson...on and on and on.

Press on, dude. Press on.

Thirty excruciating minutes later, it was up on the screen. He then realized how easily the news outlets bought it. After all, the story did come from Camano and nothing in the content or appearance would raise so much as an eyebrow. Which brought him full circle to the pivotal question: Who actually sent it, Hacker or Lopez? And how the hell could he prove it?

He copied the release to the case file along with other intel, such as the exact time the story hit the news outlets, then checked the Camano logs for unusual activity in the two hours preceding the release. Nothing. No huge surprise or revelation about that. An accomplished hacker would be over-the-top meticulous about leaving no digital fingerprint. With each new slice of information, Arnold became increasingly impressed with just how sophisticated, well planned, and well executed these capers had been. Definitely not the work of your run-of-the-mill hacker. This work was, like, Radical Dood skill level.

Okay, so how did Hacker gain access to the server?

Well, since spear phishing appeared to be Hacker's go-to attack tactic, Arnold bet that an unwitting employee had fallen for a scam and, in the process, infected the network. Thought about this a moment.

Yeah, made perfectly scary sense.

But Jesus, this meant locating the infected email so he could search for possible clues as to Hacker's identity.

He blew a long slow dispirited breath. Finding that puppy could turn into one seriously tedious time-consuming hunt, on account of it meant looking at every damn email for every damn employee in the week prior to the sabotage until he found it. Maybe even further back than a week if nothing turned up. How many emails would this require? *Jesus.* He needed to focus some serious-ass thought how best to economize the search.

He started to pace, hyper-aware that each passing second equated to more wasted time. On the other hand, one stupid mistake at this point and he would likely end up as the bull sprouting banderillas.

Proceed with caution, dude.

Hacker…Hacker…

He was forgetting something. What? He stopped, focused every amp of mental energy to backtracking his logic. What was it?

Had something to do with security…

Ah, yes.

The honeypot. He had programmed a trap into the website code for exactly this possibility. Way it worked was, the trap appeared like a simple flaw in the code—an oversight—pointing back to his network.

In reality, it sucked the intruder into a dead end, and in the process, captured their IP address. Meaning: if Hacker bit, the information he sought was already waiting for him, so there would be no need to endure the pain of scanning each freaking email.

The question now was, had Hacker fallen for it?

With eyes glued to the screen, he typed the command to access the trap and hit ENTER.

CHAPTER 27

INSTEAD OF AN IP address, the message NICE TRY GOLD flashed up on the screen.

Shit.

Arnold shook his head, disappointed at allowing his hopes to skyrocket. How could he possibly believe he'd outfoxed that canny sonofabitch? Grudgingly he had to admit he admired the asshole's foxlike cunning ability to dodge the trap. But man...

As a distraction, he worked on the list of equipment he needed to order from Best Buy and Amazon: four more servers, ten one-terabyte external storage drives, three monitors, cabling, a cheap folding chair, two more racks, and five heavy-duty extension cords.

Jesus, the process of assembling a satellite SAM from scratch was beginning to resolve into ultra-sharp clarity. How quickly he'd repressed the countless hours spent piecing together SAM 1.0's initial infrastructure. Then again, that iteration had required an extremely steep learning curve. In contrast, building SAM 2.0 at his Honolulu home had been a chip shot seeing as he already had a mirror image backed up in the cloud. What's more, he was under no pressure this time, what with SAM 2.0 up and humming along.

Piece of cake, actually.

But enough with the distractions and diversions. Time to focus on searching for the source of the damn RAT. Hmm…there had to be an efficient way to channel the search through all those emails. He decided he needed to prioritize employees based on odds. Okay, so who was *least* likely get sucked into a phishing scam? Easy answer: the software engineers and, of course, Prisha would be at the bottom of the list. He moved their names to the lowest priority. Twenty-three names remained. Okay, the flip side of the equation was, who was the *most* likely to get suckered? Another easy answer: the executives.

Done.

But this still left him with the mind-numbing task of scanning each damn email during the two weeks—an arbitrary epoch—preceding the attack. He decided, again simply playing the odds, that for his first pass, he would only scan for emails with an attachment (the most common method for delivering malware). If nothing came of this, then he was doomed to open each freaking email to look for a suspicious hyperlink, something like: SECURITY ALERT, CLICK HERE.

* * *

While sipping the dregs of his third hot chocolate of the afternoon, Arnold came across an email to the VP of Marketing from a stock analyst, asking him to complete an attached questionnaire. Alarms bells clanged.

That attachment was now toxic until proven otherwise. After isolating the email, he turned loose a malware scan on it, stood, went through a progression of stretches and eye exercises, carried his Starbucks mug upstairs to wash, having had his hot chocolate fill for the day.

How's Chance doing? Ready for discharge? There anything else I should prepare for him? He headed back downstairs.

His suspicion had been right: the attachment was indeed the RAT. At last, his first solid clue, one he intended to work as hard and as far possible to uncover Hacker's identity. Not only that, but this chunk of malware was now much more significant than the one pulled off the law-firm server this morning because this one had been employed in the hack under investigation. Any lawyer worth a damn would argue that the one found in the law firm was simple coincidence since there was, after all, a limited number of Trojans available for this kind of shit.

He copied the infected email to an empty, sanitized thumb drive banded with a strip of Day-Glo pink tape to signify that its contents contained contaminated material (his digital equivalent of the biohazard symbol).

Next, he examined the email header in-depth. The header is usually masked from the text since the information is of little interest to the typical recipient. It does, however, contain critical information, including the originating computer IP address. Assuming, of course, that the address wasn't a spoof. So, Arnold wasn't shocked to discover that the sender's address had, in fact, been spoofed. Meaning his red-hot lead had just fizzled into a massive dead end. More wasted time.

Whoa, not so fast.

On second thought, he had just verified one extremely important point: the route that Hacker used to invade Camano's network. This had to count for something, right?

Right.

Break time?

Probably.

Run over to the emergency clinic to visit Chance? He

really couldn't afford the delay, but his mental health sure could use it. And really, how could checking on your best friend be considered a waste of time? Uber? No, walk to, Uber back. The exercise would be therapeutic, he rationalized, making the lost time worth it.

* * *

Bundled in layers of cozy warm wool and down, Arnold trudged Green Lake Way to Aurora Avenue, then straight south, past Woodlawn Park toward 40th Street. Ominous, black-fringed gray nimbus clouds threatened to seep through dense gunmetal overcast with, of course, occasional annoying wind gusts. He was moving on autopilot, mentally bogged down with ruminations over the most important people in his life.

Beginning with Rachael.

How ironic: his quest to build Gold and Associates seemed to paradoxically be destroying their relationship. Why couldn't their respective careers coexist? Be symbiotic? Was that too much to ask?

A fresh bolt of gut pain struck, damn near doubling him over.

Jesus, dude, pick up some Mylanta of Tums at the first drugstore you see.

He stopped, glanced around.

Damn, dude, blew right past 40th.

After a 180, he retraced the half block back, then turned east toward Stone Way. Where the hell was the nearest drugstore?

* * *

Chance's wagging tail swayed his entire hind end as he whimpered with joy, straining against the lease held tight by the tech. He barked a single staccato hello. Arnold was overjoyed at seeing him up moving around, apparently unbothered by the cast protecting his leg. He would've wagged his tail too if he had one.

He asked the tall gangly female with a blond ponytail, "It's okay for him to be up like this?"

The tech allowed Chance to move closer to Arnold.

"It is. It's good for his lungs."

"He's not overdoing it, is he?"

The overly protective parent.

"No, he's fine. Here."

She let Chance move even closer.

"I'll let him come to you so you two can have a proper hello. Sorry, but we have to keep this a brief visit. I hope this puts your mind at ease."

She controlled the leash even as Arnold hugged him.

Chance snuggled against him, whining vociferously while Arnold engulfed him in a super-careful embrace, cautiously protecting his injured hindquarter. Chance's tail continued nonstop as he showered Arnold's face with licks.

"I'm sure Dr. Kramer will discharge him in the morning," the tech offered. "He's eating and drinking just fine and seems to have tolerated anesthesia well."

"Oh, man…"

What a huge relief, to see his best buddy looking so well and on his way toward healing. Having him home tomorrow would be incredible. Emotionally and spiritually.

"I'm sorry, Mr. Gold, but…"

"Hey, no problem. You guys are busy. Guess I should've called before showing up unannounced."

But more than that, showing up only made Chance think he was heading home.

Arnold gently handed her the leash while telling Chance, "Daddy has to go, Chance stays. Chance is a good boy."

The three phrases he always used when leaving him.

Chance's flaps turned down, accompanied by a loud protest whine. But when Arnold backed away, the pooch made no attempt to follow, apparently comprehending the situation.

Exiting the clinic, Arnold wondered who was saddest. Well, at least Chance would be home tomorrow. It would be wonderful if the bolstered bed from Amazon was delivered and waiting for him.

* * *

Outside the clinic, Arnold wondered if the impromptu visit had been selfish. The moment he saw him, Chance probably thought he would be heading home just like every other time Arnold had showed up at the vet. Made doggie sense.

Christ, add one more fuckup in a growing list.

He texted an update to Rachael.

She immediately replied with how relieved this made her, and she thanked him for the update.

A good sign? His spirits skyrocketed.

Whoa, don't get ahead of yourself, dude.

* * *

At the neighborhood Starbucks, he splurged on a celebratory Grandé latte and a chocolate chip cookie, reveling in the joy that Chance was coming home tomorrow. He settled into a table to savor the cookie and check stock prices on his iPhone but couldn't stop ruminating about Rachael.

Something was terribly amiss. He clearly sensed it. Not having a clue what it might be was driving him batshit.

He glanced around.

Why am I wasting time here? Jesus. Eat the damn cookie while you walk.

Back at his house, Arnold considered the fate of the air-gapped Camano computer. Make it a permanent isolation chamber for malware investigations? The downside, of course, was that he hated to designate any device as a mono-tasker. On the other hand, a dedicated, air-gapped, ready-to-go malware machine would economize time, right? And for only a hundred bucks...of the five Camano servers, this particular one was the most expendable due to its relatively slow speed and inferior components.

He lugged a kitchen chair downstairs until the permanent one arrived, settled in, and began to strip the machine of all software except the bare-bones operating system. Then he pulled off the cabinet and removed the Wi-Fi card, effectively converting the machine to a cyber-eunuch. He set the extra circuit board in a corner; the first spare part in a supply that would wax and wane as his duplicate SAM project progressed.

Ah, yes; order a few plastic storage bins from Amazon.

He placed the order on his phone, figured, what the hell, might as well throw in an Echo too.

The reassembled computer was now good to run an in-depth analysis of the RAT.

Ten minutes later, Arnold had an answer: the RAT turned out to be a Zeus Trojan horse; a form of malware that, when triggered, embedded in the victim's computer as a portal for the hacker.

Interesting choice.

Why would a dude of Hacker's caliber and sophistication choose to use a chunk of code that had been floating around cyberspace since Eve waved the Red Delicious under Adam's nose? On the other hand, this particular strain of malware represented a battle-hardened veteran of hacking fame.

* * *

He was in the tortuous process of deconstructing the Trojan when his phone rang. Caller ID showed Kara.

Kara? For real?

"Hello?" he said tentatively.

"What time should I drop by tonight?"

Huh? Jesus, his mind blanked.

"Uh..."

"You know, with the Trojan?"

"Oh, right, right..." he muttered, caught completely flat-footed.

"Don't tell me you forgot?"

"Well, yeah, in a way I did...I was distracted when we discussed it and totally forgot I have dinner plans. I won't be back until later."

Hmmm, not bad.

"Later's fine. Give me a time and I'll come by then. You still want it, *don't* you?"

Interesting dilemma. Truth be told, he really didn't need it now that he was deconstructing the actual Trojan employed in the hack, so why even waste the time analyzing that one?

On the other hand...

"Look, I'm really sorry," Arnold said. "Tonight just isn't going to work on account of all the things going on. Could we make it tomorrow?"

He immediately realized his mistake.

"Sure, tomorrow works," she said, enthusiastically unfazed.

Jesus, what did I just agree to?

CHAPTER 28

HE GLANCED AT his watch. He was supposed to meet Martina in thirty minutes. Factor the typical Aurora Avenue bottlenecks this time of day and he needed to ping an Uber, like, pronto.

The white Camry crept southbound pinned behind a yellow articulated Rapid Ride in bumper-to-tailpipe Aurora Avenue congestion, the fast left lane so chock-a-block that there was no way to Bogart their way around the bus.

He was shackled in commuter hell; an anxiety provoking situation for hyper-punctual Arnold. He raised his iPhone to his ear.

"Hey, bro, what up?" Chang said, when he finally answered.

"Progress, my man, progress. Did I mention I got my hands on a Camano Biopharma server?"

He didn't intend the question to be a gratuitous conversation starter. So much shit was raining on him that he flat-out couldn't remember if or when he had last updated Chang.

"How the hell you manage that?"

"Got lucky. Happen to know Camano's SysAd at the time

the shit exploded. She had it in storage."

Dead air.

Oh, shit.

Forgot. The FBI had supposedly appropriated all the servers as evidence.

Jesus, Prisha, sorry.

Explain that they're backups or just freaking clam up?

"What'd you just say? You're breaking up. Are you on your cell?"

Owe you one, dude.

"Can you hear me now?"

"Roger that, solid copy. What I was saying is, I got my hands on a copy of *backups* from the Camano network. I searched the emails for a phishing attack. I mean, that's what made the most sense, right?"

"Thanks for taking the initiative, bro. It's on my to-do list, but things are so nutzo crazy here I haven't had time to even think about the case. Sorry to interrupt. Go on."

Arnold glanced out the window at the three red-and-white towers atop Queen Anne hill, the Camry still midspan on the Aurora bridge. They hadn't moved a freaking inch since he last checked.

"Long story short is the VP of marketing opened an email loaded with a ZeuS/Zbot Trojan."

"ZeuS, huh?" Chang said, apparently reading Arnold's mind about the old dog.

"Un-huh. You have a copy of the one from the Curchfield hack?"

"Affirmatory. But like I said, I'm so deep below the surface I haven't had time for even a peek at it."

"Do you mind sending a copy my way?"

"More than happy to, assuming of course, we're talking quid pro quo."

"Sure. Hold one." Arnold paused to email himself a

reminder before it too slipped his mind. "Okay, I'm back."

He suddenly remembered the RAT they had removed from the law-firm network earlier, so he updated Chang on that part of the equation, then checked his watch. He figured at this rate he would be late and considered calling Martina, promptness being one of his things.

Chang took a moment to digest the news.

"What're you planning to do with it?"

"Seeing that I now have the one from Camano, nothing. Don't worry, I made a copy for you."

He mentioned that the address in the phishing email header turned out to be bogus.

"I'm shocked," Chang said after a sarcastic snort.

"Yeah, I was too. But I'm still running it through an extractor on the off chance I can recover something useful."

Chang scoffed.

"Like an IP address?"

Freaking cynic.

"Hey, got to admit that that'd be sweet."

"Dream on, bro. Bet you a latte it's a proxy," Chang said, meaning a fake IP address, a commonly employed tactic to mask a hacker's identity and location.

"Probably. But a friend might be able to help me leverage it into something."

"Yeah?" This seemed to pique Chang's interest. "Who?

"Oh, just a guy I know," Arnold said, purposely keeping it vague, unwilling to expose a potential source to the Bureau in spite of their history of collaboration.

Develop a rep for coughing up names and you might as well kiss any future help adios.

"Okay, bro, but remember, whatever you do, make damn sure it's legal."

"Oh, absolutely, officer," Arnold said with a grin.

* * *

Arnold beat Martina to the restaurant. Walking in, he noticed
Mr. Davidson's favorite booth was free, so as Jenny (his
favorite waitress) greeted him, asked, "Is it okay to take that
one? A guest's meeting me."

"Just one?"

She led him to the booth, transferred the two extra place
settings to a neighboring table, dealt out two menus. Before
sliding into the booth, he passed her the bottle of wine he'd
almost forgotten to grab during his dash out the door.

She asked, "You want me open now?" holding up the
bottle by the neck.

"Please."

"I get glasses."

Two minutes later, Martina hurried in, head swiveling
side to side scanning tables, made eye contact, and beelined
over. He slid from the booth to exchange cheek pecks.

"Sorry," she said slipping off her coat and tossing it onto
the seat on her side of the booth. "Denny ended up one giant
traffic jam over by Fisher Plaza."

Martina was referring to a high-rise office complex
housing, among other things, KOMO-TV and radio, the local
ABC affiliate.

"No problem." He sat back down. "Turned out I was late
too. Aurora was unusually bad and there's not even a Kraken
game tonight."

She glanced around.

"You probably couldn't be able to get a table—much less
this booth—if there were a game tonight."

"You look way less frazzled than last time I saw you,"
Arnold said. "Can I interpret this to mean Mr. Davidson's
better?"

"This booth...is Palmer's favorite," she muttered,

inspecting the table while fine-tuning her place setting, sliding her napkin and fork slightly further apart, getting them precisely positioned.

He scrambled for something appropriate to say but came up empty.

"I know. We always sit here if it's not taken."

Jesus, maybe this wasn't such a red-hot idea, what with ordering Mr. Davidson's favorite dishes while he lay in the CCU battling for his life...

Martina glanced up from her place setting as if suddenly returning to the present.

"He's stable, for now. The cardiologist said if this continues, they'll discharge him to rehab in a day or so, but that, of course, depends on if the arrhythmia remains controlled."

He studied her eyes, looking for any hint that she might be spinning this for his benefit.

She cocked her head, studying him in return.

"That's *good* news, Arnold."

"Yeah, I know. It's just..." He scrambled for appropriate words but blanked again, sighed, said, "Ah, Jesus, I thought the stents would take care of things. I mean, it's bad enough he had the attack but *this shit*...it's like a goddamn sword hanging over our heads..."

Martina leaned over the table, placed her soft warm hand atop his.

"The cardiologist said this can be typical after an attack like his. In fact, this seems to be *de rigueur*." She held the gaze a few beats before removing her hand. She sat back in the booth, still eyeing him closely. "You realize, don't you, he considers you the son he never had?"

Shocked, Arnold glanced at her.

She joking? Didn't appear so.

He shook his head.

She added, "Yes, he's mentioned several times how much he admires your resiliency, canniness, and innovation. To use his exact words."

"I think the world of him," he said. "He's a mentor and surrogate father...someone I can discuss anything with."

Jesus, can you possibly come up with any more clichés?

Arnold laughed self-consciously.

"It's an added bonus that he's my lawyer. I trust him implicitly. And it doesn't hurt that he's damn good at it." He laughed at himself again, carrying on like this, shook his head, embarrassed. "At first, I didn't think very much of him because of helping so many scumbags slither out of...the things they did, but I have to say, being involved in this has made me realize not everyone accused of a crime..."

He let it hang.

Just then Jenny, their server, materialized with two wine glasses and the uncorked bottle of Rutherford cab, Arnold's everyday wine. After serving them, she took their order for crispy walnut prawns, mu shu pork, and beef with broccoli; three of Mr. Davidson's favorites. It was probably more than they could polish off, but after a brief after-you-Alphonse exchange, Arnold agreed to schlep any leftovers home.

They toasted to "health and happiness," (Mr. Davidson's favorite), then, after a sip, Arnold said, "Okay to ask a personal question?"

She smiled.

"That, of course, depends on the question."

Arnold laughed.

"Fair enough." Tricky one. He paused, choosing words carefully. "What happened to your marriage? I mean, the two of you seem so good together." A shrug. "You're both so...caring and considerate toward each other."

She slumped against the booth, glass in hand, eyes seemingly focused on a distant point, perhaps sorting memories for an answer.

"Why do you ask?"

With a nod, Arnold leaned onto his forearms.

"Rachael and I've hit a major speed bump, so I'm just curious what happened between you two."

She glanced away another moment, finger combing her luxurious black hair, returned to meet his eyes.

"It's...*complicated.*" She paused to sip wine. "Perhaps the easiest way to distill the essence of a very complex dynamic is to say our basic personalities sometimes clash." She inhaled deeply. "As I'm sure you're aware, both of us are strong personalities with strong preferences and opinions that often are not, shall I say, *synchronous?*" Making a question of it, as if *synchronous* wasn't the precise word but would have to suffice. "That often resulted in conflicting opinions."

Arnold decided to push it.

"For example?"

A distant smile flickered across her lips, crinkling the corners of her eyes.

"The ones that immediately come to mind seem so trivial now, under the present circumstance." She shook her head sadly. "However, they certainly didn't feel so trivial at the time. I suppose if he hadn't had his heart attack, they'd still feel more significant than they actually are." Another sigh. "Here's an example: Palmer is a neat freak. I'm not. There're some things that bother him that don't so much as faze me. In some ways, he's a perfectionist. And when I say '*in some ways*', I mean they apply only to very specific picky-picky issues. Over time these rather minor differences became a source of friction blisters that refused to heal."

Jesus, she could be describing us...

Arnold shook his head and stared at the table. How sad to know their marriage had ended in divorce in spite of such clear and obvious devotion to each other. And if that weren't depressing enough, extrapolating their story to his future with Rachael...her words were beginning to drag him down.

"Would I be pushing it to ask for a concrete example?"

She pensively twisted her wine glass stem for several beats, paused, took another sip, and carefully replaced the glass on the table.

"Here's one: I clean up dirty dishes in the morning, so have no issue with leaving them on the counter next to the sink. Have you noticed that Palmer can't tolerate that?"

Arnold chuckled.

Matter of fact...

"Yes."

A curt nod.

"He'd sometimes make a point of rinsing and stacking them *in the sink* in spite of me telling him I'd get to them in the morning. This irritated me. Perhaps more than it warrants, but neither of us seemed able to capitulate. I mean, *God*, every time he did that, it would grate on me." A wistful smile tugged the corners of her mouth. "My God, it all seems so absurdly silly now, doesn't it."

Arnold shrugged. He easily envisioned this exact series of events—maybe not the dirty dishes thing, but something just as trivial—fomenting between him and Rachael. In fact, it was fomenting now, over this trip. Which made Martina's example even more frightening and real. How can such relatively trivial issues escalate to such a drastic step as divorce? This was obviously only a fraction of the irritants that, once they began to accumulate and allowed to stew, ultimately precipitated the dissolution.

"Over time, the totality of our differences created a state of constant friction. That's not to say that disagreements don't arise in any relationship whether you live together or not. They most certainly do. But when you mix together our particular personalities, this friction heated to the point of combustion." As if sensing a need to justify such a drastic conclusion, Martina quickly added, "Not one of our disputes by itself, would've been sufficient to dissolve an otherwise wonderful marriage, but eventually their cumulative effect dictated that if we desired to stay together emotionally—which we did—we quite simply couldn't live together." She shrugged as if to say, and that's it. "We agreed to divorce and live apart to save *us*. That's our story."

How sad and depressing. And way too familiar for how he saw things unfolding with Rachael.

When Arnold didn't reply, she added, "We still love each other deeply. I believe you appreciate that, yes?"

"I do."

They remained individually adrift for several seconds, Arnold finally breaking the silence with, "You're scaring the bejesus out of me...you realize that, don't you?"

"Okay, Arnold, what's going on between you and Rachael?"

He nodded, but before she could enumerate, asked, "Long as I'm sticking my nose where it doesn't belong, may I ask another personal question?"

Whether it was the wine or the distraction of conversation or the combination, she certainly appeared more relaxed than she had when first sitting down.

Another shrug.

"Why not?"

Arnold contemplated diplomatic words to probe a sensitive subject. There simply weren't any, so he plowed ahead.

"You guys didn't have children. Was that a conscious decision or...?"

"Or a physical limitation?" she finished for him with a muted chuckle. "I can see how uncomfortable the question makes you. A brief pause, then, "We discussed this the moment it became clear how serious our relationship was becoming. We agreed that we didn't see ourselves as parents."

As long as he'd opened this particular box of snakes, might as well go all the way.

"If you're not comfortable answering my next question, no problem, but what were your reasons?"

Again, she began twisting the glass stem, rotating it clockwise, staring into the dark, clear red claret.

"There were several." A deep inhale. "Neither of us felt the need to procreate. At no point in my life did I ever desire to carry or birth a child. That, of course, made me *the* outlier with the other girls. Likewise, Palmer never felt the typical male need to produce an offspring as a legacy. Instead, he believes his legacy is being a respected lawyer. After all, what's to say your child won't be born severely deformed or become a serial killer? The moment an egg's fertilized, there's no guarantee what you'll end up with, so it's a huge gamble. Most important is that we simply never saw child rearing as something we desired."

Martina's faint smile grew wistful, her eyes distant, perhaps reliving one of the discussions with her divorced husband. Arnold continued contemplating what she'd just said. She was right, of course.

A moment later she said, "Now that I've answered your questions, let's shift to you and Rachael. What's going on between you two? You're clearly upset and worried."

Arnold leaned back, lips pressed thin.

How to start?

"Only thing I know for sure is she's super pissed that I took on this job. Problem is, I worry there's something more going on that I don't know about and my work's nothing more than a smokescreen. She won't talk about it and that's so unlike her. She won't answer most texts or calls and the few times she has, she's, well, *cold?* Yeah, cold's probably the best word to describe it. I'm worried this—whatever this is—is ballooning into something..."

He shook his head, at a total loss for words.

Martina waited patiently for him to continue.

"We've never discussed marriage...I mean, *I* definitely want to but figured it'd be best to try living together first. You know...find out what the issues are. That's why I asked about you guys. I mean, you obvious really care about each other in spite of the divorce and I've never been able to wrap my head around how that works. I've always assumed divorced couples hate each other, but you two shatter that image."

Martina smiled at that.

"Why do you think she's irritated over you taking this job? She doesn't suspect you of having an affair, does she?"

Wow, never even considered that wrinkle.

"Can't imagine why. I've never looked at another woman since I started seeing her."

Really? How about your fantasies about Kara a couple months back? She pick up on those?

She pursed her lips slightly.

"Arnold, there *has* to be something to provoke her."

"That's exactly my point. I haven't a clue what it is and it's driving me batshit crazy." Shaking his head, he picked up his wine glass. "But, if I were to bet, my money would be on it having to do with her dad." He paused for a sip before elaborating. "When she and Howie were growing up, her father was on the road for weeks at a time and that was a big-time issue with her mom. I'm talking like major scenes, like really ugly ones. Screaming matches. I witnessed more than a few doozies and those were just a fraction of what went on when I wasn't around. They were embarrassing for her and Howie when they happened in front of friends and I'm sure that's had a lasting effect on her. I know for sure Howie complained about them. Problem is, when I've tried to get her to talk about this issue, she clams up. She's very closed about this matter in particular."

Martina remained quiet, still, and attentive, letting him flow.

He took another sip of wine.

"Bottom line, I'm worried about *us*...I worry that this, this whatever it is that's going on will end up destroying us."

"Why not drop the case and fly back?" she asked, eyebrows arched slightly. "What's your priority here?"

Arnold shook his head.

"See, that's the problem. You just popped the top off a jar of maggots. No way can I walk away from this." He locked eyes with her. "For a couple reasons. First, I agreed to do this. And so, for the time being, I need to be here to do the work. It's not a job I can possibly do remotely."

He raised a hold-on-a-second finger while organizing his next point.

"I know, you don't need to say it. I need an associate here and in Honolulu for exactly this type of situation, but I don't. Not yet at least. And believe me, Rachael's beaten me over the head with this repeatedly. Which brings up another reason to stay; I need to hire one for here. The good news is, I just happened to luck onto a perfect candidate. But there's an even more important reason for staying." He inhaled deeply. "Two years ago, I was floundering, stuck in neutral with no goal and no inkling about what I wanted to do. Days were just...I don't know...*days*. I hated that feeling but didn't know how or what to change. Then I remove that virus from Mr. Davidson's network for him and afterwards he makes this offhand comment about me doing this kind of work as a business. Hell, as obvious as that sounds, it'd never dawned on me, but then I got to thinking, wow, cool...but I had no clue how to go about it. So he mentions my service to a couple lawyers and a few jobs start trickling in until I caught that ransomware gig with Mr. Cain's firm. And *that* like transformed my life, hokey as that sounds. At *last*, I had a goal: build a legitimate business."

He continued, "My point is, if Rachael and I are ever going to make it, we have to be able to resolve our conflicts with rational communication and mutual kindness. No normal relationship can last if one partner tries to control the other with edicts and ultimatums. Unless of course we're talking about some sicko domination-trip thing."

She nodded, waiting, for him to finish.

Arnold glanced away and shook his head again.

"So, to wrap this up, I asked about you and Mr. Davidson on account of seeing some scary similarities to where I see this thing with Rachael headed."

Just then, Jenny, their server, materialized with two serving dishes.

"Crispy walnut prawns and Mu Shu Pork. I bring wrappers and plum sauce too."

Martina smiled at him.

"To be continued over dinner."

CHAPTER 29

SPEAKING WITH RACHEL, Arnold was propped against his kitchen counter with a glass of cab in hand from the bottle uncorked the prior evening.

"Hey, just got back from dinner with Martina."

"And?"

"If Mr. Davidson's stable tonight, they'll move him out of CCU in the morning," he said, trying to inject a positive note.

Once again, her monosyllabic reply dripped icicles.

"That's good."

Two words. Crisp. Factual. Devoid of emotion. So out of character it tied his gut in a knot.

"Look, Rach," he said, frustrated over not understanding whatever she seemed to be bottling up. "I'm doing everything imaginable to wrap this up soon as possible, but with all that's going on, I'm stuck, right? You get that, don't you?" he asked, hopefully.

Silence.

"C'mon, Rach, say *something*." He fought to keep his words even and not express his mounting irritation. "This silent treatment you're giving me doesn't help either of us."

"I don't want to discuss it, Arnold. You know how I feel

about you being away. You just admitted you have no idea how
long this'll take or when you're coming back. How am I
supposed to react to *that?*"

Well, how about being less passive-aggressive?

"All I can say is I'm working it as hard as I can under the
circumstances. What more can I do?"

Is this one of those frictional issues Martina mentioned?

"If you can't answer that, then you have a bigger problem
than you realize."

"Ah, Jesus, look, give me a freaking break. I *am* making
progress. And you'll be happy to know I just recruited an
extremely talented person for the Seattle associate position, so
at least *that* issue's taken care of. See?"

Although he had yet to formalize the deal with Prisha.

"Fine. But what about when we're in Seattle and someone
needs you *here?*"

"For Chrissake, Rach, cut me some slack. That's my
highest priority when I get back. But at least this end's taken
care of. I can only do one step at a time, and you got to admit,
I'm dealing with a ton of shit that's totally out of my control."

Man, was it a thrash to muzzle his frustration.

"Who's your new associate?"

"Her name's Prisha."

Five palpable silent seconds ensued.

"A *woman?* When were you going to tell me you hired a
woman?"

He rolled his eyes.

"Just did. Besides, what's to tell? She's competent. That's
it. That's all that matters."

Silence.

*Uh-oh. Perhaps I could've phrased that last point more
delicately.*

"Look, Rach, let's not get into this on the phone, okay? I
love you, and at the moment my highest priority is *us.* Please,

let's keep calm while I work on finishing this job so I can get back and focus on getting us back on track."

More weighty silence.

What the hell?

Suddenly, he felt he had to defend himself.

"Look Rach, you were lucky; you knew what you wanted to do. You worked hard to achieve it, and now you're doing it. I was overjoyed for you when you graduated nursing school. And be truthful, even envious on account of never having a goal like that. All my friends had theirs: policeman, lawyer, doctor, accountant...you name it. Point is, they were, like, *focused.* Me? Never. And that made me feel, I don't know...inadequate? Retarded? Out of sync? Remember when we were sitting on that hunk of lava in Maui, and I asked you to move to Hawaii?"

More silence.

She even listening?

"You said you'd only consider coming if I gave up gambling. Remember?"

"Yes, but for good reasons, don't forget."

"Okay, point made. But my point is that gambling *was* my job. Other than that and tweaking SAM, I had nothing. So, I start thinking, what can I do? Especially without any education other than one lousy quarter at the U, plus what I'd picked up messing around with computers. Okay, so, yeah, it logically had to be something with computers. Then, when Mr. Davidson suggested I start a boutique IT business, I realized that's it, that's my goal. And you know what? I love it. And I want you to be able to share this with me, Rach."

More heavy echoing silence.

"Is my business a showstopper for us, Rach?"

"I have to go, Arnold. Bye."

* * *

Moving silently from shadow to shadow, Singh snuck along the edges of the rutted compacted dirt alley to Gold's house, Finally at the security fence, he stopped and glanced around. No one was watching, though that didn't mean some nosy Nelly wasn't peeking out a darkened window.

But, he doubted it.

Why keep an eye on this graveyard-still alley?

On his toes, he peered over the wall, across an inky, shadowy back yard into Gold's brightly lit kitchen. Gold had his iPhone pressed tightly to his ear, his other hand gesticulating, apparently upset with whomever he was conversing with. Singh laughed, pleased at being witness to Gold's distress. Wouldn't it be delightful to know exactly what was irritating him so that he could effectively weaponize to use in a psych-op attack? As attractive as that seemed, savoring Gold's frustration wasn't his goal tonight, reconnaissance was. And he needed to finish before someone *did* happen to spot him.

So far, every attempt to hack Gold's network had failed. His phishing attack went nowhere. So did his attempt at dissecting Gold's website. This left only one alternative: physically lay his hands on Gold's computers, but this could only happen if he broke into the house. Tonight was devoted to assessing Gold's external security as thoroughly as possible.

Luckily, he'd just walked the three blocks from where he'd ditched his Tesla when a car pulled up to Gold's house. Singh had ducked behind a patch of shrubbery to watch Gold exit the back passenger side and walk to his front door, which he unlocked with an elaborate keyless system. From what Singh could see, he suspected it combined biometric recognition—either facial or retinal—with a numeric keycode. This double authentication made entering the home extremely difficult. Not impossible, mind you, but required some serious ingenuity and cunning. This made it an intriguing, entertaining challenge. If he was anything, he was methodical, meticulous, and masterfully blessed with patience and persistence. And certainly up for this contest.

Once Gold shut the door, Singh had hurried around to the alley and straight to the rear of the property where he was now standing. First impression? Gold's security measures were impressive. Definitely far exceeded what a typical homeowner might employ. Singh suspected the not-so-subtle cameras at the corners of the second story were intended to intimidate. Even more interesting was this security wall. What could possibly necessitate such elaborate measures? This was, after all, no war zone. To Singh, such outlandish security became an attractant rather than a deterrent. Why go to such expense unless you're protecting something extremely valuable?

Yesterday he'd downloaded copies of the house-building permit and architectural plans from the City of Seattle Permits website. This had required a bit of effort but no exorbitant degree of finesse. He now knew, among other things, that the house had been constructed recently. He suspected that whatever Gold was protecting in this fortress was in the specially equipped basement room that included dedicated surge-protected electrical circuits complete with emergency backup power and temperature control. Given Gold's computer-centric business, it made sense to conclude that this was where Gold housed his network.

He watched Gold end the call in obvious frustration. With a chortle Singh turned his attention back to the task at hand. His cellphone identified the router for Gold's Wi-Fi. Good; he now had something to work with. One obvious method for breaking into the network: return with a laptop and hack the router directly. However, given Gold's paranoia for security, he suspected this would prove difficult and time consuming, requiring more hours than was worthwhile or safe. Though given enough time, he *would* prevail. During which time, Gold would continue investigating, and with the Trojan now no longer providing updates from the law-firm network, Singh's intelligence source was gone. Which was making him extremely nervous. No, he must disable Gold's network soon as possible.

He spent a few moments evaluating his surroundings more carefully. If it weren't for the brightly lit mercury vapor bulb on the nearby utility pole, this spot would be an ideal workplace. But that light made the location risky, especially given Gold's obvious paranoia. And if a car just happened to turn into the narrow passage...

It would be problematic to attempt the hack from a stationary car. First, finding a parking spot near enough was unlikely. Not only that, but an unusual car out front would be immediately obvious to any neighbor who glanced out a window or walked past. Perhaps there was a more satisfactory option...

Smiling, he walked out of the alley. He would return tomorrow during the day to examine the area in front of the house in greater detail.

* * *

Arnold studied the ruby pool of wine in the wine glass, acutely aware of how deeply he missed Chance. But this only triggered the image of the poor pooch slamming helplessly into the tree trunk, and that flooded him with guilt. Should've been more vigilant, especially under such godawful conditions. The accident wouldn't have happened if Chance had been on-leash. But Chance hated being on-leash. And besides, it was late, the streets deserted...

Chance, Rachael, Mr. Davidson. What the hell was happening to him? His life seemed suddenly besieged by calamity upon calamity. Had he somehow pissed off God? Or was this some sort of karmic retribution thing? If so, for what? What had he done to deserve this?

All right already. How can I dig out of this quagmire?

Drop everything and fly home to devote all his effort into righting their relationship? Nope.

Yeah? Why not?

For exactly the reasons you gave Martina.

Far as he could was see, the only viable option was to work his ass off, wrap up this tar baby, fly back and hopefully convince Rachael to buy into couples counseling. It seemed clear to him they needed help from an impartial, objective professional. Yeah, *he* understood that, but counseling would be a humongous hard sell for such a private person. It was very unlikely that she would agree to go.

Oh, shit.

He doubled over, both hands pressing his stomach. After a moment, the wave lessened enough for him to pop a Tums. He glanced at the wine. Man, the cab would taste like garbage what with the chalky residue in his mouth. He tossed it down the drain and then put a mug of chocolate milk in the microwave.

Butt propped against the counter, waiting on the microwave, he wondered what to do if Rachael refused counseling. See a therapist solo? Naw, that wouldn't resolve squat. Perhaps seek a short-term pharmaceutical bridge to navigate this emotional crisis? Xanax or an equivalent?

He Googled *Xanax side effects*. Nope, couldn't risk the drowsiness, not during this job. Well, so much for drugs.

Where was he? He checked his notes for a clue, but the last entry didn't click, so backtracked one earlier note. Ah, yes, the malware, hoping to find a lead on Hacker's identity. Had he already started the extraction? He double-checked his last notation and, once again gave thanks for compulsively maintaining a step-by-step report. Yes, the extraction was running. Okay, so back to work.

Hmm…was doing *any* work given his present state of mind such a red-hot idea? Good question. Delaying until morning, however, would waste even more time. Then again, what would be the cost of a mistake? He absentmindedly finger-combed his hair, weighing the issue.

Best err on the side of caution.

He tossed the hot chocolate down the sink and poured another splash of wine, tucked a rapid-release melatonin under his tongue, opened his Surface, started the next episode of *Halt and Catch Fire.*

He was just settling in when a phone alarm chimed; an infrared sensor had just picked up activity in the alley. Arnold switched from Netflix to the appropriate camera. Nothing. He burned another minute watching and waiting. False alarm? Maybe. Probably not. His gut agreed. The security wall was too high to be triggered by a random dog or cat in the alley. Had to be a person. Hacker? Or was he funneling himself into a paranoid trap? Maybe. Maybe not. After all, there was no doubt the RAT had been embedded in the law-firm network. What's more, someone *had* snooped the back end of his website. These were stone-cold facts, not paranoia.

No, someone was definitely scoping out his place. He dumped the TV series and rechecked SAM's firewall. No attacks. Not yet. But how long would that last? He'd done everything possible to limit his exposure to cyber-threats, but a hacker as clever as that asshole could—given enough time and skill—ultimately slither into his world.

It was simply a race to see which of them would nail the other first.

CHAPTER 30—Thursday

ARNOLD SCHLEPPED ON autopilot, heading home from Starbucks, mind ensnared in an endless loop, mechanically munching a classic breakfast sandwich. Dense gray overcast threatened as annoying gusts out of the north burrowed through the slightest opportunity. The only good news of the morning was that his latte should be at a perfect drinking temperature by the time he sat down to work.

At the kitchen table, Arnold tried to dial back the chatter fogging his brain. A classic chess strategy was to simplify a position for tactical advantage; it had served him well. Why not apply the same tactic to his present situation? Couldn't hurt. Resolving the Prisha thing would remove one issue from his ongoing emotional melee. He needed her, that's for sure. Plus, she was smart and more than willing to help.

What's not to like?

Okay, but what about Rachael's sensitivity about her? Like, why fan the flames? Okay, but he did need Prisha and she would cover the Seattle associate position perfectly. Question was, was the upside worth it? Certainly seemed like it, but...

Jesus, this inertia was so un-him. He hated it.

At least do something.

He checked his stock positions, which, for him served as a touchstone of normalcy in a sea of indecision. No recent trades and no outstanding orders. He disconnected from SAM.

Where was I? Oh yeah, the Trojan.

With various versions of Zeus malware so well-documented over the years, ten extractors—software that unravel the underlying program code—had been published on the Web. The trick was to find the version that would unlock this particular edition; in other words, he needed to try each one until he found the key. He'd previously downloaded all ten editions to a clean flash drive, transferred them to the air-gapped Camano server, and began to systematically eliminate one after another. He'd eliminated four already.

Time to resume work.

On the sixth one he hit paydirt. Excellent. He typed instructions for the extractor to disassemble this part of the malware. If he got incredibly lucky—something that never seemed to happen—and it yielded the hacker's legitimate IP address rather than a proxy (as Chang had predicted), he would blip over to the 7-Eleven to pick up a five-buck Lotto ticket.

Yeah, right.

Ten minutes later the extractor coughed up an IP address. For close to a minute, he stared at it.

What were the odds?

Low. Definitely low. But he had to test it, right?

And if it's real, buy a $5 Lotto.

He zoned out momentarily, fantasizing about all the cool things he could buy with the present jackpot. Like charter a jet to bring Rachael and Chance here for a minivacation. Something totally frivolous.

Assuming you get things back on track with her.

He ran the address through three verifying databases.

Chang was right. It was a phony.

Shit, back to reality.

He did the same with the Trojan from the Curchfield Technologies computer. Turned out to be identical to the one from Camano. Both spoofs. Huh. What, if anything, did this tell him? Well, this was, perversely, good news, for it was his first confirmatory evidence linking the two crimes. Which, of course, upped the odds that the same hacker committed both hacks. Okay, it was interesting finding, but did diddly-squat to uncover Hacker's identity.

He was back to square one.

* * *

Singh studied the spec sheet for Gold's elaborate security system. This wasn't your average afterthought add-on favored by most homeowners. No, this design was the bespoke product of a serious commercial design integrated into the architectural plans. Translation: cracking this mother would require some serious planning and finesse, a challenge that both delighted and turned him on.

He faced a choice of two broad approaches: brute force or finesse. Brute force went like this: break a pane in Gold's French doors, reach in to open it, run to the basement to infect the computer network. This might give him a minimum of ten minutes before the police responded. Assuming they did, considering their present staffing shortages. Would ten minutes suffice? Yes, but would this route be effective? Oh, it would be enough time to implant a Trojan all right, but Gold would instantly be alerted to what had just happened and he would respond appropriately. Moreover, a man of his talent would never stoop to such Neanderthal antics. No-no-no, brute force was simply too boorish. Singh would, instead, devise a devilishly elegant and brilliant attack, something worthy of his capabilities.

Eyes closed, he concentrated on the elements necessary

to satisfactorily humiliate Gold. First, he shouldn't discover he'd been hacked until *after* Lopez was convicted. Only then could he find out he'd been so elegantly played. The perfect garnish would be when he realized that his expensive, elaborate security system had been solidly defeated. Yes, this would serve as a crowning blow. Singh now had direction and a plan that seemed eminently suitable.

The construction blueprints and other downloaded materials made clear that the security system was installed as the house was being built. In addition, it provided the system specs. As with all high-end security, it included battery-powered backup and cellular communication capability should the need arise. It offered remote video access in addition to door and window sensors.

In other words, all the usual bells and whistles.

But, every security system has an Achilles' heel. In this case, the master control unit communicated with the entry points wirelessly. Basically, Singh could capture the system key by tapping into that wireless connection and recording the access code in real time.

* * *

Arnold was mired in a memory black hole. There was an insanely cool trick for pulling Hacker's IP address from the malware, but for the life of him, couldn't remember it. The answer danced teasingly on the fringe of recall, whispering, *hi, I'm here, but you can't catch me.* Had something to do with conning the Trojan into...

Shit-shit-shit.

What?

He downed the hot chocolate in three long gulps, started to pace again, and finally threw up his hands. Time to call for reinforcements.

"Yeah, yeah, I know...there's a wickedly wicked trick out there, damnit, but for the life of me I can't dredge it up *either*," Prisha admitted with a stitch of irritation.

Damn.

Arnold palm-thumped his forehead.

"Okay. Thanks. Sorry to bother you."

"No bother. In fact, I'm grateful for a break. I was getting a little tense."

"Well, if it comes to mind, call me immediately, okay?"

He glared at his phone, fighting the urge to hurl it against the floor. A totally stupid counterproductive urge, he knew, but the frustration was pushing his limits.

His father, a recovering alcoholic, had adopted a creed from AA that popped to mind: God grant me the serenity to accept the things I cannot change, courage to change the things I can, and the wisdom to know the difference. That definitely sounded lofty and wise and applicable, but at the moment was of absolutely no help.

Dammit.

He slipped on his parka, walked out the front door and started around the block to calm and clear his mind (hopefully). Threating rain had become light drizzle but not enough for him to flip up the hood. With both hands thrust deep in the coat pockets, he continued to struggle with recalling the trick. One dude who for sure knew would be Radical Dood, the high priest of cyber-wizardry. But Arnold still harbored a serious issue with him.

Yeah, okay, but you really need his help, right?

Absolutely. Yet the nasty aftertaste still lingered from when Dood remotely drove Naseem's car over the edge of a steep ravine, killing her. Well, that *did* happen, *but to be fair, you have to admit it did remove the crazy woman who was trying to kill you.* Yeah, but doing her that way? Man, that was, well, *cold.* Like, stone-cold cold. Did he really want to deal with the devil on this? Not really. But...

The problem with this hacker shit was how difficult it usually is to discriminate the good guys from the bad. No doubt Dood knew the trick, but at what cost? Round and round he went, before bingo, an amazing realization slapped him upside the head; for the first time in, oh, forty-eight hours, he'd been able to concentrate on a topic for more than five or ten seconds. So, applying obtuse logic, he owed Dood at least some credit. Sort of.

All right already. Stop wasting time, get on with it.

The answer he desperately needed was more valuable than a few moments of sanctimonious indignation. Just man up and ask the asshole. He glanced around. Where was he? Wow, he'd circled the block and was now mere steps from his front door. Unbelievable.

* * *

After tracking down Dood in an internet chat room, he asked him to migrate to a private room. Once securely linked and free of eavesdroppers, Arnold explained that he'd deconstructed a Zeus Trojan, but that the IP address was a proxy.

"I know there's a super-sick way to trick it into giving me the sender's real IP, but for the life of me I can't remember it. You know it?"

"Of course," Dood answered, as if this exceedingly ridiculous question brushed the boundaries of insult.

Arnold waited for him to continue but heard only silence.

Three seconds later, he asked, "Mind sharing?"

"Maybe."

Uh-oh.

"Okay...?"

WTF?

"Why do you want it?"

What, you've suddenly grown a conscience?

Arnold's antennae began vibrating.

"What difference does it make?"

"Because it sounds like you want to use it against the brotherhood."

"The *brotherhood?* The fuck's that supposed to mean?"

Arnold immediately regretted not choosing more, ah, diplomatic words. The last thing he wanted was being a lightning rod for Dood's wrath. No telling what that asshole was capable of conjuring up.

"Hey," he continued, "look I'm sorry, man. Like *really* sorry." Then, before Dood could respond, added, "It's just that my life's turned into a steaming vat of shit, I mean my girlfriend just dumped me and my dog got hit by a car..."

Well, the last part was true. Although he *was* righteously worried about Rachael. And besides, it *did* add a nice touch of realism.

"Sorry about the dog, dude." Pause. "The thing is, I worry you've switched sides."

"Switched sides? The hell you talking about?"

"I'm floored you have to ask? Last time you asked me to help, you were pillow-talking with the FB-fucking-I, Massa."

Yep, and you offed Naseem.

His phone beeped. Another call. Glanced at the screen.

Prisha.

"Hey, look, dude, I need to take another call. Sorry to bother you."

"No problem, but just so we're clear, don't *ever* bother pinging me again if you're winging it with the Evil Empire. And don't even think about trying to con me, man. You can be damn sure I'll find out about it, and I don't think you want that. In fact, I fucking guarantee it."

* * *

"Know what?" she said. "Damn thing just kept bugging and bugging the shit outta me, so I snooped around, asked a few questions and got the answer."

Gratitude welled up in Arnold's chest. He would've hugged her through the phone if he could've.

"Thank you, thank you."

"Look at it this way: consider that Trojan as a beacon that's constantly sending Hacker's C-2 messages—"

Of course.

"Therefore," he said, completing the punchline, "if I make it think I'm the C2, it'll send me Hacker's IP." The C2 is the malware Command and Control software. The Trojan employed in both capers allowed Hacker to control the infected computer just as when you allow a Dell technician in, say, Bangalore, India, to remotely take control of your machine when resolving a problem.

"Right on." Prisha said. "Meaning, if you can dissemble the—"

His phone beeped.

"Hold that thought," Arnold interrupted, "Have an important call coming in. Call you right back."

He disconnected with Prisha to answer the veterinary clinic.

"Mr. Gold?"

"Yes?"

Shit, hope it's not bad news.

"Your boy's ready to go home."

Arnold's heart soared.

CHAPTER 31

A FEMALE VET tech in pale blue scrubs, pink cross-trainers, and a dirty-blond ponytail choked by a red rubber band, led Chance—securely restrained on a short, blue, braided-nylon leash—into the waiting room. The moment Chance saw Arnold, he bolted forward. An inch. The leash snapped taut, the tech having anticipated this reaction. Tail furiously fanning, the leash levering his front paws off the cement floor, he began to whine plaintively, the cries quickly growing in intensity and frequency.

Arnold dropped to his haunches, face to face with him, and started in with a barrage of choobers, repeating, "Calm down, boy."

Chance, in turn, showered him with doggie kisses.

Reunion complete, Arnold exchanged the clinic's temporary leash for the black nylon halter and leash he'd thankfully remembered to stuff into his rucksack.

"Thank you for taking such wonderful care of him. Please pass along my heartfelt thanks to Dr. Kramer."

He made a mental note to post a glowing five-star review on Yelp.

"He's an awesome doggie. It's clear to all of us just how

smart he is."

"I couldn't agree more, but then again, I'm obviously biased." He leaned down to give Chance more choobers. "So, how do I care for him? And when do you want to see him again?"

"Basically, he needs to take it *very* easy for the next *two* weeks to let the wound and bone have a good start at healing before they're stressed at all. Feel free to take him on walks, but *please* keep him on a short leash like you just saw me use so he doesn't bolt. In particular, we don't want him making tight turns or pivots that'll stress the healing bones. For the first couple of days, expect him to sleep more than usual as the anesthesia clears his body. We'll want to see him back in two weeks for a wound check and cast change. That's about it."

"No antibiotics or anything for pain?"

"Nope. He's done remarkably well without any sign of pain." She reached down to pat his head. "He's an awesome doggie, but I'm sure you're well aware of that."

Her words instilled a momentary flush of pride, which was immediately shouldered aside by the thrum of guilt for having walked him off leash...

* * *

The Uber he'd arrived in was waiting in the parking lot as Arnold carefully shepherded Chance through the front door and into the back seat, slid in next to him, then wrapped him in a protective arm for the short ride home.

"Thanks for waiting," he told the driver.

He planned to slip him a five-dollar bill in addition to the tip he routinely added on the app.

As they exited the parking lot, he marveled at the grace with which doggies jettison the past to seemingly live in the present. He wished he possessed equivalent mental resiliency, but this thought only incited another wave of guilt for allowing

Chance to be hit by the bike.

He also was amazed at how well Chance appeared to be recovering. All due to Dr. Kramer's skill. Which not only awed him but twanged another string of guilt. Why couldn't he have done something more productive with his life instead of putzing around playing computer games? How short-sighted stupid was that? Why didn't he consider becoming a vet? Or an MD? Even a lawyer, like Mr. Davidson? Why had he allowed himself to slide down the slope of least resistance? Okay, sure, his present work provided clients with a service, but nothing as meaningful as what Dr. Kramer or Mr. Davidson do.

Why beat myself up?

Good question. He sucked in a deep breath and tried to bury the counterproductive mental debate consuming him.

Yeah, easy to say.

* * *

The driver dropped them at the Evans Field parking lot where Arnold exercised overly protective care transferring Chance from the back seat onto the wet asphalt, making sure he didn't jump down as he normally did. The earlier rain had puddled the glistening black surface with rippling, abstractly shaped grayish pools, the park grasses saturated and sad looking.

After wrapping excess leash around his hand to shorten it, Arnold moved Chance several feet from the car before it drove away. Saturated flannel clouds melded into threatening darker ominous patches, worrying Arnold they might get caught in a downpour and soak the cast. Something he should've thought to ask. Oh, well, nothing he could do about that now other than hightail it back to the warm kitchen as soon as Chance did his business.

Oh, Jesus, they were only feet from where the accident had occurred.

Another wave of guilt washed over him.

He led Chance onto the grass and shrubs bordering the pool house and opened a blue poo bag to toss in the trash on the trip home, figuring Chance would have a chance to sniff shrubs along the way. Took another look at the ominous clouds as a drop of rain splashed against his forehead.

"C'mon, boy, time to go," and started toward Green Lake Way.

* * *

"How's he doing?"

"Better," Martina said.

A single word, but Arnold heard a genuine spark of relief in it. Good. He was at his kitchen table now watching Chance snooze, curled up in a compact ball, having immediately settled into the new bolstered bed beside the French doors. Felt wonderful to have him back. His fuzzy little ball of Prozac.

"Is it okay if I pop up for a quick visit?"

"Yes, but I'd appreciate it if you make it brief. He's eager to see you, but desperately needs rest. He couldn't sleep worth a damn in CCU, so it's important he catch up now."

"No problem. I don't have much time anyway. Just brought Chance back from the vet and don't want to be gone too long."

CHAPTER 32

ARNOLD STOOD ONE step inside the hospital room, looking at a complete stranger. Mr. Davidson was sitting on a sheet draped over a high-back, sickly green vinyl recliner beside his unmade hospital bed, a white thermal blanket wrapped over his legs and abdomen. Martina occupied a similar chair facing him. Yes, here was his attorney, his friend, but then again, this person verged on the unrecognizable. Arnold had never seen Mr. Davidson so worn out, so old, so vulnerable. A rush of embarrassment flooded him for invading an extremely guarded person's intimate compromised state.

Turn and leave? Try to forget what he's witnessing? Then again, why? Did removing Mr. Davidson's pedestal humanize him? Should he be honored to be allowed a glimpse behind the meticulously crafted public persona, and in so doing, be treated as family? Regardless, Arnold was overjoyed to see his mentor in a more normal environment than surrounded by monitors and crash carts.

Martina looked up and smiled.

"Oh, there you are."

They exchanged a knowing glance, silently tightening their recently forged bond.

"Looks like you finally got some sleep," Arnold told her.
Oh, shit. That didn't sound right.

"Yes, thank God." She turned to her ex-husband, "Now that this guy's on the mend." She bent forward and briefly grasped his hand. "Loving someone and being able to live with them are two different things calling on two completely different sets of feelings and skills. Love is forever; relationship maintenance is daily work."

Her obvious deep concern for him only boosted his bewilderment over their divorce. Especially given their frequent displays of reciprocal tenderness. Why on earth couldn't they have reconciled their differences and stayed married? Then again, emotionally, they still were.

Mr. Davidson gently squeezed her hand in return, then turned his gaze back to him.

His words were spiked with sarcasm.

"See if you can find another chair. My apologies for not being better prepared to entertain."

"Naw, I'm good. I've been sitting all day. Besides, I need to bounce. Just wanted to zip in and say hi and see how good you're looking."

"Thanks for your concern." Mr. Davidson glanced at Martina. "Moreover, I want to thank you for looking after M during this...ordeal."

"Actually, we've sort of been looking after each other."

Davidson smiled at that, obviously pleased.

"Any progress on the case?"

"Some, but not as much as I'd hoped," Arnold admitted with a shrug, avoiding any mention of his other distractions. "But I've finally dug up some pretty solid evidence that another hacker other than Carlos sent out the press releases. Problem is, I haven't been able to identify him yet. Whoever he is, dude's like scary good. But what I do have so far is very encouraging."

Perhaps this last bit was a stretch, but it at least contained a whiff of validity.

"I have faith in you, son. Just keep digging and you *will* find him."

"Thanks, Mr. Davidson, that's the plan." Arnold paused, grateful that so far, he hadn't tripped up by saying anything about Chance or Rachael. Better to eliminate any further risk by leaving. "Okay then," he said with one step back toward the hall. "I need to get back to work. I'm just very happy"—*and relieved*—"to see you doing so well."

* * *

His Uber dropped him at the PCC market where he scored a box of doggie biscuits, and then browsed the deli for dinner.

"May I help you?" a counter woman asked.

With an affirmatory nod, he opened his mouth to order two thick slices of their killer meatloaf to slather with his favorite marinara sauce and sliced mushrooms when the image of Davidson in the hospital gown flashed into consciousness.

"How about a serving of vegetarian lasagna."

Well, hell, I can still use the marinara sauce.

* * *

Sheltered by the metal awning, Arnold zippered the wool sweater to his chin and flipped up the hood of his coat. Damn November wind. Of the twelve months, this one epitomized Seattle's most annoying weather, bar none. At least, for him, it did. Especially this goddamn wind. Pacific Northwest Octobers were often deceivingly temperate, lulling you into hoping *this* Fall and Winter might play out differently and maybe, just maybe, a bit less obnoxious.

Then *wham*, November hits.

Just one more reason his Honolulu home was, for him at least, essential to his mental health. Sufficiently bundled, he lowered his head and stepped onto the glistening black parking lot asphalt for the miserable slog home.

* * *

Chance was still snoozing in his new bolstered bed when Arnold entered the kitchen. Totally out of character, but exactly as the vet predicted. Arnold couldn't remember a time when Chance—the quintessential guard dog—hadn't been at the door to meet him, tail wagging, doing his happy dance as if he'd been abandoned for a month instead of an hour.

"C'mon, boy, let's go for a walk."

Chance sprang up—a bit awkwardly with the cast—yawned, stretched, then trotted enthusiastically to the front door.

They remained outside only long enough for Chance to drain a very full bladder.

In the warm kitchen again Arnold rewarded him a Bully Stick, then washed his food dish, stocked it with a cup of kibble, and refreshed his water.

With break time now over, it was time to get back to work. The first order of business: check in with Chang.

* * *

"How are Davidson and Chance doing?" Chang asked.

Arnold updated him on their conditions.

"Don't take this the wrong way, bro, but how's your head? Still in the game? I mean, seriously."

"Yeah, yeah, no problem," he lied. "What's your point?"

"I'm worried, is all, considering the shitstorm you're going through…"

Arnold surprised himself by actually considering his response. Lie?

Naw.

"Yeah, truth is, I *have* been a bit distracted." A few

seconds ticked away. "It's slowing me down for sure, but I compensate by being super cautious and double-checking every step as I go. Yet I still can't help but worry."

"Good. You *should* worry." Pause. "Just as long as you're being careful." Chang paused for an audible inhale. "Finally came up for air long enough to do some digging on our case and duplicated your finding for both Trojans. The good news is you're right: we now have our first objective evidence that one hacker is very likely responsible for both hacks."

"We have a third one too," Arnold said.

"Oh? Do tell."

Arnold explained the RAT that Kara discovered in the law-firm network.

"Kudos to her. Does it match the others?"

"Haven't had a chance to check it out thoroughly but guess it's about eighty percent likely."

Oh, shit. Speaking of which...

Kara was planning to drop off the RAT this evening.

"Good to know. I'll put that in Sentinel."

Sentinel, was the FBI's digital case management system developed to replace the paper workflow during investigations.

"Long as we're on the subject," Chang continued, "we need to list everything we know or suspect about our unsub. Why don't you start?"

Arnold considered this for a moment.

"Well, one thing that stands out is the dude clearly knows the market. In particular, he's familiar with short selling. That's not a particularly common practice for the average investor. Besides, that's how the SEC targeted Lopez so quickly, right?"

"Duly noted. Go on."

Arnold could hear the background clickity-clack of a keyboard and figured Chang was on speakerphone.

"So, it makes you want to ask," Arnold continued, now getting into the exercise, "why'd he target those particular companies? Did he have some sort of vendetta against them? If so, what's the common thread here? He ever work for either of them?"

"Hold on, you're going too fast." More clicking. "Doing great, bro, keep going."

"Then, of course, how's this all work into targeting Lopez?"

"Wait. I'm not with you on that one."

"Okay, let me put it this way: was the attack directed at framing *Lopez* or was it directed at doing damage to those two companies? If Lopez was the primary target, why? I mean, far as we know, he's never worked for them, right?"

"Right. The SEC cross-referenced that angle right out of the box and couldn't find one single employee who had been employed by both parties in any capacity."

Silence.

"The only other thing I can come up with is the dude must've done some serious-ass research, so...guess that implies he's meticulous. In other words, these jobs weren't spontaneous or capricious."

"We already have that in the report," Chang said. "And for what that's worth, they both happened on the heels of their IPOs."

"Which happened to be in their lockup periods, which lowers the odds of him being an employee." Arnold's tank was dry. "Your turn."

"Because both companies were small potatoes," Chang picked up, "we're discounting this to be the work of a large, organized group of Russians or Chinese. Those douchebags don't waste time with such petty-ante shit." He added, "In summary, everything indicated that the attacks were targeted and very *personal*, which strongly indicates there *is* a connection between Hacker and those companies, and we're flat-out missing it."

"Agreed."

"Because I'm tied up with these two higher-priority cases, I can't devote time to this yet, so I'm hoping you'll continue to try IDing his IP for us," Chang said with a glimmer of hope. "That'd be a massive help. If you were to get that, I could bump the priority and run with it."

You have to ask?

"Hey, no problem. I planned on doing that anyway."

"Thanks. Owe you one." Pause. "Have a strategy worked out?"

"Funny you should ask, that's the main reason I called," Arnold said, bringing the conversation full circle. "I'm going to try to trick the Trojan into coughing up the IP."

"How, by messaging the C2?"

"Exactly."

"It's worth a try, I guess." Chang's voice held a clear note of skepticism. "Just keep in mind that if this eventually points to a computer, that in itself proves nothing. We'd still need evidence he actually did the hack."

"I realize that, but at least it'd be a toehold. Hey, if you got a better suggestion, I'd love to hear it."

Chang snorted sarcastically.

"I wish." Pause. "Pretty sure I know the answer to this but have to ask anyway. What are your thoughts about trolling a few close colleagues? A bro with Hacker's creds must've been around the block more than once and, in the process, undoubtedly has pissed off a few people. Maybe someone'll recognize the MO and dime him."

"Seriously doubt anyone would chance it, dude."

Arnold quickly summarized his earlier exchange with Radical Dood.

Chang snickered, muttered, "Yeah, I'm shocked I asked."

* * *

Arnold stood beside the sink, tapping his iPhone against his palm, wrestling with what to do next.

Walk Chance or start coding the Trojan?

Chance was snoozing, so why wake him? On the other hand, how much did he trust his ability to code in his present state of mind? After all, Hacker wasn't some fourteen-year-old wannabe Radical Dood who would allow himself to fall prey to the trick. No, Hacker was one seasoned grade-A formidable threat. He was probably up there at Primal Fear level. Maybe even close to—if not at—Dood's exalted status. Which meant that leaving just one digital breadcrumb for him to latch onto could end up being disastrous for SAM.

In his present mental state was he really willing to take such a high stakes gamble?

CHAPTER 33

ARNOLD WALKED CHANCE toward North 80th Street, the stroll more about rebooting his mind than giving Chance another potty break. But organizing his thoughts was proving impossible. On top of everything else zinging through his brain was the fact that it might take over twenty-four hours to weaponize the Trojan. And that was only if he worked straight through. Jesus. With all his other diversions, it might take even longer. He could imagine Rachael's reaction to the news. But there was no way to put lipstick on this one. He simply shook his head at the anticipated blowback.

By now, Chance had marked just about everything he had sniffed and was peeing air with each leg lift. Okay, diversion over.

* * *

Arnold listened to Rachael's phone play the "Leave a message" recording.

Seriously? It's escalated to this? Try again?

A hunk of ice crystallized in his gut. She never ignored his calls. Never. And this was his third unanswered call in the past ten minutes. He texted, asking her to call.

The microwave beeped. He stirred his hot chocolate and waited. Five minutes dragged past. Nothing. Busy at work? Come to think of it, was she even on today? No idea. Or was this some sort of statement? Yeah, somehow it was feeling like one. Discouraged, helpless, feeling a bit sorry for himself he slumped into the chair.

Hold on...

Had something happened to her, making her physically unable to answer? An accident? A sudden illness?

Arnold burned the next half hour calling her employer and then every hospital on the island. Not at work. Not at a hospital. Where was she? Good question. Now what? A vaporous gut premonition warned him that this uncharacteristic radio silence was a prelude to some, like, *really* bad news.

He suddenly realized Chance was whimpering and nose-nudging his elbow. He looked down at the pooch. Doggies know. He gave him a reassuring behind-the-ear scratch.

"Everything's good, boy. Everything's good."

But Chance wasn't buying it; his whimpering increased.

Doggies know.

Shit. Now what?

Mr. Davidson would know what to do. But under the circumstances, seeking his advice was a non-starter.

Yeah, true, but how about Martina?

* * *

"I'm sorry to bother you, but do you have a minute?"

"For you?" Martina said. "Always. What's wrong? You sound upset."

He hated to ask, but...

"Is there any chance we can talk? In person?"

"Oh, my God. Has something happened to Chance?"

He sighed.

"No. It's Rachael. You still at the hospital?" hoping that if she were, it might diminish the inconvenience of an impromptu late evening call.

"Yes, but I was about to leave. Palmer's heart has done well enough that the cardiologist said if this continues overnight, he'll be discharged tomorrow. Why?"

An idea hit.

"You eaten yet?"

"Not yet, but plan to."

"How about dropping by? I was just about to run over to Flavio's for pizza, so…"

"How can a girl pass up an offer like that? Tell you what, I'll pick up a salad *en route*."

"Excellent. What toppings do you prefer?"

"Anything but pineapple. Whoever decided pineapple belongs on pizza should be sentenced to life without the possibility of parole."

Oh, shit.

Kara was intending to drop by the malware copy tonight. He called her, said he was running late, and could she put it off until tomorrow? She said she was also working late, so, "What time should I come by?" She sounded suspiciously eager.

Bad idea, dude. You're playing with fire.

Was she due in the office first thing in the morning? Probably. Perhaps throwing out a late hour would dissuade her.

"Oh, jeeze…won't be free until oh, eleven o'clock?"

"Fine, I'll see you then."

Shit.

"Okay but call first…just in case."

"Later."

Seriously, dude? Why not tell her you no longer need it, so just go ahead and delete it? Why green-light a visit? Well, a quick look wouldn't hurt, right?

Oh, give me a freaking break, dude. You like that she hits on you. You like the gamble of playing with fire. You find it exciting, the titillating allure, the curiously visceral temptation. Especially now, with Rachael seemingly pushing you away.

* * *

"My god, you look in worse condition than you sounded," Martina said, breezing through the door, a plastic container of green salad in hand. "I've never seen you look so stressed."

"I can only think of one other time," he replied, referring to a few years back, when he had regained consciousness as the original house was burning down around him, his wrist handcuffed to a heavy oak desk, coughing his lungs out from thick black smoke. Yeah, that experience definitely qualified as *The Mother* of all stressors.

"Let's see if talking will help." Martina set the salad on the counter before stripping off her coat to toss over the kitchen chair opposite his workspace. "It smells good."

"Flavio's. They're the best. May I pour you some wine?" he asked.

She was heading for the counter, peeling the plastic lid off the salad container.

"Might as well get the chill off this. Yes, I'd love one."

"Where did you pick it up?"

"Zeek's. They're premade and ready to go. Their Greek salad pairs beautifully with pizza, I believe."

Arnold held up a bottle, his everyday Rutherford Cab.

"You okay with this? Sorry, but I don't have a Chianti."

"If it's red and alcoholic it's fine by me tonight. I'm not as finicky as Palmer about wine." She shook her head. "Sorry, under the circumstances I suppose that's insensitive and uncalled for, and I'd retract it if I could."

Arnold flipped a dismissive wave before popping the cork

and pouring their glasses, which he carried to the kitchen table. He handed Martina hers before settling into the opposite chair, pushing the Surface aside. The pizza was in the warming oven while the salad remained on the stainless-steel counter by the sink.

Glass raised, he said, "To health and happiness."

It was Mr. Davidson's favorite toast.

After clinking, Martina took an appraising sip, nodded approval, returned her attention to him.

"Whatever it is, Arnold, it can't be *that* bad. You look as if you're in emotional crisis."

Arnold slumped, shaking his head, forcing himself to verbalize his fear.

"I'm worried that Rachael's about to do something drastic. I have no idea what that is, but can't shake a dread in my gut, and it's eating me alive."

Martina set her glass on the table and began rotating it by the stem.

"Do you know this for fact, or do you *suspect* it?"

"I suspect it, but, for good reason."

"Why? Because you're here on business?" she asked, appearing genuinely bewildered.

He nodded. "I know…that sounds so trivial, but for her it's, like, massive."

She stopped rotating the glass.

"Is there any chance you're over-interpreting?"

He shrugged.

"Guess so, but that's part of the problem. I'm not sure what she thinks. She's still not answering calls or texts and that's so not her. Yeah, sure, we've had our disagreements from time to time just like all couples, but we've always been able to talk through them. But not this time. That's what's so upsetting. This feels way different."

A nod of acknowledgement.

"Are you sure nothing else has happened to her? An accident or illness?"

"No, not *for sure* sure. But I've checked every place I can think of. She's not at work or in any hospital or ER either. What I do know for sure is she's royally pissed at me." He pressed both palms against his temples. "It's starting to feel like someone's stuffed me in a food processor and pushed the High button."

"Oh, Arnold..." Resigned sadness filled her words, "why stay here? Why not go back? Noah can easily hire another investigator."

"Nope." he said with an emphatic head shake. "Can't do that."

Her eyebrows raised in a nonverbal ask for an explanation. He sipped wine, burning a moment to assemble a clear explanation.

"See if this makes sense. There's just too much going on right now, what with Mr. Davidson in CCU and Chance recovering. There's no way I can leave until both of them are out of the woods, right? Plus, I need to lock down the Seattle associate position. I mean, that alone is reason to stay." He raised a hand, silencing any rebuttal until he finished. And God forbid he lose his train of thought again. "Did I tell you her reaction when I told her about Prisha?"

This appeared to surprise her.

"No."

Didn't think so.

Good, he hadn't completely lost his mind. Yet.

"She was like super upset. I mean...almost to the point of accusing me of sleeping with her. I was shocked."

He'd never given her cause to question his loyalty.

With a smile, Martina said, "Think about that, Arnold. That's jealousy. You don't feel jealous over someone you don't care strongly about."

"Hang on, I haven't gotten to the most important point." He inhaled deeply. "If we're to have any prayer of a future together, we have to support each other's careers. In grade school, when all the other kids wanted to be, I don't know…long-distance truck drivers, cops, heart surgeons, whatever, all I focused on was being the world's best gamer. I mean, *really,* gaming? When I was in, oh, ninth grade maybe, I totally got into AI. Okay, cool, that's great as a hobby and all, but not a *career.* Didn't matter. I kept at it and I cobbled three computers together and was blown away by what that could do. That's how SAM was born."

His voice had the ring of a proud parent.

"That sucked me right in. I became, like, obsessed with refining it. But in truth, all I was really doing was intellectually escaping adulthood." He thought about what he'd just said, shook his head. "I know, but there's no other way to describe it. Then one day Mr. Davidson puts this bug in my head when he suggests I start an IT business, and *boom*, I have a goal: Gold and Associates. My own business. *My* company," pausing to savor the concept, "and I love it."

He continued, "The point to this little rant is that I refuse to let Rachael force me to abandon my commitment to Mr. Cain and Mr. Davidson. Not only that, but I won't allow her to force me into giving them an inferior product by doing a half-ass job just so I can get back quicker. That'd not only damage my business reputation, but it'd seriously damage *our* relationship on account of I'd always blame her. See what I'm saying?"

Martina was rotating her wine glass again.

"That's a valid point. It's interesting that Palmer has never mentioned your devotion toward the business. Perhaps it's because he's as unaware of it as I was." Pause. "I believe you're saying this is a critical test of your relationship. Yes?"

"That's one way to put it."

"Have you tried explaining this to her?"

"I've *tried*, but she refuses to discuss it. Now, with the Prisha thing fanning the embers, she's gone flat-out radio-silent."

Martina started to say something, then appeared to back off.

"What?" Arnold asked.

"Then I hate to admit that I share your concern. But if it's any consolation, I agree to not allow her to dictate your business decisions. It's good that you ask for her opinion, but ultimately those decisions are yours to make. Otherwise, like you say, you'll eventually regret it and that may create repercussions."

* * *

Three pieces of pizza and only a few bites of salad remained by the time they pushed their grease-stained paper plates away and polished off the dregs of the wine.

Sighing contentedly, Martina stretched.

"There're times when I crave comfort food and pizza is right up toward the top of the list." She stifled a yawn with her fingertips. "Sorry, but the combination of fatigue and wine taking their toll and not any indication of your company. I'm mentally and physically exhausted. This evening was precisely what I needed. For the first time since Palmer's attack, I feel relaxed enough to suspect I can sleep through the night." Pushing back her chair, she opened her cellphone. "The time had come for Sir Uber to whisk me home."

* * *

Arnold and Chance walked her to the waiting car.

After she slipped into the back seat, Arnold leaned down, one hand on the roof, the other holding the door open, said, "Thanks for listening. I feel better now, it's been...therapeutic."

"I can't thank *you* enough for the emotional support you've provided these past days. As you can certainly agree, I've been a complete mess. Knowing you're there when I needed strength has been more help than you realize."

"Thanks for such kind words. Okay," he said, straightening up and closing the door, "sleep well. I'm sure we'll be in touch sometime tomorrow."

In the kitchen, Arnold stared at his Surface, unsure of which task to start next. Although he too needed a good night's sleep, he was too on edge to retire just yet. He poured a small glass from a previously opened bottle of cab, then settled into his chair, pondering the Rachael dilemma. His phone rang.

Oh, shit, it's Kara.

He'd completely forgotten.

CHAPTER 34

KARA GLANCED AROUND as Arnold shut the door behind her.

"Wow, nice place," she said.

At least the wind had died down. Somewhat.

"Let me take your coat," Arnold said, hand out.

Big mistake, dude. Should've just asked for the flash drive.

Then again, he suspected they were both toying with the same game and she might've parried that request. He watched her slide from a heavy, black thigh-length North Face jacket revealing tight stone-washed jeans, black cashmere V-neck sweater, and Adidas cross-trainers; a noted change from the typical business suits she favored at work. Her red hair was particularly dramatic against the black sweater. Looking good. Sexy. Like, *treacherously good.*

"Did you have any problem finding this place?" he asked, hanging her coat in the closet to distract from ogling her.

Jesus, just get the freaking thumb drive and get her gone.

"Nope. That's what GPS is all about. Where's your computer so we can get to work."

All business, even teasingly holding up the flash drive, a

coy smile tugging her lips.

Arnold found her statement appropriate yet curiously disappointing while at the same time provocative.

Jesus, dude, don't even think it.

"Perfect. Let's do this. I need to get some rest."

"On one condition," she quickly added, slipping the thumb drive into her skin-tight rear pocket with a strange twinkle in her eye.

"What's that?" he asked, hoping for... *what, dude?*

He picked up a kitchen chair to take with him.

"That you let me watch," she answered, tailing him down the stairs. "I want to see how you handle the transfer. Dealing with malware can be dicey."

Hmmm.

"No problem. Here," he said, setting the kitchen chair to his left. "Oh, before we start, would you like a glass of wine?"

Seriously dude?

"I'd love one."

"Right back."

A moment later he handed her a glass, which she immediately set on the floor. Then she slid her chair closer until their thighs brushed each other, the small act turning him on.

"Okay," Arnold said, trying to suppress the stirring in his groin. "If I had to bet, this'll turn out to be the same as the other two." He inserted the drive into a USB port, typed the command to copy it to the Camano server under a unique identifier. "Cheers!" he said, raising his glass, purposely avoiding Mr. Davidson's favorite toast.

They clinked and sipped. As he returned his attention to the malware, her hand slid onto his thigh.

She murmured, "This is so *exciting.*"

He swallowed but said nothing.

"How long you think this'll take?" she said.

"The comparison? Depends."

"It gets so hard waiting," she whispered, cupping his bulging crotch. "I have a feeling you agree."

Arnold opened his mouth to say something but blanked. Instead, he reached down and simply removed her hand.

A minute later he said, "Yep. It's identical to the other ones."

"Show me."

He showed her. Although he hadn't done an in-depth comparison, it appeared to be the same version of Zeus used in both corporate espionages. Case closed.

Kara departed shortly afterward, having consumed all of two minuscule sips of wine. Arnold was back at the kitchen table, grappling with fresh anxiety over Hacker. Not a premonition exactly, but close enough to make him hyper anxious.

Why? What the hell was provoking this?

It hit him. After a flurry of activity—probing his website then triggering his perimeter sensors—the offensive activity suddenly settled into nothing but eerie hollow silence. Which could only mean one thing; something was brewing. What? There was no way to know. Meaning, there was no way to prepare a defense other than making goddamn sure SAM was as secure as possible without taking it completely off-line.

The one thing he *did* know with conviction was that Hacker was out there on the side of the road with his rattler going like crazy.

Friday Morning

Arnold was programming a bot downloaded from a nefarious Dark Web site known for providing very cool hackerware. A "bot"—short for robot—was a chunk of software designed to execute a specific task any number of times.

Arnold reprogrammed the instructions so that immediately after embedding itself into Hacker's C2, this bot would send back the account name and IP address and then—more importantly—self-destruct, thereby eliminating a trail back to him. All this in a matter of two seconds. The ultra-short life reduced—but didn't eliminate—the risk of it being detected and captured. Yet the simple act of sending the bot to Hacker's computer for even two seconds *did* place Arnold at risk. If—God forbid—Hacker had built a defense for such an attack by installing a trap capable of capturing and neutralizing a bot, he would have a conduit straight back to him. Meaning, if Arnold's instructions weren't perfect and the bot malfunctioned...

Jesus, he didn't want to even think about it.

So, the big question—the one accounting for his present emotional shitstorm—boiled down to a critical question: was his coding absolutely perfect? For if he had unwittingly committed even the tiniest error, Hacker would pounce without hesitation and destroy him.

C'mon man, it's good enough. This ain't Coding 101.

Oh, yeah? Are you one-hundred-percent sure about this?

Especially considering the freaking truckload of distractions messing with your brain? Put another way, how can you be so sure your judgment's not impaired if it's impaired?

Pertinent question, don't you think?

Okay, so what to do about it? Get a second opinion?

Yeah, probably. On the other hand, time was blurring past at rabid bat speed while Hacker continued to lurk in nearby water like a hungry shark. Each additional minute fiddle-farting around playing *what-if* mind games was, well, wasting time.

Aw, shit, go ahead, send the damn thing.

Or run it past a second set of eyes?

Yeah, a second opinion was prudent.

Okay. Who?

Scratch Dood. Ditto for Fear. Same with Chang. There was no way he would be complicit in any act carrying the slightest whiff of illegally. Even for a CI.

Leaving him one choice: Prisha.

* * *

Prisha answered the phone call saying, "Weren't you supposed to call back yesterday when we discussed the C2 thing?"

"Oh, crap," Arnold said, palm-thumping his forehead, "You're right. My bad. Sorry. Look, it's that I've had a ton of shit going on that makes it hard to remember things."

"Yeah, I sorta got that impression. What up?"

"I need a quick reality test on this thing I'm doing, but in the spirit of full disclosure it's, ah, not exactly kosher. Got a problem with that?"

She hesitated long enough to be concerning, but eventually said, "Guess that all depends on what you want. If it's to troubleshoot a computer, hey, no problem. If it's to stick up a 7-Eleven at gunpoint, well dude, I'm out. Just so we're clear."

He laughed. He liked her attitude.

"I want you to double-check a bot I wrote to make sure I'm not messing up."

"Yeah? What's this bot do?" she asked suspiciously.

Tell her?

Hell, why not? What did he really have to lose?

"Okay, so here's the deal."

He explained the case in detail, going through his reasons for believing Hacker set Lopez up to take the fall for the stock sabotages.

"Hey, no problem. Wanta send me a copy or just talk through a checklist?"

Having her actually read the code would be ideal but too time-consuming. He needed to stay ahead of that damn shark circling closer and closer.

"I'll settle for a checklist."

She sounded as if she was already distancing herself from any potential repercussion.

"Are you sure?"

"Look, I know it's not the best option, but I've got this really bad feeling that asshole's zeroing in on me, so..."

"Okay, but just so we're clear, I take no responsibility on this." Pause. "For starters, how long is it in his computer?"

"Only long enough to send back his ID and IP. Two, maybe three seconds, max."

"Okay, check." Pause. "Then what?"

"Then it's supposed to self-destruct."

"Supposed to? You don't sound all that confident on this point."

Arnold hesitated. Exactly. Here was the crux. Mess this part up and it's *hasta la vista, baby.*

Screw it. Don't waste time having her line read the code.

He shook his head, feeling the pressure of time evaporating quickly.

"Guess I'll find out."

"Dude, that *really* doesn't sound all that encouraging." Silence. "Okay, assume the worse, assume he miraculously snags the bot *before* it destructs. Is there *anything* in the code that'll point to you?"

"Yeah, of course. My IP."

She'd just scored a ton of points for asking the right questions. He liked her style of analysis, of breaking down a situation into essential points. Organized. Clear. Even more importantly, she was eager and able to work collaboratively. Besides, she was devilishly smart, nonjudgmental, and had a network of connections.

What's not to like?

"You willing to risk it?"

Although not absolutely convinced his code was flawless, he decided to take the gamble.

"Don't think I have any other choice."

"Oookay," she said, disconcertingly dubious.

"Yo, Prisha, it's cool. Seriously."

"Oh, yeah? Why's that?"

"On account of I'm sending it from a Curchfield Technologies machine. So if he—"

"You *asshole.* Why didn't you just say that?"

When Arnold didn't answer, she asked, "How the hell did you—"

"That's classified."

She laughed.

"Guess you know what you're doing. Lemme know how it plays out."

"Indeed." Pause. "As long as we're talking about work, how'd you like a job as the full-time Seattle Associate for Gold and Associates?"

"You serious?" she asked with a clear note of excitement.

"Utterly."

"Whoa, that's seriously sick. But before we get ahead of ourselves, what exactly does this entail? And, what sorta compensation package you talking about?"

Compensation package? Well, yeah, dumb shit.

He hadn't given it a thought on account of paying Fear on a case-by-case basis. Which, now through the 4K UHD clarity of retrospect, had been his only wise decision concerning the asshole. But for an Associate position, he needed to draft an actual agreement. In contrast to Fear—who he never believed would contribute to company growth—Prisha would. In other words, her agreement would require some careful and significant planning.

Suddenly, being CEO of Gold and Associates was becoming way more complex. Especially if it meant having to deal with such annoying details as setting up accounting software and payroll and all the other numerous nuts-and-bolts details that would rob him of enjoying the fun stuff, like business development. Why can't managing a business be fun too?

Well, because of the pure unadulterated drudgery it required, that's why.

Whoa...a lightning-bolt idea zapped him: *Rachael.* These were precisely the kind of administrative minutia she would thrive on. Besides, involving her—if that was even possible—might just be the secret ingredient to make the business more palatable to her.

"Arnold?"

"Sorry, I needed a moment is all...okay, how's this: twelve hundred a month base pay plus a percentage of the prior month's collections based on your percentage contributions to that month's billings? This way you can keep your present jobs if you want." Another idea flashed to mind. "*Or* you can roll them into the Gold and Associates' case load to count toward your production."

He liked how his plan was sounding as the words were flowing off his tongue.

"It sounds exciting, but when you say percentage of the prior month's collection, what exactly do you mean?"

His brain cycled through some calculations.

"Okay, as of now, you're our only associate. Previously, I subcontracted a job here and there to a few friends."

Friends? Wouldn't really label Fear a friend.

"But nothing regular. That outsourcing stops now unless we need extra help."

Jesus, you wish.

"Moving forward you'll receive forty percent of our

collections. Keep in mind that the moment I get back to Honolulu, I'll start looking for an associate there. From then on, we'll only add techs or associates as needed. Then, once we grow to more than two associates, we'll establish a mutually agreed-upon profit-sharing plan that still covers the overhead. But I haven't planned that far ahead yet. Does that make sense?"

He cringed at the work this newly unleashed monster would require.

"Wow that sounds amazing. I'm totally down with it."

"So, we're good? You're on board?"

"Most definitely!"

Whew. Maybe locking down a Seattle associate would help smooth things over with Rachael. Assuming, of course, she would speak to him once she'd learned he'd hired Prisha.

CHAPTER 35

ARNOLD PACED TIGHT circles in the small basement room, vacillating between hitting SEND or asking Prisha to actually lay eyes on the code, hyper-aware that each second of hesitation was another second down the drain while Hacker moved ahead with whatever attack he was preparing. The shark's presumed presence kept tingling his tailbone.

Jesus, do it. Stop procrastinating.

He stopped and stared at the keyboard, thinking, worrying.

You love to gamble, right? Well okay, here's a biggie. Roll the freaking dice.

His index finger hovered above the ENTER key. Once pressed...

He swallowed, slowly withdrew his hand. What were the odds of Hacker capturing the bot? Zero? That was a total unknown, for there was no way of even getting a handle on it. They were low, but how low? Everything hinged around having a trap built into his system and how probable was that? Big question. Round and round...but...someone always buys the winning Powerball ticket, right? Improbable as that is. *And it's* never *me.*

Worst-case scenario? Well, that part of the equation was easy: Hacker somehow is able to worm his way into his network and retaliates by completely annihilating SAM. Or worse, discovers that SAM controls his portfolio. Then what? How disastrous might that be? A cyber-reprisal shitstorm of biblical dimensions.

Oh, for Christ sake, just do it, get this shit over with.

He punched ENTER, then quickly withdrew his finger as if it'd touched an ember. There. Done. No going back now. What time was it? He checked. Now what? Wait, that's what. Okay, but...

He couldn't concentrate or sit, so resumed pacing. Nuke a hot chocolate?

Upstairs, he reconsidered. Nope, he'd already downed too many today. Another glance at the time. If the bot worked, the results should back. Go ahead and check? He was afraid to, but knew he had to, that each passing second was only amping his anxiety.

Arnold's vision suddenly became hyper-sharp, images of vibrantly intense colors and razor edges, his sense of smell more sensitive, more potent. Heart racing, he realized he was hyperventilating.

Jesus, chill, dude, chill.

Only way to chill would be to settle the issue by checking. He blew a long breath, figured what the hell, dropped into the chair, then froze, eyes closed, mouse in hand...

Wait.

If Hacker *did* intercept the bot, would he send back a trap? Well, that *could* happen. In theory. But realistically? The odds weren't great. And besides, this wasn't the time to be getting all paranoid and shit. The prudent thing to do would be to see if the bot responded to a command. For, if it blew itself up like it was supposed to, it couldn't reply, right?

Right.

He pinged the bot, sat back, watched five sloooow seconds tick past on his watch. No response. Just for drill, he waited another ten seconds. Still nothing.

A wave of relief reverberated within him. Convinced that his caper had been executed as programmed, he exhaled a long sigh of relief. Holy shit, he might've just pulled off the riskiest part in his whole plan. A jolt of adrenaline struck, jacking his heart, sending his brain into the euphoric stratosphere.

He jumped up, yelled, "God*damn!*" and fist-pumped air.

A sharp bark came from upstairs.

Cool it.

He didn't want Chance to try climbing downstairs in a cast.

"It's okay, boy. Stay." He ran upstairs. Chance stood in the doorway peering down at him. Arnold dropped onto the top step and began to pet him, cooing, "It's okay, boy, it's okay."

What an absolute unadulterated rush. Hadn't experienced one of these puppies since his gambling days. No wait, that's not entirely true; he'd experienced one while fleeing Bundy Phillips' yard the night he hacked the asshole's router. Oh, man, he loved feeling so hyper-alive and jacked. Yes, but a crash inevitably followed these rushes.

Hmm…maybe Rachael was smart about demanding he stop gambling.

But had he really stopped?

Wasn't it a gamble to send the bot?

Or when he crept Phillips' property to hack his network?

Admittedly, these escapades weren't the quite same as betting the spread on Sunday's Seahawks game or a hand of Texas Hold'em. But they were gambles nonetheless. Still, somehow this shit felt more, well, respectable. Her issue had been with his flat-out online, Las Vegas-type shit, like poker and sports. In distinction, weaponizing a bot was a super-cool sophisticated tactic for hunting a criminal (in other words, righteous), so yeah, he could rationalize it. Still...

All right already.

Did he have Hacker's IP address?

He sucked a long slow calming breath and steeled himself to look, then clicked the mouse button. Holy shit, there it was, the whole enchilada: IP address, internet provider, plus some additional intel of lesser significance. He high-fived the wall.

Totally tubular, dude.

Now came the difficult job of leveraging this into identifying the asshole behind the address.

CHAPTER 36

ARNOLD LEANED, FOREHEAD against the wall, eyes closed, working through his next moves step by step. It was a simple enough goal in concept—use the IP address to identify Hacker—but much more difficult to actualize. He would begin by researching several databases. The tricky part: the closer he got to the asshole, the riskier his exposure would be.

He would need to dance a delicate ballet.

So, he had spent the past hour polishing his strategy into one as straightforward and foolproof as possible. But he knew too well that even the most meticulous plans always have unanticipated glitches. Hell, that's why they're called *unanticipated*. He just prayed that whatever curveball came zinging his way wouldn't be catastrophic.

Question was, was *he* ready?

Thought so. Okay then…

He ran Hacker's IP address through an online database of present and past registered domains looking for anything relevant, such as a website. Nothing turned up. Then again, he hadn't expected a dude of Hacker's caliber to actually have one. But hey, no need to get sloppy and overlook a point just because it seemed like a longshot.

Next, he ran the IP address through a database capable of localizing the computer to within a three-mile radius. Bingo. Holy shit, the machine was in *Seattle.* That was interesting. Perhaps relevant. After updating his case file, he backed it up again. At this point, he planned to back up each new finding as it occurred. You never knew when a small bit of intel could prove pivotal.

Though narrowing the hunt to a three-mile radius represented clear progress, being a high-density vertical city meant he was looking at one shitload of computers per square block. He needed way more granularity. A second—more expensive—database refined the radius to within two-blocks. Nice! Now *this* was progress. He fist-pumped air.

He was up, pacing again, phone to ear, waiting for Chang to answer.

"What up, bro?"

"Drum roll please...." Arnold's free hand was nervously raking his fingers through his curly black hair. "I've got Hacker's IP to within a two-block radius. Guess where it is?"

He smiled in self-satisfaction.

"Truly? You're asking me to fucking guess?"

Out of force of habit, Arnold nodded even though Chang couldn't see him.

"Unbelievable. You really want me try?"

Silence.

"Okay then, Gaborone."

"*What?*"

"Gaborone."

Arnold frowned.

"Where the hell's Gaborone?"

"Botswana."

After a moment of silence, Chang added, "It's a joke, bro. I mean, asking me a question like that... C'mon."

Arnold felt a slight tingle of victory surge though him.

"Seattle, dude. He's right here in this freaking city."

"Whoa. And you've got it down to a couple of blocks?"

Arnold smiled proudly.

"Yep."

"How did you manage that?"

"I ran it through Digital Element."

"That's impressive. You pay for that, or did you...?" leaving Arnold to fill in the blank.

"I'm legit and it's worth every dime. Besides, I can write it off as a business expense."

"Yeah, but last I checked, subscriptions run almost a hundred K per year."

Arnold paused for emphasis. What was coming should really blow Chang's socks off.

"Then I put it through MadX."

"You have *got* to be shitting me. Like, 'See your network the way an adversary would,'" Chang said, quoting their website's tag line.

"I shit you not. Besides a server and a few other machines, he's got—get this—a home weather station inside his—

"Say what?"

"A home weather station."

"Yeah, I heard that. But seriously, it's *inside*? I mean, why inside?"

"Who the fuck knows? Maybe he's obsessed with living-room carbon-dioxide levels."

Chang guffawed at that one.

"But here's the real kicker: I have his GPS coordinates." Arnold said proudly.

After a moment of stunned silence, Chang said, "How the hell did you manage *that*?"

Was that a hint of awe in his tone?

"From the weather station, dude," Arnold said as if the

answer should be self-evident.

"Unfuckingbelievable. Give them to me and I'll do a rundown on the location."

"Whoa, it's not ready for prime time just yet. Turns out it's a twelve-story condo. He could be in any of the apartments."

"Knew it was too good to be true," Chang muttered. "Go ahead, give 'em to me anyway and I'll see what I can come up with, but don't get your hopes up. I'm still underwater on these other cases so will have to sandwich it in whenever. In other words, it'll suck hind tit."

He could certainly use the Bureau's help, but he knew it would be fruitless to try to push. Then again, he wasn't counting on their help at this point anyway.

"Understood."

"You're doing a great job, bro. I can't emphasize enough how much help this is. Fisher's going to love this."

* * *

"How's he doing?" Arnold asked Martina.

"It's been seven blessed hours without a problem. If this continues, they'll move him to rehab."

The good news lifted Arnold's spirits.

* * *

Rachael's cell rang until it finally rolled over to, "I'm unable to take your call right now, so please leave a message after the beep."

Shit. She never didn't answer. Well, hardly never. Even when she was pissed at him. But this…this new *thing* felt, well, different. Foreboding kept gnawing his gut like a freaking beaver. This disagreement—or whatever you wanted to call it—seemed to be escalating into something more than a simple hissy fit.

Shit. Don't even think it.

"C'mon, boy, want to go for a walk?"

Chance rocketed from his bolstered bed, skittering toward the front door.

Jesus, dumb shit. Don't mess up Dr. Kramer's good work.

* * *

His worry over Rachael was destroying the concentration needed to maintain pace. Yeah, okay, he *was* plodding along, making *slow* progress, but he was losing the race. Two hours ago, SAM's firewall had been probed. Hacker. There was no other explanation—meaning he'd correctly interpreted Hacker's silence as a harbinger of something bad on its way.

But, this also raised a couple of key questions, like how the hell did the asshole discover SAM? And this was very concerning. SAM's firewall remained intact for now, but eventually...

He took Chance for a short walk. The break was just what he needed: despite his constant background brain cacophony, he'd been able to concoct a rough plan for teasing out which of the hundred and forty-some units was Hacker's.

CHAPTER 37

ARNOLD SUPERIMPOSED THE GPS coordinates on Google Maps. Yep, they intersected right over Seatown Lofts condominium.

Switching from the Map to Street View, he studied the building and its immediate neighborhood, then ran intensive Google and Bing searches for every scrap of information available on the building: its developer, architect, general contractor, structural layout, and any additional intel that could be dredged up.

The initial owners had begun moving into the newly opened building in the waning months of 2008. An in-depth search of relevant city databases yielded a string of permits and allied information and, ultimately, the building's floor plans. Three basement levels served as the parking garage along with a handful of storage lockers. The ground floor contained a lobby and three commercial spaces. The second floor included additional storage and maintenance rooms.

Floors 3 thorough 11 comprised fifteen stacks of apartments. The floor plan for each unit within a stack remained identical to the one above and below, but subtly different from the others on that floor; all variations on a one bedroom plus den configuration. The only exceptions were the two-bedroom twelfth-floor penthouses.

Okay, now we're getting somewhere.

Superimposing the GPS coordinates on the building pinpointed Hacker's apartment to the northwest corner stack; a total of ten units if you included the penthouse.

Could Hacker afford a penthouse?

For some reason, Arnold doubted it, but for the sake of completeness, he included it in the list.

He began pacing again, totally amped, smelling the coppery scent of blood, convinced of finally closing in on Hacker. He stopped, pressed both palms to his temples.

Think.

A problem this complex couldn't be solved by working things out mentally but instead needed to be organized step by step in a logical progression. In other words, graphed out in a flowchart to make it easier to identify errors and logic traps.

At the top of a fresh sheet of a yellow legal tablet, he printed *Stack 8 Inhabitants* in large block letters. Directly underneath he wrote, *names?*

Good question, and a real bitch to answer.

Under that, he jotted, *Find list.*

Hmm....how the hell could he do that?

Well, various city and county departments had lists: the tax assessor's office, for one. But getting his hands on a copy would not only be problematic but time-consuming. Not impossible, just problematic. And most likely, illegal. The more he considered this route, the more he became aware of the drawbacks. A major issue, for example, was that the property records listed unit owners but not necessarily occupants. Most condominiums contain units purchased solely to be rentals. What's to say Hacker wasn't renting? Still, finding a list of unit owners would at least be a start.

Okay, so say he got his hands on a list. Then what? How

Allen Wyler

could he leverage that information into the names of actual residents? Hmm...sitting back, tapping the mechanical pencil against his incisors, he thought of the various condominiums he'd visited, like Mr. Davidson's in Honolulu.

Didn't they all have a lobby desk manned by...what's that person called? A concierge?

Yeah, that seemed about right.

A Google search gave him a phone number for Seatown Lofts. After putting it in his file, he dialed.

A voice answered, "Seatown Lofts, Michael speaking."

"Sorry, wrong number." Arnold disconnected. Okay, the front desk was a definite starting place. All he needed now was to gin up a plausible scam to score a list of residents. How would that work? What about their administrative infrastructure? Don't buildings have a property management company for services like collecting monthly maintenance fees?

An internet search led him to the DCW Property Management website.

Interesting.

The site contained a directory devoted to each Homeowner Association under management. Each directory should contain building-specific documents such as the HOA's declaration, rules and regulations, etc. Unfortunately, directory access was restricted—an obvious security precaution—to property owners. What were the odds the Seatown Lofts folder contained a list of current owners and renters?

After jotting a few critical notes on the flowsheet, he began to pace again, noodling a sellable tale to access their directory. The obvious, most direct route would be to skip any attempt at social engineering and just crack the freaking website. But, depending on its security, this would burn an unknown amount of time while exposing him to unnecessary risk. And besides, a direct hack would definitely be illegal, and

Mr. Cain's warnings to stay within the law reverberated loudly through his brain. If even a just teensy-weensy speck of illegal work wound up in subsequent prosecution, it could potentially expose the Cain/Davidson team to very real jeopardy and he wasn't about to gamble that.

Back to square one. The only alternative he saw was to finagle the password out of DCW. Which would be extremely tricky. For sure, it would most definitely require some serious-ass planning. After noodling on it for a couple minutes, he zeroed in on an idea.

* * *

As the microware heated a fresh mug of milk, Arnold mentally played out various slants on a common theme before, *boom*, he had *The One*.

A quick scan of Zillow gave him the two most recent sales in the building. He selected a likely candidate that had closed just last week. Perfect.

* * *

"Hi. I'm wondering if you can help me? I just bought unit ten-o-five in Seatown Lofts and need to review a copy of the declaration. Could you please give me the website password so I can access it? My realtor suggested I get it from you."

After a brief hesitation, an abnormally deep baritone said, "Your agent didn't give you hard copies of the declaration and CC & Rs? That's *always* part of the sales process."

Oops.

Arnold scrambled for an answer.

"Ahhh, no, she didn't. Why? That a problem?"

"What'd you say your name is?"

Luckily, he'd prepped for this, but additional questions might quickly mire him in quicksand. He gave him the name on the sales record.

"That squares. Do you have something to write with?"

"I do!"

You have no idea how grateful I am, dude.

Arnold repeated the password.

"Anything else?" the baritone asked.

"No, that's it. Thanks. Can't tell you how much this helps."

Careful, dude, don't spread it too thick.

Five minutes later, Arnold—now totally jacked—had a list of unit owners by ascending floors. So amped, in fact, that he decided to take a chill break before barging ahead full steam, and potentially tripping up.

"Hey, boy, want to go for a walk?" he said, giving Chance some choobers, so he could restrain him if necessary.

* * *

Fifteen minutes later, at the table again with Chance curled up, snoozing, Arnold dialed the owner of unit 308. For no particular reason, he had decided to start at the lowest in the stack and work up. Among the motherlode of intel his bot provided was Hacker's Internet Service Provider: Astound, formerly Wave Broadband.

"Hi, this is Alex from Xfinity Broadband," he announced in his cheeriest salesman voice. "We're offering Seatown Loft owners a free three-month trial of our amazing two-gigabyte internet plan so that you can experience firsthand our blazing-fast download speed."

"That's my renter's responsibly, not mine," the respondent said flatly.

"In that case, would you be comfortable giving me their number so I can extend our amazing offer to them?"

"Dream on."

The phone went dead.

Oh, well, on to the next one.

* * *

Forty-five minutes later Arnold had whittled the list down to three units using Astound Broadband. Sitting back, sipping the dregs of his now-cold chocolate, he struggled with how to sort out which was Hacker's.

From the MadX info, he knew the dude used multiple computers in addition to at least one server, most of which were probably laying around in plain sight. Meaning, if he could finagle a peek inside the units in question, the answer should be obvious. So, the problem now was to find a way to engineer that.

He sat back, fingers interlaced behind his head, mulling it.

Single-family homes were chip shots. He had a vast portfolio of battle-hardened scams for scoping those puppies out: pizza delivery, Jehovah's Witnesses, Comcast repair man, ad infinitum. But a hyper-security-conscious downtown condo building?

Man, those were waaay more problematic.

First you had to scam your way past the concierge. Then, of course, you had to access each floor, which undoubtedly required a fob to access the elevator and/or stairwells. Finally, you had to con a way into the unit. Was this even possible? He seriously doubted it.

A phone alarm chimed. Didn't even need to check the freaking notification. Someone was trying to mess with his home security.

Shit-shit-shit.

Hacker. Jesus Christ. Who else had even the remotest cause to screw with it?

Arnold went straight to SAM and was massively relieved to see that the firewall remained intact. *Okay...*after initially probing SAM's firewall Hacker probably realized that breaking through such a Fort Knox defense would waste too much time. On the other hand, if he could *physically* enter the house…shit, Arnold didn't want to think of the consequences.

Options?

He began to mentally grind through them. The ultimate defensive move would be shut down SAM completely until Hacker had been effectively neutralized. Assuming he *could* neutralize the bastard. Okay, sure, shutting down SAM would eliminate a risk but doing that also meant suspending its programed stock trading with all the allied ripple effects. The financial consequences would suck. His only other option was to press on in the hope that he could nail Hacker's ass before Hacker nailed his.

Focus. Get that sonofabitch. Don't let this slow you down.

Where was I? Oh yeah…

Hacker's condo. How to access the building? Okay, say through some miraculous scheme he conned his way into the building. Then what? Sell himself as an Astound tech? Hmm…nope, too risky for a slew of reasons, but mostly lack of intel. He had no idea, for example, if a tech had recently been to the building for any reason. Or if Astound assigned a designated tech to each building under contract.

And, say through some miraculous good fortune he *did* manage to con his way inside a unit. Surely the manager or concierge or homeowner would be standing next to him. Then what the hell was he supposed to do? Glance around, say, "Okay, I'm done here," and leave?

How would that play?

Lame. Super suspicious. Nope. Scratch that approach. And, as long as we're on the subject, scratch any attempt to enter the building.

Whoa, not so fast…so if I can't look from the inside, why not look from the outside?

Boom.

It slammed him like a sixty-mile-per-hour eighteen-wheeler.

If I had RAID...

Well, you don't. So what? Buy an off-the-shelf, less sophisticated drone that'll live here for whenever you need it. After all, if Gold and Associates continues to grow...

Since building RAID from scratch, commercially available off-the-shelf drones had skyrocketed in quality and features while plummeting in relative cost, making the hassle of building one from scratch senseless. Besides, now that the business required his full-time attention, he simply didn't have the bandwidth, or inclination, to repeat the process. What's not to like?

Why even debate this?

Five minutes later he ordered a fully loaded Holy Stone 2-Axis Gimbal Drone from Amazon, even ponying up the extra dineros for expedited delivery. With that item taken care of, what's next?

Time for some on-site reconnaissance, that's what.

CHAPTER 38

ARNOLD AND CHANCE stood on the northeast corner of Broad Street and Denny Way, checking out the neighborhood, the Space Needle at his back, a ratty red-and-white Union 76 dump to his left, a biting chilling wind blowing freaking eddies between his shoulder blades in spite of having his pea-coat collar up and every button secured. Not only that, but he'd zippered his wool sweater into a modified t-neck.

Freaking November winds.

The twelve-story Seatown Lofts was a half block away, beyond a parking lot, looking exactly like the photo on the website. The stop light turned green, so they hoofed across Denny to the north side of the almost-empty parking lot, then crossed Third until they were standing in front of the white, four-story, KIRO-TV building.

He paused to survey their surroundings, absorbing a more granular feel for the area than provided by Google. A small Wells Fargo bank branch chewed up the far corner of the triangular lot, but the lot itself remained empty except for a clot of Zip cars in another corner. The lot was a perfect spot for launching and flying the drone.

The first floor of Seatown Lofts was clad in reddish-beige brick, while the remaining eleven floors glass and concrete columns and black-painted steel I-beams. Small grate balconies jutted from each apartment. Contemporary and sleek. And, given the proximity to companies like Amazon, Microsoft, and Google, was likely inhabited by a fair number of techies. Was Hacker one? Was this how he'd gained his chops?

Arnold led Chance southward along the sidewalk to the corner directly opposite the building, pausing to snap several pictures of the northwest stack with his phone. Once home, he'd enlarge them to look for a telltale sign of Hacker's unit—a weather station component, for example. At the moment, nothing noteworthy jumped out at him.

They crossed the street, continued along the sidewalk, and eventually circled the entire block that housed the condominium. They even walked the alley forming the spine of the block but saw nothing remarkable. The parking lot was by far the best spot for the mission. The downside, of course, was being conspicuous as hell working from there where God or anyone could see if they happened to glance his way. On second thought, what's so weird about seeing some dude fly a drone in the middle of an empty parking lot? Especially in *this* city.

Well, at least Phase One Recon had been completed. However, it was now very clear that Phase Two would require serious-as-shit planning and would be way iffier.

CHAPTER 39—Friday Afternoon

"THAT WOULD BE wonderful," Martina said. "Palmer would love the company. In fact, I'm with him now."

"Cool. Can I bring you guys anything?"

"Just yourself, Arnold. Oh, and I have a proposition for you. Will you join me for dinner at my place this evening? After all, I was your guest the other night."

Hmm…still had a ton of work pending, but a break would be welcomed. And well deserved. But…

"Love to, but here's the problem; I don't want to leave Chance too long. Is it okay to bring him? If that's a problem, I totally understand."

Chance wasn't a big shedder, but some people get really twitchy about allowing pets in their home. She'd never mentioned one…

"He's no problem at all. Then that's settled. My next question is do you eat pasta?"

"Love it…assuming it's not too much trouble."

He'd never learned to cook pasta of any type, but always enjoyed various dishes.

"Pasta's never any trouble. Preparing dinner will be a much-needed distraction from constantly worrying about

Palmer."

"In that case, I'm in. What time?"

"Sixish? Will that meld with your schedule?"

As if my schedule was packed.

"Perfect. But I'm still on my way up to visit now. Oh, and what can I bring tonight?"

"Just yourself and Chance. There's a good chance I'll be gone by the time you arrive. In any event, see you for dinner."

"Oh, before I forget, where do you live?"

Minor item.

She chuckled.

"Yes, you would need to know that, wouldn't you? I live in the 2200 Westlake complex. So you know where it is?"

Took a moment to zero in on the location but was able to dial it up.

"Yeah, the three-tower condominium complex at Westlake and Denny directly over Whole Foods, right?"

"That's the one. Mine is the building that includes the Pan Pacific Hotel, the one directly above Whole Foods. If Uber drops you on Westlake instead of the courtyard, just take the stairs up the south side of the store and you'll be right next to the lobby entrance."

"Got it."

He knew the store, though seldom shopped there.

* * *

It was a relief to see Mr. Davidson's color and alertness almost back to normal. He was in a high-back chair, wearing a standard hospital gown and bathrobe, a white thermal blanket draped over his legs, reading from a Kindle.

The lawyer's face lit up with apparent pleasure as Arnold entered the room. Martina was still there, camped out in a similar chair, paperback in hand. Smiling, she dogeared the page and closed the book.

"M mentioned you were on your way," Davidson said, setting the Kindle down, giving Arnold his full attention.

"Man, oh man, you're looking better, Mr. Davidson. A *ton* better. Feeling better?"

"Indeed. I am happy to be alive, and that, son, is no theatric exaggeration. I would not wish anyone to experience this. It scared the holy hell out of me. Have a seat."

He extended a palm toward an empty chair to Martina's right. Arnold sat.

Davidson spoke before Arnold fully settled in.

"Now that you are here, any progress on the case?"

Wow, nothing like getting right to it.

"Unfortunately, progress is slower than I'd hoped, but I *have* made definite progress. At this point, my next steps require some, ah, seriously creative planning."

"Whatever it takes," Davidson said, spreading his hands. "Assuming of course, you remain within legal boundaries. I do not wish to represent you in court again."

"Don't worry about that, Mr. Davidson. I'm not looking to get jammed up on this."

He said this more to placate the lawyer than to restrict himself. He planned to do whatever was necessary to finish the job while minimizing any risk of exposure. If this meant bending the rules a touch, well, so be it.

"Good. How are Chance and Rachael?"

Arnold caught himself from glancing at Martina and cleared his throat instead.

"Doing well, thanks." He saw no upside to being truthful at this stage of his recovery.

The fewer things to worry or upset him, the better.

"I apologize to Rachael for stealing you away from her, but Noah and I put a great deal of faith in you, son. If anyone can help Carlos, it is *you*."

"Don't worry, sir. In fact, being in town gave me the

chance to finally hire my first associate," he said with a note of pride. "At the first convenient opportunity, I'd like you and Mr. Cain to meet her. Her name's Prisha's and she's uber-talented and competent. I hope you'll give her a chance to prove herself to you."

"If you took her on as an associate, we may only assume she is top-notch. However, I prefer it if we continue to initially contact you when requiring your services?"

He asked this with a slight cock of his head and in a tone that implied only one answer.

"Exactly."

Although he hadn't given this aspect of his operations any thought. Yet.

Made sense, though. At least for Mr. Davidson and Mr. Cain. Other clients, well…

"I assume Rachael is happy with your decision?"

"Oh, you have no idea," he said wryly.

Friday Evening

Arnold entered Martina's eleventh-floor apartment—a fifteen-hundred-square-foot, two-bedroom, two and a half bath unit—and paused to take it in, Chance obediently heeling. Beautifully stained oak floors, minimalistic contemporary furniture, a prominent glass-top dining table set for two complete with linen napkins and honest-to-God silverware, topped off by a killer view over Denny Way and beyond to Queen Anne Hill with her iconic crown of three red and white communication towers.

"Wow," was all Arnold could muster. He loved it.

"May I take your coat?"

"Sure, but first, here," he said, handing her a bottle of Antinori Marchese Chianti Riserva.

"Grazie." She paused to inspect the label. "Lovely. This

should pair nicely with the marinara sauce I'm preparing."

After setting the bottle on the corner of a hall credenza, she held out both hands for the pea coat he was shedding. With the jacket in a coat closet, she motioned toward the living room/kitchen area while collecting the bottle.

"Chance is free to settle wherever he chooses."

"Thank you," Arnold said, unclipping the leash from the halter. Chance trotted straight to the window and dropped onto his belly to take in the view. "You sound as if you know that particular wine."

He followed her into the kitchen area and set the black nylon leash on the gray quartz counter.

"Of course. Tignanello vineyard is near the area where I grew up."

"Really? Where's that?"

He slid onto a counter chair on the living room side of the large white quartz island defining the kitchen area. Since first meeting her in Honolulu, he'd wondered about her nationality, but for whatever reason had never had an opportunity to broach the subject.

She slid the bottle toward him along with a corkscrew and nod to open it.

"Americans call our beautiful city Florence, but to us it's *Firenze*."

She pronounced it with an exaggerated Italian flourish complete with a hand gesture.

Ahhh…

"You grew up there."

"I did," she said with an unmistakable note of pride.

Arnold slit the red foil with the opener blade then peeled it away as she pulled down two wine glasses from a cupboard to set on the counter.

"Did your whole family come here?"

"No, just me. I came for college."

She began transferring a variety of ingredients from the counter to the island stovetop.

Arnold twisted the corkscrew deeply into the cork then began working it slowly from the bottle.

"Where do you want the wine?" he asked, suspecting she would say on the table.

She shot him a bemused expression.

"In our glasses, of course. You can just leave the bottle here until dinner's ready."

* * *

On his toes, fingers on the top of the rough stucco wall, Singh studied the back of Gold's darkened home. Faint, anemic light filtered into the kitchen from somewhere toward the front where the blueprints indicated the living room was. He'd been watching the back windows for five minutes and apparently Gold was out, providing him an ideal opportunity.

The primary objective for tonight's visit was to glean as much information as possible about his security system. Gold wasn't being coy or secretive about the CCTV cameras covering the property.

Quite the contrary. They were obvious.

Perhaps this was precisely the point; display the cameras as a deterrent, an unequivocal statement of just how secure this home was. For Singh, though they had the opposite effect. To him, they simply underscored the value that Gold placed on the computers—computers that he now felt certain occupied the custom-designed basement room.

Singh exited the alley to 80th then moved around to the front of the house. With his hood over his head, black face mask, dark glasses, and black gloves, he strikingly resembled the Unabomber. Briskly, purposefully, he marched straight to the front door, camera out, ignoring the motion-sensitive lights now flooding the yard. He snapped closeups of the security keypad and embedded faceplate camera, paying particular attention to all identifying features. After making sure the pictures contained as much detail as possible, he turned and walked straight back to the sidewalk, turned left to continue the three blocks to his car. Undoubtedly the security system notified Gold of his presence—the Jew was probably looking at a picture of him now—but, hey, good luck with *that*.

The pictures of the security faceplate should provide sufficient information to identify the system make and model. Once he knew this, he could research the specs to decide the best method to defeat it without Gold ever knowing how it happened. The thought delighted him.

* * *

On a counter stool, leaning on the cool polished quartz, Arnold watched Martina sauté ground meat in olive oil to a golden brown, then drop in several cloves of freshly sliced garlic, diced red peppers, onions, carrots, sun-dried tomatoes, and red sauce. The enhanced sauce looked and smelled mouthwateringly delicious, especially the savory garlic.

"Thanks, by the way," she said without glancing up, "for not mentioning a word to Palmer about Rachael or Chance. It'd only cause him worry, and that's the last thing he needs at this point in his recovery." She gave a short dismissive laugh. "At the moment, keeping him from fretting about work is enough of a difficult challenge that he really doesn't need any other distractions to deal with." She glanced up. "As long as I just raised the subject, what *is* the status with her?"

Arnold sighed, glanced at the expansive view while trying to rein in his rampaging emotions.

"The worry's eating me alive. She's been completely radio-silent for, like, forty-eight hours. I don't have a clue what's going on with her other than she's seriously pissed." He paused. "I've been having this horrible premonition she's...I don't know...going to do something weird...my imagination's running totally out of control."

"I've already asked this, but are you sure she hasn't had an accident or an illness that would account for it?"

He shrugged.

"Of course. I checked but came up with nothing. And anyway, I know for sure she's pissed. I mean, I'm pretty sure she's making a statement of some sort with this silent treatment. What really worries me is where she's headed with it. I keep getting this godawful feeling that whatever it is, it's *bad.*"

Martina turned the burner down, moved to the side of the stove, arms straight, leaning forward, palms flat on the counter, locked eye onto his.

"I understand how upsetting this must be. My only advice is to just keep trying to communicate with her."

For a few blessed moments, watching Martina doll up the red sauce had been a glorious distraction from the topic, but there it was again, front and center in his consciousness, dragging him down. He'd really wanted to enjoy this evening free from the endless ruminations over an issue for which he had no control.

"Know what? Let's please change the subject. I need to focus on something more positive."

Martina gave an *it's-your-call* shrug.

"Sorry. I thought maybe you wanted to discuss it. I meant no harm."

She returned to her cooking.

Ah, shit...

He hoped he hadn't hurt her feelings.

"What were you studying when you came to the States?"

She paused, gazed into the distance again, a faint fleeting smile on her lips.

"Law." She continued staring, perhaps reliving a moment. "My father—a man I greatly admire—is a lawyer." She returned to her cooking. "While growing up, I was what you might call a 'daddy's girl,' so it surprised no one in my family—nor anyone who knew me—when I choose to follow his footsteps." Another pause, another distant wistful moment. "However, that's where all career similarities cease. I vowed to never—even remotely—appear to compete with him *or* his career."

Interesting.

"Because?"

She seemed to be momentarily taken aback.

"That, Arnold, is a dynamic far too complex to synthesize in a casual conversation. Also, it's personal. Suffice it to say, I made the very conscious decision to study a field of law as far afield from his practice as possible."

"Wow, had no idea. What? Do you do criminal defense work, like Mr. Davidson?"

This prompted a hearty, dismissive laugh.

"No. Far from it. Father was with the *Ministero della Giustizia* which, in the U.S. legal system, is roughly equivalent to a district attorney. I wanted to practice in an area far removed from criminal law. Luckily, in my third year, intellectual property law began to intrigue me, so I specialized in that."

With the sauce simmering, Martina dropped two handfuls of ravioli into a pot of boiling water, then pulled a wooden salad bowl of premade Caesar salad and a Saran Wrap-covered bowl of dressing from the fridge. She handed it to him with instructions to set them on the table while she grated a chunk of deliciously fragrant parmesan cheese into a dish to sprinkle over the salad and pasta.

His phone alarm sounded.

"Whoa, I need to take this," Arnold said, grabbing his

phone, "it's my home security system."

He opened the security app to a video recording, thumbed play and watched a fish-eye distorted view of a hooded masked figure step onto the front porch, crouch, and shoot pictures of the system faceplate with his phone. Although heavily disguised, the stride and movement convinced him the creeper was male.

Hacker. Had to be.

Like, who else would pull off shit like that?

Martina spoke from across the island.

"What is it?"

When he finished explaining, she shook her head sadly.

"And now this, on top of everything else. I'm so sorry, Arnold."

* * *

Arnold's first action after locking the front door and tossing his parka into the closet, was to call Rachael. After ten rings it rolled over to voice mail. Interesting. Given the number of messages he'd left over the past thirty-six hours, her mailbox should be overflowing. Unless she was deleting them.

Whoa, just a minute, idiot. If she's listening to your messages, why not say something more than "we need to talk."

Propped against the counter, he rehearsed his message until satisfied with the words and tone, then dialed.

"Look, Rach, I know you're picking up my messages and I *get* that you're pissed, but your petulant silent treatment is juvenile, and more importantly, it's destroying everything we have as a couple. Please don't damage us irreparably. I love you, sweetie. Bye."

During the trudge upstairs to the bedroom, his phone pinged a text from her; the single letter *K*.

Was this their first step in reestablishing détente?

CHAPTER 40—Saturday Midday

THE HOLY STONE drone turned out to be way cooler than anticipated, plus it came loaded with several seriously sick features like the capability to transmit blast-your-socks-off high-def video. And the flight time? Like, totally off the chart, dude: a tad over thirty minutes. Not only that, but this puppy weighed in at a mere 1.25 pounds, making it chip-shot easy to lug around in a rucksack with the other necessary equipment.

After carefully inspecting the exterior for imperfections and other obvious issues, he dedicated a good thirty minutes to acquiring a "feel" for the controller. Both drone and controller came with partially charged batteries, so Arnold had them charging as he got a feel for the joystick limits. Specifically, he intended to be as proficient with this controller as he was with RAID's. The big-ticket challenge: adapting his skill to this strikingly different weather; specifically, the nasty Seattle wind, compared to Honolulu's mild breezes. It would require a ton of practice, what with these seemingly random freaking gusts. Better start now in spite of the partially charged batteries.

After ensuring that Chance was behind the French doors—the last thing he wanted was an inquisitive nose sniffing at a spinning prop—he took the new equipment into the back yard. Chance, on the other hand, appeared to not give a flip, probably having grown blasé about drones after countless hours watching Arnold fly RAID.

Arnold began with a simple take off to two feet, holding the aircraft steady for a minute in the unpredictable gusts, then landing it. Each successive try buttressed his confidence enough to increase altitude. Satisfied with being able to take off and land, Arnold focused on flying a steady path back and forth between the property lines.

So far, so good.

Next came some trickier lateral maneuvers and corrections. Pleased with such rapid progress, he transitioned from the relative wind-protected back yard to the street in front until the battery indicators began flashing red.

Back inside, he sipped hot chocolate, rewarmed his hands, and mentally rehashed his plan while the batteries sucked up juice. Warm again, he took Chance on a leisurely walk around the block. By the time they returned, the lithium power packs had enough charge to resume practice. He repeated this routine throughout the day and on into early evening, honing his skills, gaining confidence.

Saturday 9:31 PM

Hood up, head bowed, Arnold stood at the entrance to a high-rise condo three blocks from the target watching the Uber's red taillights be gobbled up in southbound traffic. He'd purposely worn dark clothes: Fjallraven olive parka, black jeans, black knitted cap, black Adidas kicks. Now alone, he trudged through chilly drizzle to the empty parking lot across from Seatown Lofts.

As expected, the lot served as a perfect spot to scope out the units. Amazingly, the shades for the targeted windows were up. Perhaps urbanites didn't give a rip if neighbors spied on them. But, of course, this would mean they had nothing more interesting to do, something he seriously doubted.

He ran into no problems readying the drone on glistening black asphalt, stepped far enough back to clear the props should a gust blow the craft toward him during liftoff, then, for good measure, dry-ran the controller joy sticks again.

Good to go.

He powered up the rotor and *voila*, the drone was airborne, gaining altitude quickly, Arnold flew it straight to the northwest corner stack. Once it reached the desired location, he gained altitude until it was hovering an estimated twenty-five feet from the penthouse, its onboard camera aimed straight horizontally into the unit's largest windows. Arnold glanced at the high-def image on his iPhone attached to the controller.

Perfect.

All devices were working as planned, allowing him to concentrate on keeping the aircraft's props well away from the balcony railings. One gust, clip a prop, and game over.

He settled in, focusing on the job ahead. He began by videotaping the darkened penthouse, then carefully worked down the stack, pausing at each unit only long enough to glance at the screen, confirm he had a good image, then lowered it to the unit below, working slowly, methodically unit by unit.

Suddenly the wind tapered to an eerie calm. Creepy. But it allowed him time to for a more than cursory glance at the image. Did a double-take. Seriously? The motherlode? He used the onboard camera zoom to check out what looked like...

Are you shitting me!

A goddamn weather station?

Yep. Right there, in all its geeky weirdness. He was looking in the window of the sixth unit down from the penthouse.

Working quickly now, taking advantage of the lull in wind, he snapped three closeups before backing off the zoom to survey as much of the interior as possible given the angle limitations. Ah, there was the Samsung TV against the north wall. A nice correlation with his MadX findings. A young dark-skinned male was hunched over a keyboard apparently using the TV as a monitor. Arnold snapped two shots of him at three different magnifications.

He had to be Hacker.

It felt dissociatively weird to finally attach a face on the heretofore faceless enemy.

Thrilled unbelievably, Arnold backed the drone away from the railing far enough to not worry so much about clipping a prop, and carefully counted floors from street level up to the target. Then reversed the process, counting from the penthouse down. Yep, they matched: Hacker's unit was on the sixth floor, making it 601.

The wind suddenly kicked up again. In spite of the ten-kilowatt-tingling jazzing him, he was able to fly the drone in for an elegant landing just five feet away.

* * *

Arnold studied the property records for Seatown Lofts apartment 601. Ramesh Singh owned it. Well, the name fit the dude inside. He was finally beginning to feel upbeat and optimistic about the tempo of the investigation. And it felt like he'd just gained some serious traction.

Okay, fine, but what's the next move?

Share the intel with Chang—and by default, Fisher—or dig deeper for more intel? After all, Chang's and Fisher's full attentions were focused elsewhere. Ergo, this new information would probably remain inactive, right? Maybe. Maybe not. Didn't Chang allude to a potential change in priorities should

Arnold find a name? He tossed that around for a moment.

Okay, but before calling Chang, he needed a come-to-Jesus talk with Rachael.

This shit can't continue.

* * *

"Yes?" came a monosyllabic greeting encrusted with ice.

"Thanks for answering." Arnold paused. "I need you to explain why this silent treatment?"

After a long pause she said, "I was out, Arnold."

Again, with a decidedly frosty tone.

Uh-oh. A veiled threat?

Sure sounded like one. Arnold's gut knotted.

"Look, we're both in and out during the day, but we've always made time to answer messages. I'm asking why you're going to such great lengths to ignore me? What's your message?"

After a resigned sigh.

"No message. It's simple. I was hunting for an apartment close to the hospital and I didn't want to get into an argument over it. That's why."

Boom.

Every molecule of air suddenly felt sucked from his lungs. His gut dropped onto his Adidas.

"Jesus, Rach, *please* tell me you're joking."

"Why would I joke about this, Arnold?" she said flatly.

Silence.

Say something. Anything.

All his mental circuit breakers seemed to blow, flatlining his brain into a catatonic stupor.

Finally, Rachael asked, "Did you hire *that* woman?"

Jesus, dude, breathe.

He gasped, filling his lungs with much needed air, blew through pursed lips while palm-wiping his face. And there it was, the line in the sand, the blow he'd sensed was on its way. A brief pause to steel himself, then.

"Yes, I did, but what's the issue? You know I need coverage here. What's her gender have to do with anything?"

Yeah, he remembered Martina's words about this, but needed her to say it—if that was the issue—so he could at least put her mind to rest.

"Has she been to your house?"

"C'mon, Rach, you know damn well she has. I told you, she drove me here from the storage unit. Why make such a big issue about this?"

No answer.

"Look, this is totally nuts. Please don't do anything that drastic until I get back and we've had a chance to discuss this like rational adults. I *am* making significant progress. I might even be able to wrap this up in a few days."

"Good for you, but my old apartment was available, so I signed a one-year lease and have already moved my clothes. I need to go now."

"No, wait—"

But she was gone.

CHAPTER 41

ARNOLD BECAME AWARE of something nudging his elbow and glanced down. Chance stood next to him, whining, nose-bumping him.

Doggies know.

They read your moods with an uncanny sensitivity he wished more humans possessed.

He slid from the chair, knelt in front of him, held his head nose to nose, and said, "I love you, boy." He buried his face in the pooch's forehead fur while giving him a serious dose of choobers. Chance angled his snout away from his hands to lick tears from his cheeks, whimpering louder now. Arnold wrestled him playfully to the floor, rolled him onto his back, belly up for a serious dose of rabber-de-jabber tummy rubs, murmuring, "Chance is a good boy. Yes he is. A good boy," in that silly high-pitched baby-talk voice he reserved for moments like this, when he knew no one could see him.

Minutes later, with his emotions under some semblance of control and Chance calmer, Arnold stood, poured a glass of wine from a previously opened bottle. What could he possibly do to convince her to move back in? From a distant corner of his mind a voice whispered.

What difference would that make?

Which shocked him. Then, after a moment of objectivity, he resigned himself to the undeniable answer: not a damn thing.

Sunday Morning

Arnold ushered Prisha into the kitchen, where an assortment of Starbucks pastries and a skinny Grandé latte, with her requested shot of vanilla, waited for her on the table. He and Chance had timed their return from Starbucks mere minutes before she curbed her car.

"If your latte's too cool, I can nuke it," he offered.

Settling into the chair across from his, she unzipped her coat, then sampled the coffee.

"No prob, it's perfect."

He remembered Martina's hospitality from the other night, so offered, "If you want, I can hang up your coat?"

Need to polish your social skills, dude. Especially with the company growing.

"No, I'm good, thanks. I'll slip it off as soon as I warm up," she said, briskly rubbing her palms together. "That damn car heater works like crap as you've undoubtedly found out. I mean, it sucks more than a Dyson."

After studying the goodies, she set the slice of banana bread on her white paper plate, broke off a chunk, popped it into her mouth. Arnold took the blueberry scone.

"It's your meeting, Boss. What up?"

"In the spirit of full disclosure, I'm going to be totally upfront," Arnold said making direct eye contact. "This place," he said with a sweep of his palm, "is mine. Sorry I fed you that bullshit about it being a friend's, but..."

Flashing him a dose of squinty side-eye, she waited a few beats.

"But what? Why lie?"

Arnold glanced away, his face doing the space-heater thing. She wasn't about to cut him an ounce of slack.

Well, it was, after all, a self-inflicted wound. Might as well man up.

With a shrug, "I felt guilty about having such a nice place, what with you guys struggling financially."

Arms crossed defiantly, she leaned back in the chair, coagulating his retinas with lasers.

"Are you fucking serious?"

He shrugged.

"Uh…"

She gave him a disgusted headshake, then made an exaggerated glance around the kitchen before zapping him again with those lasers.

"Dude, let's get something straight. That's *our* problem, not yours. As of this minute"—she stabbed an index finger on the tabletop—"if we're gonna be partners, we *will* be totally—I'm talking brutally—straight-up with each other. No matter what. If that isn't acceptable, then I'm out. Got it?"

He nodded.

"Yeah, got it. Sorry. It won't happen again."

A pause, then, "So, we're good?"

She shrugged.

"No reason not to be."

She nonchalantly broke off another chunk of banana bread.

"Okay then, down to business."

He worked her through the evidence he'd accumulated that pointed to Singh as the hacker for the Camano and Curchfield hacks, then showed her the pictures of Seatown Lofts and described Singh's apartment in as much detail as he had been able to accumulate. While studying the photographs, she asked well-targeted questions. When he finished, she nodded.

"Man, he sure looks like he's our guy. What's our next step?"

"Our next step,"—he loved the sound of *our*— "is to construct a bullet-proof strategy to obtain enough evidence to prove—I'm talking unequivocal here—that he's the hacker."

She nodded thoughtfully.

"You've obviously put in some serious brain time on this. Why not just lay it on me so we can smooth out the kinks?"

"True. That's all I've been able to think about since reconning it."

Well, except for Rachael.

He continued, "Any evidence—if any remains—must be on his computer, right? Which means, we need to figure out a way to access it."

Her reply was a staccato sarcastic snort.

"Just like that, huh? Hack a world-class hacker?" Then, "If he's as good as you imply, that'll be, like, massively difficult if not impossible."

"Difficult yes. Impossible no. But there's a catch."

Another sarcastic snort.

"Always is."

"Keep in mind we're doing this for criminal-defense lawyers, so our evidence has to be, like, totally Mr. Clean clean. Know what I'm saying? I'm talking not even the slightest whiff of illegally, nothing that has the faintest chance of being challenged in court. *But...*" He raised a hold-on-a-minute finger. "If forced to do something, ah, sort of *on the fringe*, we need to make damn sure we minimize our exposure."

"You mean, like lie our asses off," she said flatly.

He smiled.

"Guess that's one way to put it."

"Put another way," she said, "*if forced* to do something

illegal, we need to make damn sure we're not caught."

What could he say?

He simply nodded.

"I'm totally down with this, so go ahead, lay it on me, Boss."

Having her dissect the plan for potential traps was enormously reassuring, especially given they were about to lock horns with a dude of Singh's caliber. He loved her commitment to going all-in on a caper that had only a fifty-fifty shot at success.

"I plan to drop a Hak5 Pineapple right here," he said, tapping a picture of Hacker's balcony displayed on his Surface. The device, a flat rectangular black box sprouting three angle-adjustable antennas, was a staple for any committed serious hacker. They sold online for $100 to $150, depending on which bells and whistles you wanted, and intercepted the Wi-Fi signal between a router and computer, making it a cyber-equivalent of a phone tap. Arnold's master plan was to capture Singh's password with it. Strategically an easy concept but difficult as hell to actualize. "The totally cool and clean part of this is that—if we can pull it off—any information we capture is legal on account of it being *broadcasted*, right? Broadcasting it makes it public domain and no different than, say, listening to FM radio."

Prisha's face morphed from a broad smile to a sneaky grin.

"Your classic Man in The Middle attack. I love it." She clapped applause. "It's a terrific idea, but how you plan to put it there?"

Arnold grinned.

"Fly it in on a drone."

Prisha sucked on a tooth, studying the balcony shot closely, cocked her head a couple beats, then shook her head no.

"Oh, man, I dunno…that's a pretty tight space." She sighed, sat back in the chair, looked at him skeptically. "All I can say is it'll be interesting."

"Especially at night."

She flashed an abrupt dose of side-eye.

"Are you serious? At night?"

"I know, but the drone's less likely to be seen in the dark."

"I'm just saying…"

Compelling him to explain, "Look, there's a bigger issue at play. I calculated the balcony width. That's fine, but the depth is what's going to be a bitch. It's *doable*, but it also means it's crucial to control it from the best viewing angle possible and that ain't the parking lot, not by a long shot."

She studied him a long moment.

"Okay, I give. Where you plan to fly it from?"

Ah, Jesus, just discussing it was causing some serious sphincter pucker.

He started to pace, rubbing his palms together.

"Look, we need the shortest possible flight path from the highest possible viewing angle, right?"

She cocked her head.

"Are you asking, or is that rhetorical?"

He looked at her, dead serious.

"I'm asking."

"Yeah, of course." Another shrug, like, obvious. "The shortest distance, best viewing angle. It's a no-brainer."

"Okay, so we're left with two possibilities, both rooftops: the TV station and the building across the street from the target. Scratch the TV station. No way in hell we're conning our way onto *that* baby. *Especially* at night. I haven't seriously scoped out the other place but strongly suspect it's our only possible option." He stopped pacing. "There *is* one other remote—I mean, like, Azerbaijan remote—possibility: a high-rise apartment a block south. It'd be within *radio* range but, man, that baby's far enough away and has such a lousy angle that even with magnification, it's a nonstarter." He looked at her. "Any thoughts?"

She stood, latte in hand.

"I can't give an opinion until I've scoped it out. C'mon, let's take a ride."

CHAPTER 42

ARNOLD, PRISHA, AND Chance strolled the sidewalk just to the north of Seatown Lofts. Just an ordinary couple walking their pooch. Across Third was the white, four-story fortress TV station. Prisha agreed it was a scratch. They stopped at the corner, looked around.

Prisha slowly shook her head.

"I see what you mean about that balcony. *Man.* In this weather it'll be a bitch no matter what time of day you pick, so I agree about needing a high viewing angle. The higher, the better if you want to improve any shot of not hitting that railing. I don't see a ton of options."

"There're only three possibilities: this parking lot, that roof"—he nodded toward the three-story building across Third Avenue—"and that one."

He pointed to a high-rise one block south.

She studied the building directly across from the target.

"Whatdaya know about that place?"

Arnold laughed.

"Nada."

"Guess that's why we're here, then. We'd best check it out."

The building occupied about a third of the block with an alley in back. They started down the gently sloping side street toward Second Avenue. Arnold paused at the alley to scope out the rear of the building: blue recycling and green garbage bins flush against the wall, a breeze rippling random black puddles in cracked concrete potholes.

"Hmmm, look at that," Arnold said, referring to a narrow, enclosed walkway two stories above the alley connecting the target to another, architecturally different three-story structure fronting Second Avenue.

"Huh, I never noticed it before," Prisha muttered. "Then again, I never had a reason to look down there until now."

"Let's see what's up with it."

They took a right at the corner, sauntered past the main entrance of what turned out to be an insurance company. They hung another right at the next side street, heading back uphill toward Third. Approaching the alley again, Arnold noticed a heavyset black dude in a dark uniform with a shoulder patch and neon-chartreuse vest eyeing them from a driveway spiraling down to an underground garage.

Arnold waved.

The guard casually returned the wave, calling, "Nice dog."

"Thanks." They kept moving, Arnold whispering to Prisha, "See that? They even have security. The dude must've just come from the main building. Wonder if they've been watching us on camera?"

"Do you have any doubt?"

Arnold nodded.

"Tells you something, doesn't it."

They kept moving, trying to be as inconspicuous as possible, especially now that the insurance company certainly had them on video. Soon they were back on Third, having circled the block. They stopped in front of a small coffee shop, out of view of the main building.

Had they drawn suspicion? Or was the guard's appearance a random event?

They were the only pedestrians on this sidewalk at the moment and vehicular traffic was minimal, so…

"Let's move down there," Arnold said, motioning toward a large metal garage door into the target building and directly across the street from the Seatown Lofts lobby.

"Well, that answers one of our questions. This has to be additional parking for the other building," Prisha said with conviction.

"With a few offices thrown in. But not many."

Arnold inspected the building's only pedestrian entrance.

A moment later, she asked, "What's so interesting?"

"That door needs a pass card or fob to open, so scratch that as an option."

"Yeah, noticed that too."

Arnold shook his head in frustration.

"The only logical place to launch from is this roof, but I can't see an easy way to get inside." Then quickly added, "*Legally* that is."

"Nope." Prisha nodded. "They ain't going to make this one easy."

Arnold shot an impassive glance over her shoulder, weighing just how far over the line he could go and still be comfortable with protecting Mr. Cain and Mr. Davidson.

As if reading his mind, Prisha offered, "You know, we haven't actually ruled out that apartment building yet." There was a shrug in her voice. "Personally, I'm not willing to scratch it unless we check it out first." She studied him a moment. "I'm just sayin'…"

No way.

Arnold shook his head.

"Ah, man…in better weather, *maybe*. But in this shit?"

He kicked at a cigarette butt squashed on the sidewalk. "It's for sure in radio range but…a night landing in these dicey conditions at that angle…"

"No doubt." Sigh. "Look, just for grins, humor me. I need to know for sure we're not overlooking a possibility, slim as that might be. Or do you disagree? After all, you're the one gonna be flying it."

Arnold glanced around once more.

"No, no, you're right. We need to give it a fair shot."

They paused at the corner, scoping out the building in greater detail. Arnold looked from it to the target, back again. Huh. Maybe, just maybe there *might be* a workable angle. Not ideal by any stretch, but conceivable. The range was certainly doable if not for such shitty weather. Especially at night. But…everything hinged on the angle. Prisha was right: the only way to know for sure was to actually look.

An A-frame sidewalk sign boasted, APARTMENTS FOR LEASE. Through the large plate-glass lobby windows, he could see the door to the leasing office was open.

"Follow my lead," Arnold said as he started across the intersection, heading for the entrance, Chance on-leash beside him.

* * *

Gold's security system ranked right up there with the best Singh had ever encountered in a private residence. Hell, it might even give a few business systems a run for their money: wireless technology, high-def normal and infrared imaging, window and door sensors, and smartphone or computer accessible anywhere in the world with internet access.

Absolutely First Cabin.

It didn't surprise Singh that his few attempts at cracking the password failed. Although he could eventually brute force his way in, a system of this caliber would probably alert Gold after the first failed attempt. This forced him to dig into his trick bag.

His solution went like this: the system's brains spoke to the various components scattered throughout the house via simple Wi-Fi technology. Specifically, the front-door access panel—which housed the video camera for facial recognition and the numeric keypad—communicated with the system brains via packets of encrypted code sent as radio signals.

By planting a portable computer with a decent antenna near Gold's front door, he could intercept and record those signals while Gold was using the system to open the front door.

Then, when Gold was away, he could simply transmit the code to the brain and *voila*, the door would unlock.

Piece of cake.

Once in, he'd head straight to the basement and if, as suspected, it contained computers, he'd infect the network.

Because the computer required for this job needed to be as tiny as possible, he selected a Raspberry Pi 4 powered by a lithium battery pack that would provide enough juice to run it for several days. Okay, that part was now settled. He pulled up pictures of Gold's house and the surrounding properties to look for a good spot for hiding the equipment. Gold's extensive CCTV coverage made putting the equipment anywhere inside the property line impossible.

However, the house directly across the narrow street was hidden behind a large embankment thick with years old ivy, trees, and other foliage, making it perfect for concealing the equipment. The downside, of course, was the distance from Gold's home made an already feeble Wi-Fi signal even weaker. To counterbalance this, he would use a high-gain directional antenna for capturing it.

He had in his collection the perfect solution: a parabolic dish spray-painted black as all-purpose camouflage.

* * *

A pinch-faced, fiftyish woman with squinty eyes looked at Arnold from a small, suspiciously uncluttered tidy desk in the leasing office.

She wore a smartly tailored blue pinstripe suit, sensible shoes, and stylishly coiffed gray hair welded into place with enough sickly-scented Aqua Net to withstand fifty-knot winds. A tasteful choker of black pearls adorned her sun-weathered slender neck.

"May I help you?"

"We hope so," Arnold answered. "Are any units available on the northeast corner or close to it on the north side? We're particularly interested in ones with a balcony."

With pursed lips, she considered his request a moment.

"Yes. I happen to have one fitting those specifications."

"Is it possible to have a look?"

* * *

"We're definitely interested," Arnold said, stepping back across the threshold from balcony to living room, then sliding the glass door snugly shut, cutting off the chilly wind. Prisha was in the kitchen inspecting cupboards, doing an excellent impersonation of a domesticated wife.

"Wonderful. Shall we go back down to the office to begin the paperwork?" the leasing agent asked, as if a lease was a given.

"Not yet," Arnold said, with another glance toward Seatown Lofts. "As I said, we're *interested*. Before we consider signing a lease, we need to visit at night, oh, say around nine o'clockish?"

The agent's plastic smile quickly mutated into a sour-lemon pucker.

"What an unusual request. In fact, in all my years of

renting apartments, I've never encountered this one and am not inclined to even entertain it without greater commitment on your part."

Arnold nodded sympathetically.

"I realize it is unusual, but here's the thing. We love our present place over on First. In fact, we love Belltown in general. The only reason we are looking to move is our present bedroom is directly across from a cluster of bars and restaurants. Which isn't an issue until about midnight till two in the morning when almost every night a fight breaks out or some yahoo's car alarm goes off or a drunk starts screaming and wakes us up. We both work at Amazon and need to be in the office early. The only reason we're looking to move is to find a quieter place within walking distance of work."

He flashed his best hopeful smile.

"I see." She appeared to seriously consider his story for, oh, maybe two seconds, tops. "Frankly, there's no way I'll accommodate a showing at that hour. However, I *can* assure you we've never had a single complaint of street noise since the building opened seven years ago and I should know. I've been the sole leasing agent for this building from day one."

Shit. Hmm...

Lease it for a month and chalk it up as a business expense?

"Fair enough. In that case, how about a short-term rental?"

She cocked her head questioningly, lips pursed a beat.

"What do you consider short term? Our minimum is twelve months."

Well, that's a non-starter.

"Why twelve months, if you don't mind me asking."

"To discourage subleasing units as Airbnbs, especially during tourist season when, as I'm sure you're well aware, hotels are booked to capacity with cruise-ship traffic. Transient leasers are a major security issue for downtown apartment buildings, to say nothing of the additional maintenance issues it necessitates. Our building does everything possible to discourage transient traffic and I assure you our tenants wholeheartedly embrace this policy."

He didn't see how a twelve-month minimum discouraged the Airbnb issue but decided to not press it.

"In addition, we require a two-month damage deposit that, if the lease is broken, is non-refundable," she said painting him with a suspicious once-over, as if reading his mind.

Well, shit, that was his next brilliant idea, but the deposit thing just made leasing it too expensive.

* * *

On the sidewalk again, Arnold reluctantly admitted, "Looks like our only option's the insurance garage."

"Agreed. Unfortunately, that sucker strikes me as almost as tight-ass secure as the TV station. Any ideas on how we're getting in?" Apparently, as an afterthought, she added, *"Legally."*

Arnold simply smiled and headed across the intersection toward the building.

CHAPTER 43

THEY STOOD ON the sidewalk just in front of the slatted metal garage door, hammering out details of his plan. Wouldn't be easy.

And definitely not legal, but hey, what other choice was there?

And if, God forbid, they were caught in the act...Jesus, he didn't even want to think about the repercussions.

"Know what?" Prisha said. "We haven't walked the alley yet."

She threw it out hopefully, as if they might stumble across a mind-blowing unlocked door or something equally astronomically improbable.

Arnold leaned back, flashed her his best you-got-to-be-kidding expression.

With a shrug, she mumbled, "Hey, ya never know..."

He gave a sarcastic snort.

"True, but we're dealing with a freaking insurance company that has security guards walking patrols, right?"

"All I'm sayin' is I've seen some pretty bizarre shit in this line of work."

Arnold hiked his shoulders.

"Won't hurt to look if it'll make you feel better. But just so you know, I'm officially on record as skeptical."

* * *

Alley access to the building was limited to two steel pedestrian doors, both sans handles and with quarter-inch thick tempered steel flanges welded securely along the unhinged edge, top to bottom, to prevent crowbarring them open.

So much for a miracle alley entrance.

* * *

The Third Avenue possibilities boiled down to the roll-up metal-slat garage door and one solid metal pedestrian door, both street-facing, both directly across from the Seatown Lofts concierge who routinely manned a desk with a view straight at them.

"These're our only possibilities," Arnold said.

Hands in her coat pockets, Prisha appeared to be studying the sidewalk.

"Don't look now, but a dude across the street, about third-floor center, seems to have taken an interest in us."

Arnold casually bent down to give Chance a choober and cast a casual glance that direction.

"Yeah, caught him just before he ducked inside."

She kicked at nothing on the sidewalk.

"Don't like it."

He straightened back up.

"I'm with you on that one, but with our hoods up…"

"We should move."

"Not yet. If we move now, we'll be acting even more suspicious. Besides, I want to clarify a couple things."

Arnold checked his watch, not for the time, but to give the impression of waiting for something.

"Since these are our only options," Arnold continued,

referring to the two doors, "depending on which one we
choose, we'll either need a proximity fob or a garage-door
opener, right?"

"Right."

Prisha turned her back toward the condominium.

"Cloning a proximity reader isn't a big thing but it
requires a blatantly obvious move like bumping into someone
wearing one. I don't know about you but given we're up
against a group of certified paranoids, making such a blatant
move like that isn't very appealing. And so far, we haven't
seen a soul use that door, so we could be standing out here till
freaking Christmas."

"When you're right, you're right. What I'm hearing is
we're talkin' garage door."

Prisha reached down to scratch Chance behind the ears.
He responded with enthusiastic tail wags.

"Okay, move closer."

Arnold sidestepped to the metal roll-up door, Prisha
sticking close to his right.

Eyes shielded with cupped hands, he peered between the
metal slats into the brightly lit interior, toward the ceiling. He
caught the corner of a red door opener partially obscured by a
cement ceiling beam. Ho took a half-step to the right for a
better angle.

"Take some notes for me, okay?"

"You got it, boss."

"Okay..." he said, adjusting his line of sight slightly,
zeroing in on any identifying markings, figuring to hell with
anyone watching.

By the time police responded—assuming someone even
bothered to call—they would be long gone.

"The opener's red, rectangular, and looks...like...okay,
got it. A LiftMaster 5.0."

"Roger that."

* * *

Singh drove slowly past the spot where he'd concealed the parabolic antenna and battery-powered Raspberry Pi. Wonderful. The ivy camouflaged them perfectly, making them invisible even to the knowing eye.

Now the question was, was Gold at home?

He ditched the car in the usual spot three blocks away, then approached the house through the alley to look for signs of Gold. He peered over the security wall at the back of the house and saw no activity inside. This being the middle of the day, he didn't linger; he would return after dusk to swap out the memory card to check for recorded activity. Admittedly, it was a cumbersome process, but he couldn't think of a quicker method for stealing the security system access code.

* * *

"I'll take the lead on the opener if you bear down on catching us up on pending work orders," Arnold said, justifiably worried that the turn-around time on their routine work was taking a hit because of their total focus on Hacker.

From the standpoint of growing his business, an enlarging work backlog was nice, but also underscored how woefully understaffed they were. Nailing down a qualified Honolulu associate ASAP was now a top priority.

If you start pissing off customers, the company bugler might as well blow taps.

* * *

Minutes later, as he slid back into the front seat, she said, "I just thought of a couple other things you'll probably need, so I plan on a quick detour by my place. Any problem with that?"

"Not at all. Out of curiosity, what are they?"

After she told him he was even more convinced he'd

made the right decision about hiring her. Now he just needed to convince Rachael.

* * *

With a mug of chocolate milk heating, Arnold settled into the kitchen table to check on SAM and was shocked to see no further probes at the firewall. Come to think of it, no alarms from anything. He'd been too preoccupied to notice the silence.

Hmm...the stillness stoked his paranoia.

Hackers—especially ones as vindictive as Singh—don't just throw in the towel that easily.

Failure isn't part of their rubric. Tough firewalls do nothing but whet their appetites for Putinesque dominance. Same with security systems. But this sudden All-Quiet-on-the-Western-Front thing was fueling his anxiety.

Had something taken Singh out of action? *Or*—and this was huge—had Singh actually breached SAM's firewalls and was already inside his network? Palms pressed against both temples, eyelids scrunched tightly together, he began inhaling slow deep breaths.

Do not panic. Not now. Think.

After several measured breaths, his anxiety began to tamp down to a level that allowed him to think more rationally. No way could Singh—or anyone else for that matter (including Radical Dood)—have penetrated SAM's firewall without leaving some evidence, but just to be absolutely one-hundred-percent certain, he began a step-by-step analysis of SAM's security levels.

Thirty minutes later, Arnold felt certain SAM's integrity remained intact.

Okay, where was I?

The garage-door opener, that's where. He carefully reviewed the plan he'd mapped out in flowsheet form. He couldn't see an obvious error.

Okay, but before implementing it, call Rachael.

No answer. His gut knotted.

Shit. What the hell was going on?

The pragmatic truth was, there was nothing to be done to rectify their issues if she continued to ignore him. But the glaring question remained, why be so...so what? Childish? Merciless? What?

Shit.

He downed the chocolate, washed the mug, inverted it in the dish rack, leaned against the sink edge, then struggled to regain focus.

Don't let this derail you, dude. Press on.

Not with your brain this fractionated.

What he needed was a mindless task to chill with.

What?

Amazingly, in spite of all the crap raining down on him, his stomach was telegraphing hungry signals. And besides, he should eat *some* time tonight, right?

"C'mon, boy, let's take a walk."

Flavio never seemed to mind Chance walking into the small restaurant with him; just one more reason to totally love this place.

Back home, halfway through the pizza, he realized the distraction had worked its magic; he was ready to build the device.

CHAPTER 44

"YES?" WAS RACHAEL'S frosty monosyllabic greeting when she finally answered the phone.

"Yes?" One word? That's it? Seriously?

"Look, Rach, please stop this silly game of yours. You're obviously pissed, but you haven't explained what it's really about, which leaves me helpless to do anything to resolve this. Please give us a chance to discuss it like adults, okay?"

Several seconds of frigid silence elapsed, Arnold waiting her out.

"How're Chance and Mr. Davidson?"

"They're recovering nicely. Don't avoid answering my question, sweetie."

"I don't want to discuss this over the phone. We can talk about it when you're back."

Not good enough.

"No, we need to discuss it *now*."

If she hung up on him, so be it, but he wasn't terminating this call until there was some clarity.

"I doubt that'd be helpful."

"Why's that?"

"Because you're too damn preoccupied with your

precious business, that's why. Besides, I don't want to get into an argument over the phone and I know that's what'll happen."

As if she wasn't arguing already.

Well, shit, in for a penny...

"So, what're you saying about *us*? That we're finished?"

She hesitated one beat.

"No, not that."

"Well then what *are* you saying? I need clarity. I need to know where we stand. You owe me that."

She sighed, paused, sighed again, as if picking just the right words to break some really bad freaking news.

"For the time being, I think it's best if I have my own place. We can still see each other like we were doing before I moved in...it's just that I don't think we should be living together."

And there it was.

"Why's that?" Becoming a bit defensive. "Because I'm trying to build a future for *us*?"

Intense pressure was building in his chest, making him feel like it would explode, and he was completely helpless to prevent it.

"No. That's your interpretation, Arnold. It's just, I think it's best to hit the pause button until we've had time to sort a few things out. I mean, maybe you pushed me into moving in with you."

He recoiled.

Pushed?

He glanced at the phone in hand, then put it back to his ear.

"*Pushed* you? For real? It sure didn't seem like you were being pushed."

That's crazy bananas.

Or is it?

Three or four people can see the very same event yet

everyone will describe it differently.

The ensuing silence prompted him to add, "You know I love you and want to marry you. Are you saying you don't love me anymore?"

"No, I'm not saying that at all. I *do* love you. *That's* not the issue."

He blew a long hard breath of frustration.

"Then what *is* the issue, Rach? Please...I need to know."

Does she even know?

No answer. Which, in itself, was an answer. Of sorts. But not at all illuminating. Arnold was pacing again, phone to ear, the initial shockwave subsiding to the point of giving him...what? Perspective? No, that wasn't the right word. Hmm...at least the situation didn't sound like a total disaster. At least she was dangling a shred of hope for their relationship. Had no idea how, but instinctively knew it would take a ton of work. Even then...

"Okay, look. Do whatever you need to do, Rach. And pleases don't take that the wrong way. It sounds like you need to resolve a few things. Just wish I knew what they were so I could help you, but I don't, so I can't...in the meantime, I'll continue to work on finishing my work here. Just realize this will not change the effort I'll be putting into building our business. Hopefully once I'm back, we can work on getting things back to where they were. But I'm sure you realize that that'll be impossible if you have a problem with my work."

There were certainly more eloquent words to express how he felt but he was at a loss, so...

Silence. Well, hell, might as well go ahead, make the pitch.

"Look, Rach. I'd love for you to be our business manager." He paused two seconds for that to sink in. "Your skills are perfect for it, and I guarantee you'd have time to continue nursing. I'm convinced you have the bandwidth to do both, no problem. It'd be wonderful if you could join us, and I bet you'd really get into it. I'm not asking for an answer now, I'm just putting it out there for you to think about. Just know I think you and your skills would be perfect for us. Will you at least *please* consider this?"

More hollow silence.

If she intended the silence to make a point, it was completely lost on him.

But by now he was too fed up with her lack of engagement in the conversation to care, so he said, "I love you. Good night."

"Good night."

Shit.

* * *

Singh glided silently along the shadowy side of the street, toward the curved embankment of dense ivy and thick trees and into the densest shadows. He stopped, remaining dead still, listening for sounds—footsteps or an engine—eyes scanning the sleepy bedroom street of homeowners engrossed in *American Idol* or their favorite podcast. Thank God no dog walkers were out at the moment.

After several seconds of hearing only the distant freeway hum, Singh believed it was safe enough to click on and aim a red penlight at the camouflaged equipment. Excellent. It appeared untouched. Holding the light between his teeth, he swiftly exchanged the memory card for a fresh one, replaced the computer, and backed up two steps. The camouflage looked perfect.

* * *

"How's he doing?" Arnold asked, his back against the kitchen sink, phone on the counter set to speaker.

Martina said, "The cardiologist will discharge him in the

morning pending no issues overnight."

The news seemed to levitate him off the polished concrete.

"Whew!"

"You can't imagine how incredibly relieved I am. This is the first time since Medic One took him that I'm convinced the worst is behind us."

Arnold nodded, reassured by the news, yet still down over Rachael's decision.

"What's going on, Arnold? Has something happened with Rachael?"

How could she interpret his voice so cannily? Was he that transparent?

Apparently.

He quickly summarized their conversation.

"I realize this will sound trite, but if you two truly love each other, this will sort itself out. Believe me."

Oh, yeah?

She didn't know Rachael that well. And besides, how well had she and Mr. Davidson sorted out their differences?

* * *

Singh slid the SD memory card into the reader and studied the screen. Ah, files. Excellent. Not only that, but after opening one, he found a string of packets. Singh's face exploded into satisfaction approaching infantile glee.

This *had* to be Gold's security-system key. If he transmitted these packets to Gold's security control when at the door, the lock should open. Assuming, of course, he knew Gold wasn't home. It was presently too late tonight to bother looking, but what about tomorrow? He considered this a moment.

Why not?

He'd wait until dark when the risk of neighbors spotting

him was minimal. His past surveillance told him Gold routinely shut off all but one living-room light when he left home, so a quick peek from the alley should indicate if he was gone.

Yes, indeed, if Gold left home tomorrow evening, he would strike. From start to finish would require less than five minutes; just enough time to walk in, go straight downstairs, implant the Trojan, then straight out the front door.

No muss, no fuss, no problem.

CHAPTER 45—Monday Morning

ARNOLD, PRISHA, AND Chance stopped to the right of the slatted garage door. Once again, a gust of surprisingly chilly wind swirled annoyingly down his spine straight through his heavy wool sweater and peacoat.

He shivered.

A dense low ceiling of saturated gray threatened to open up, making the weather feel shittier than it looked.

"We can't hang here too long, or someone'll get suspicious," Arnold said, casting a truncated nod toward Seatown Lofts.

"So how about in there?" Prisha said, referring to a small café in the adjoining building.

"Naw, can't get back out here and in position fast enough."

They continued to loiter, acting out their lame charade.

Three gusty minutes later Arnold muttered, "Please let this be it."

A silver Toyota RAV4 slowed, approaching from the north, its right side turn signal winking. Arnold readied the garage-door opener as Prisha stepped aside, purposely blocking the driver's view of his hand. The heavy-duty door opener clanked as gears engaged, then began a grumbling groan as the metal slats slowly started up, sliding into the horizontal ceiling tracks. The SUV nosed into the garage, came to a complete stop, brake lights now bright red embers, the driver making certain the door slowly groaned back into position until the metallic lock plates in the concrete driveway clacked tight. Once the door secured, the vehicle disappeared.

"Exemplary security practice," Arnold remarked offhandedly, as the vehicle vanished. "Exactly what you'd expect from a tight-ass insurance company employee. Sort of gives us a prelude of what to expect."

"Did you get it?" Prisha asked, nervously glancing around.

"Believe so. C'mon."

They headed south to the corner, did an about-face, returned on the reverse of the path they'd just walked, Arnold thumbing the cloned opener a few steps before they came abreast of the door, but without breaking stride, the metal gate groaning into action.

They passed the heavy lumbering door without as much as a sideways glance. At end of the block, they stopped, turned to watch the heavy door settle onto back onto its magnetic locks.

"Yeah, we're good," Arnold said, flashing a satisfied grin.

A block later, tucked into Prisha's chilly car, Arnold asked, "Does eight work for you?"

She shrugged.

"Works fine, boss."

Monday 8:17 PM

Turning from the side street onto Third Avenue, Arnold noticed a clot of four figures huddled a few feet from the closed coffee shop, about fifteen feet down the block from the garage door.

By the hunch of their shoulders and their inadequate clothing in the brisk wind and light rain, he figured they wouldn't be loitering in this shit *that* much longer.

"Don't slow," he whispered to Prisha as they approached the group.

He wished he could've worn his black pea coat instead of the olive parka, but the shade of olive was dark, and the hood held a definite advantage over the Navy coat. His backpack, jeans, and shoes were black. As planned, Prisha also had on dark clothes and a black rucksack.

For this trip Chance remained home. He was probably in the kitchen, snoozing snuggly in his bolstered bed, hopefully enjoying a satisfying dream of chasing a squirrel. Or, better yet, a cat. Regardless…

Arnold pegged the assembled group for late teens, perhaps pushing early twenties. One of the four, a gangly, tatted, pockmarked punk, glowered as they passed. Arnold ignored him but kept his thumb on the Mace in his coat pocket just in case.

When they were far enough past to not be heard, he told Prisha, "Let's circle the block. Odds are they'll be gone by the time we get back."

After an abbreviated headshake, she said, "You might be giving them more credit than's due."

They took their time rounding the block, allowing the loiterers sufficient time to grow thoroughly miserable in the chilly, gusty, drizzle. Turning the corner back onto Third again, Arnold's prediction proved accurate: the group was gone.

"Slow up," he said while scanning the immediate surroundings.

No pedestrians. Minimal vehicular traffic. So far, so good. He prayed their luck would hold.

When they were about fifteen feet from the garage door,

he thumbed the opener, heard the metal slats clack taught a faction of a second before starting their laborious grind upward. They had timed their approach perfectly.

"There's an alcove to the left, about fifteen feet inside the entrance," he said. "Head straight there, okay?"

"Got it."

* * *

Singh peered over the security wall, across the back yard, at the French doors to the kitchen. The kitchen, bathroom, and TV rooms were dark, the second-floor graveyard black. Rays of anemic light filtered in from the living room. Gold was gone.

The perfect opportunity.

Two minutes later he was on the front porch, using a small transmitter to send the disarming signal to the security-system's brains.

A small LED just above the viewing lens in the face plate changed from red to green. *Voila.* The alarm system was now disarmed. With a victorious smile, Singh confidently thumbed the door latch, heard the satisfying metallic click of the lock disengage, stepped boldly inside the house; the floorplan indelibly committed to memory.

In the inky darkness he was greeted by a deep-throated, menacing growl.

* * *

Hidden from the street, their backs pressed against a cold metal alcove door, Arnold listened to the metallic groans of the heavy garage door lumbering down, then the solid *clank* as the magnetic locks engaged.

They remained statue-still for thirty seconds, scanning the eerie harsh echo of a cement cavern for footsteps, but Arnold heard only the wet sloshing swoosh of vehicles passing outside on Third Avenue.

The garage interior was squint-inducingly bright from harsh overhead fluorescents. The bare cement floor was spotless, the air hinting of motor oil and damp concrete and a feeling unnervingly vacant, with nothing but empty parking stalls. At the far end, a ramp ascended to a second level.

About halfway there a set of doors.

An elevator?

Inching from the alcove, Prisha began scoping out the surroundings.

"See a stairwell?"

"Not yet."

Arnold trotted to the elevator.

"Shit, it needs a fob," he said, not at all surprised. "Hey, is that a stairwell behind you?"

"Whaaa—"

She spun around. They'd had their backs to it in the alcove.

"Shhhhh," Arnold whispered, finger to lips, suddenly aware of how badly he'd messed up: no doubt the garage door was under video surveillance.

Neither he nor Prisha had had thought to scout for a camera during their reconnaissance but he did now. Nope, couldn't see one, but that didn't mean one wasn't hidden, for one undoubtedly was. Not only that, but he bet that a security guard patrolled both buildings at night.

Then he heard the soft metallic click of a door latch.

From?

He quickly reviewed his imagined floor plan. No doubt the night guard devoted the lion's share of their shift to the mother building across the alley; the most direct route here would be straight through the skybridge, which would put him on the floor directly above them.

Frantically, he surveyed their surroundings.

Shit, no place to hide.

Their only escape routes were back out the garage door or through the metal fire door to the stairwell. But would the guard be coming down those stairs or take the car ramp? Was there another flight?

No way to know and he wasn't about to wait around to find out.

Had to play the odds and assume whoever was coming would take the ramp.

"C'mon. No sounds," he whispered to Prisha, hurrying back to the fire door, which unlike the elevator didn't require a fob or key.

Carefully, slowly, he depressed the latch lever and prayed the hinges didn't squeak. With the door cracked only enough to squeeze through, first Prisha then Arnold slid into a bare cinderblock stairwell smelling of decades-old concrete dust and stale air.

Arnold allowed the door to ease closed until the latch began to engage. With his left hand flat against the latch and his right hand gripping the handle, he slowly seated it, then released the lever with a barely discernable dull click.

Blowing a breath of relief, he backhanded sweat from his forehead, then motioned to the stairs while mouthing the word *slowly*. They started up, creeping as stealthily as possible, Arnold thankful for having chosen his Adidas. Prisha was wearing a pair of black Nike Air Max with the reflective white swoosh masked by black electrical tape.

On the second floor landing they found—no big surprise—the door entry required a fob. Just then, the ground floor door latch clicked. Jesus, the goddamn guard was earning his goddamn pay tonight. Silently, Arnold jabbed a finger upward.

They continued creeping up to the third floor. But again, this door required a fob.

Dammit!

Trapped.

Arnold shook his head in frustration then glanced around in desperation. The final flight of stairs undoubtedly led to the roof where the open expanse would expose them. He heard the jangle of keys relentlessly climbing their direction. Well, shit, no other option than the roof.

He started up, Prisha on his heels, moving more quickly now, certain they were being actively pursued. Would the guard follow them onto the roof? Was there any possible hiding place up there? If so, the guard surely must know about it, right? What if they were apprehended? Was the guard armed?

They reached the door to the roof. Unlike the others, this one didn't require a fob. Quietly as possible, he and Prisha stepped out onto a—surprise surprise—a dirty white membrane. Freaking *white*, man. Damnit. Although the overcast cloistered the moon, enough city light was reflecting from buildings and clouds to make them, like super obvious in their dark clothes.

Fuck it.

What choice did they have? Using the same technique as on the ground floor, he began to carefully allow the door to shut, then stopped. Though exiting the stairway didn't require a key, what about getting back into the stairwell? Most likely it did. Basic security 101: any interior access required a security measure. If so, they would be trapped.

Damn.

Hadn't thought to check and now there wasn't enough time, not with those footsteps closing in on them.

Think.

He whispered, "Got any paper on you—Kleenex, receipt, *anything?*"

Prisha began frantically fishing though her coat pockets

and came up with a wad of Kleenex.

"Here," she said, shoving it at him.

He packed the wad tightly into the strike plate receiver, inspected it. Yeah, *might* work but he didn't have enough time to test it, so quietly shut the door then glanced around frantically. No place to hide either.

Unless...

Was there room behind the small rectangular stairwell housing? The problem was, the back wall of the housing abutted the two-foot-high parapet. He glanced over the side at the three-story drop onto the concrete.

Shit-shit-shit.

He took one last glance around. Nope, nothing. Another look at the parapet. A foot wide? Maybe. Awfully goddamn narrow, that's for freaking sure. Too narrow?

Choices? Stand here looking stupid and get caught or chance it.

He swallowed hard, inhaled deeply, and stepped up onto the parapet, left hand pressing the wall, eyes straight ahead.

For Christ's sake, *do* not *look down.*

Freaking rucksack was forcing him to lean forward. Precariously. No way to get up there with it on his back, so he stepped back onto the roof, quickly slipped it off. Prisha was staying stone-cold silent, watching him.

With the rucksack straps in hand, he stepped back onto the parapet, Prisha anxiously ready to follow suit. His back against the wall, eyes locked on the building directly across the narrow alley, he slid his left foot laterally along the parapet, heel against the wall to guide it, left hand against the wall for balance.

He slid his right foot up against his left, repeating this process as quickly as possible without losing his balance.

One look down and you're freaking toast, dude.

Inch by inch he worked along the parapet, taking only

enough time to assure as-solid-as-possible footing, Prisha to his right. He crabbed like this until convinced they were hidden from a cursory view.

Unless, of course, the guard was anal-retentive enough to peek around the corner at them.

Then they would be totally hosed. But he was counting on the guard seeing an empty roof and simply assuming no one was insane enough to even consider such a stupid-ass stunt. He carefully angled his wrist far enough to check the time without looking down. What were the odds the guard would actually check the roof?

Guess we'll find out.

CHAPTER 46

THE RAIN HAD picked up since Arnold and Prisha had entered the garage ten minutes earlier. Ditto for the freaking wind. Hoods up, backs to the stairwell housing, Arnold and Prisha stood, legs stiff as rebar, eyes riveted straight across the alley at the parent building, ears searching for the slightest sound of the guard, but the waxing and waning gusts were making subtle discrimination impossible, leaving them to simply sweat it out, hoping like hell they didn't see a face poke around that freaking corner.

How long should they wait?

Five? Ten, fifteen more minutes? Heart hammering his ribcage, breaths coming in ragged gasps, Arnold's stamina for holding this dicey position was fueled by a bizarre amalgam of anus-puckering fear atop of skin-prickling excitement, the same schizophrenogenic adrenaline rush he'd experienced during the Bundy Phillips router hack.

He hated yet loved the high. But, like everything in life, it exacted a price.

Well shit, if rent-a-cop hasn't shown by now, fuck it.

Besides, his leg muscles were becoming so damn shaky that he seriously doubted he could manage much longer and live to tell.

Canting his head slightly toward Prisha, he whispered loud enough to be heard over the wind, "Start inching back."

Jesus, why bother whispering?

"Thank God."

She started crabbing toward safety.

The moment his feet landed firmly on the white membrane, Arnold dropped into a crouch to massage his cramping leg muscles, then glanced around. No guard. They were alone. After a few more moments of relished relief, he moved to a spot behind the parapet with a direct view across to Singh's apartment.

Crouching, he shrugged off his backpack, plopped it next to him, and studied the target. Their vantage point was pretty damn good, infinitely better than the parking lot. Not perfect by any stretch, but well enough situated to fly the drone. Using an extended finger, he counted from the penthouse down to the sixth floor. Singh's windows were dark.

"Maybe he went out for a late dinner?" Prisha said hopefully, having apparently counted too.

Nice to have confirmation.

"Don't know. Could be anyplace, but he was definitely in there the other day. Hope he didn't just leave for a two-week vacation to Maui or is spending the night at a girlfriend's. Hate to sit here two, three hours for zilch."

"Which begs the question, how long *do* we wait?"

Arnold shrugged. Hadn't considered it till now.

"Oh, man...until eleven, maybe? We'll just have to see what happens. We can always come back tomorrow, but Jesus..."

Didn't even want to consider it now with the building's security people aware of their entry.

She inched the jacket zipper up tight against her chin, her hood over her head.

"Let's hope he's just out to dinner."

He liked the way she said that. Committed. No hint of disapproval.

"Well, shit, we might as well go ahead and set up, in case he comes back."

Arnold carefully unpacked the drone, extended the rotor arms, making certain the blades cleared the Pineapple that was securely Velcroed to the top along with the burner phone that would transmit the Pineapple's signal back. The additional weight of these devices made the drone's maneuverability sluggish, in particular when rapidly adjusting to unpredictable gusts, severely taxing the aircraft's power, which, in turn, would drain the battery at a phenomenal rate.

The only upside—if you could even consider it as such—was that the extra weight stabilized—somewhat—the aircraft in gusts. Good thing he had practiced like crazy with the additional load attached.

Finished preparing the drone, he set up the Glasshawk spotting scope and tripod on the wet membrane and focused it on Singh's balcony. At night, with the interior lights off, focusing on the dark railing was difficult but what he could see provided a clearer assessment of the limited landing space.

Man, the combination of a small target, railing, and rapidly changing conditions...

"What's wrong?" Prisha asked.

Arnold simply moved aside so she could look.

Eye to the scope, she studied the image a few seconds before whistling.

"Lordy! You have your work cut out for you. Glad I'm the one spotting. Bring that mother in just a hair off, clip a rotor, and this turns into one ginormous shit sandwich."

Arnold nodded, mind churning through various iterations, trying to balance how best to do the job while mitigating the substantial risks. He could feel Prisha's eyes on him but said nothing.

"Hey, we can come back tomorrow night," she offered with a shrug to her tone.

He scoffed at the suggestion.

"You check out the seven-day forecast?"

"Ahhhh, noooo…"

"This's the kind of shit we're getting all week. Nope, tonight's as good as it gets. In fact, it's our best shot."

"Ouch."

"Besides, I have business that needs tending to back in Hawaii."

"How 'bout this? Since he's out at the moment, why not go ahead, take your time, and set that baby down on the deck now? Bet he's back soon, so why not go ahead and get it over with now that you don't have the pressure of him being on the other side of the window?"

He rolled her suggestion around for a moment.

"Good idea. I like it."

After assuming her position at the scope, she said, "Ready when you are."

Arnold placed the drone five feet away, powered up the burner and Pineapple, double-checked their battery indicators, and returned to his spot at the parapet. He sat cross-legged, soaking the rest of his 501s. Trying to ignore the resulting chill, elbows on knees to stabilize his hands, he dry-ran the joy sticks just for drill.

Okay, I'm good to go.

Man, this better be perfect. Only enough juice for one shot.

He thumbed the ON switch, the props immediately whirring at speed, spinning off a spray of mist.

At least the controller and drone communicate.

Slowly, carefully, the aircraft raised from the glistening white membrane while he struggled for enough confidence to fly it safely onto the postage-stamp target. To capture its "feel" again, he hovered it three feet above the roof before scooting it side to side and through one tight square. Maintaining control in these harbor gusts was noticeably more challenging than in his tree-protected neighborhood, forcing him to struggle as precious power drained from the batteries.

"Time?" he asked.

"Five minutes."

Jesus.

His elapsed budgeted flight time seemed to be evaporating at warp speed.

"Fuck it, here goes."

"I'm on it," Prisha said, monitoring the drone's location with the scope as it crossed over the parapet and over the sidewalk three stories down.

He flew it directly across Third Avenue to a few feet above the railing, to a point directly in front of where the two sliders joined at the middle of the small balcony. Rather than fly by direct sight, he was navigating off the image from the drone's high-def camera. Although this gave him excellent detail, like any two-dimensional image it lacked crucial depth perception, making critical Prisha's second-by-second coaching—especially the proximity to the railing.

"You're doing great," Prisha said. "You're now at eleven minutes and counting."

"Goddamn lighting's killing me."

"I know. It sucks. But you're doing fine, dude, just fine. Now bring it toward the sliders about one foot."

Cautiously, he jockeyed the drone closer.

"More…more…"

Inch by inch, he edged it closer to the building, still aiming for the center seam of the opposing sliders, mentally trying to track the power consumption to ensure enough juice to bring the critical payload back. Assuming, of course, they captured anything useful, which would only happen if Singh returned.

"Perfect. Now lower it straight down."

Now came the most critical maneuver of the flight. Clip a railing and, *boom*, game over. He angled the camera straight down at the balcony deck, then began lowering the craft.

"Good, good, almost there. Good, okay, touchdown!"

He cut the drone's motor, then checked the craft's position through the telescope. Although it'd been a major goddamn thrash in the air, it was well positioned for a straight vertical lift-off. Satisfied, he blew a lung-exhausting breath and allowed his muscles to relax as much as possible in his cold, soaked clothing.

"Here, want it back?" he asked, with a nod at the telescope.

She cinched her hood more tightly around her face.

"Not until we need it," and began hugging her knees, curling into a small ball, all the while keeping her eyes on the apartment.

After shaking water from the scope, he slipped it into the rucksack, then checked the connection between his phone and the burner on the Pineapple. Solid.

He huddled, arms around knees, mimicking Prisha, fighting to conserve as much warmth as possible, what with his jeans thoroughly soaked.

"Thank God I'm wearing wool," she offered.

"Still, it's goddamn miserable."

"Just saying..."

Arnold turned to her.

"Are you from New York?"

"Why?" she answered, not taking her eyes from Singh's darkened windows.

"Your accent, it's like what, Bronx, Manhattan?"

"Naw," she said with a laugh, "Brooklyn."

"Huh. Well, at least I was close."

They sat in miserable cold silence, watching Singh's darkened apartment, each second taking what felt like a minute, the wretched wet chill relentlessly seeping into his marrow stem cells.

Yeah, you've definitely turned pussy, dude. That's what Honolulu winters have done to you.

"Know what?" Arnold asked rhetorically. "Cold and miserable as this shit is right now, I'm sort of getting off on it. Know what I mean?"

Prisha laughed.

"You mean skulking around, figuring out ways to pull this sorta shit off?"

"Yeah. But not only the planning, but also the actual doing. Of course, this assumes we don't get busted."

Yeah, wouldn't that be a bitch.

"Weird, huh," he said.

"Yep, know *exactly* what you mean. To tell the truth, I get off on it too."

Silence.

"Yo, Prisha, wouldn't it be hyper cool if we could pick up a few gigs doing this shit? But, like, legally?"

She giggled.

"Most definitely."

Arnold dropped back into deep thought, juggling possibilities, excited by the prospect.

Thirty seconds ticked past.

"What?" Prisha asked, sensing his thoughts.

"Okay...okay...just throwing this out for consideration, but what if we expand our services to include pen testing?" Penetration testing tries to foil a customer's security systems—physical and/or digital—to uncover exploitable vulnerabilities. "I mean, it'd make doing this type of caper totally legit, right? I mean, like, we'd get *paid* to do this without such a huge legal risk, right?"

She laughed.

"Never thought of it that way but yeah, that'd be, like, like crack-smoking insane. I'd be totally down for it."

"*Plus*—and get this—we'd still keep busy with our other routine shit," Arnold added, getting hyper-cranked as each new aspect of his emerging plan gelled. "I mean, it's like putting a few drops of Tabasco on your scrambled eggs, right?"

She nodded thoughtfully.

"Totally."

Arnold was getting even more jazzed.

"We'll need to add a couple of team members with specific skills...maybe build a dream team capable of dealing with whatever situation gets thrown at us. But for now, we'll be the core group. We wouldn't even need to hire the others full-time, just contract them as needed for whatever the job required, right?" His mind was hitting Mach II rabid-bat speed. "Over time we'd have enough depth on the bench to tackle just about any job comes along."

What would Rachael's reaction be to this business expansion? Resent the extra work?

Don't get ahead of yourself, dude. Focus on nailing down the business manager thing first.

"Yeah, utterly," Prisha said with a broad smile, eyes still riveted on Singh's windows.

"What do you think about Lopez?" Arnold asked, unable to let it go.

"Dunno a thing about him. He any good?"

"See, that's the point; we don't bring someone on board—certainly not at associate level—until we've had a good opportunity to evaluate them. For starters, we'd hire him to help out with the day-to-day grunt work, like piecework. Follow?"

"But he's already got a job, doesn't he?"

"Yeah, but it doesn't hurt to ask."

"Yeah, definitely like the built-in vetting process. And for sure we need help with the routine work, so yeah, more I think about it, more it makes sense. Seriously think he'd be interested?"

"Have no idea but I'll jump on it first chance I get, try to lock him down."

She was beaming now.

"I can see that working for Gold and Associates is definitely gonna be interesting. You're just a damn fountainhead of ideas. One of these days soon, we need to sit down over a beer and map out just where you see us taking the business. But yeah, adding pen-testing to our services is crazy cool."

They both dropped into separate thoughts, fighting to conserve as much body heat as possible. Arnold's initial adrenaline rush was beginning to slip-slide into a deep funk over how Rachael might react to the news. Especially with their relationship so up in the air rocky.

Prisha, asked, "What's going on, dude? I mean with you personally."

He turned to her, but she was focused on Singh's place.

"Nothing. Why?"

"You're, like, totally not yourself tonight, going all bipolar yo-yo on me, dude. Like right now. One minute ago, you're all hyper and shit and now—"

"Personal issues," he said, abruptly cutting her off.

Then immediately regretted his tone of voice.

"Rachael?"

Just then the lights in Singh's unit came on.

"Game time, dude," Prisha said, opening the laptop to monitor the Pineapple.

Arnold focused the spotting scope on Singh's living room.

"Okay, get ready...he's taking off his coat...okay, he's

going into the bathroom."

They waited.

After three minutes, she asked, "The hell's going on?"

"Don't know, but I do see three computers in there. One desktop, two laptops…"

They waited another two minutes.

Prisha finally muttered, "He's been in there a *long*, long time, dude."

Arnold shrugged, eye to the scope, watching, waiting, aware that the floorplan showed only one bathroom door, so Singh had to reemerge at some time.

Three minutes later, Arnold said, "Okay, he's out and his shirt's off. Jesus, he's got one mother of a bandage on his right arm. Whatever happened, dude must've really hurt it. He's not moving that arm too well either…okay, he's in the kitchen, opening the fridge…grabbed a beer. Man, I'm looking at one seriously pissed-off dude."

"Just as long as he gets on his computer soon. I'm freezing my ass off up here."

So am I.

"Patience, Grasshopper, patience."

"You're not freezing?"

"*Whoa*, you're on. He just landed on the couch and is opening a laptop."

"Roger that."

"Okay…he's typing…and now's doing something." He turned to her. "Looks like he logged in. We get it?" he asked, hopefully.

"Not a goddamn thing," she said, shaking her head sadly.

Arnold punched his other palm.

"*Goddamnit.*"

Prisha gently nudged his shoulder.

"Just fucking with you, dude. Yeah, we got it."

She began wiping down and packing up the laptop.

He turned to her.

"You're not shitting me, are you? We got it?"

"Well, yeah, we captured something. I can only assume it's what we're after." Her hands continued to work as she spoke, clearly in a rush to get going. "Now let's get the hell outta here before I die of hypothermia."

He handed her the scope.

"Let me know when you've got a good bead on the drone."

Sitting cross legged she adjusted the scope.

"Ready when you are."

"Okay, here we go."

Arnold thumbed on the power, watched water spray from the rotors then waited for vibrations to shed as much additional water from the body as possible before carefully raising the drone straight up off the small deck to an altitude above the railings.

"We good?" he asked.

"Yeah, yeah, you're clear. Now bring it straight to us."

He beelined the drone toward them, this time flying by direct vision instead of the onboard camera since landing here would be a piece of cake. Soon as the craft came back over the parapet to the safety of the roof, Arnold began lowering it to a landing site several feet away. About a foot off the roof a sudden gust caught the craft, tossing it sideways, a prop biting into the surface and flipping it into a crash.

"Shit." Arnold muttered, running to the wreckage.

"Electronics okay?" Prisha asked, joining him.

Arnold knelt in a puddle to collect the ruined drone, no longer worried about getting wetter, since that seemed impossible by now.

"Can't tell until we get them back and can look, but this drone's officially junk. Are our recordings solid?"

"Far as I can tell. They're already backed up to the

cloud."

"Then we're good," he said, ripping the Pineapple free of the Velcro to stow in the backpack, turned his attention back to the damaged drone, shook his head. "Sure would be nice to have a replacement on tap for whenever we need it. Especially if we diversify."

Zipping her rucksack closed, Prisha simply nodded, the rain and wind having picked up even more, cranking up the dial on the misery factor.

From the edge of his vision, Arnold caught flashing red-and-blue lights reflecting off of several windows across the street.

"Shit," he muttered, pointing toward the flashes.

"Cops?"

Arnold peeked over the edge of the parapet. Parked directly in front of the garage door was a dark blue SPD SUV, misery lights flashing.

CHAPTER 47

"COPS," ARNOLD CONFIRMED, fighting the panic suddenly inflating his chest.

"Lordy, they coming up *here?*" she asked, slinging her pack over a shoulder.

"Beats the hell out of me, but you can bet they're here on account of that security guard." He quickly finished packing and muttered, "Shit."

Their fantasy of diversifying into pen-testing had just lost all of its brilliant luster. He glanced around to make sure they weren't leaving evidence.

"Hear that?" Prisha asked in a hoarse whisper.

"What?"

"Footsteps. Coming up the stairs."

Arnold grabbed his rucksack.

"Quick, back onto the ledge."

He rushed toward it, but Prisha was already ahead of him. His mind was scrambling for any possible spin for being up here if the unthinkable happened. Couldn't come up with of one. What he *did* know for sure was, they would need a damn good lawyer. And that tapping Mr. Cain or Mr. Davidson wouldn't be an option.

Then he was back on the ledge going through the same slow carefully choreographed moves as last time, sliding his left foot leftward, then meeting it with his right foot, back flush against the housing, face and eyes straight ahead, inching sideways fast as his nerves and Prisha allowed.

Arnold heard the stairwell door bang open, saw a flashlight beam sweep across the parapet to his right. He froze, tip of his right Adidas exposed, but he dared not risk the slightest movement for fear any motion would draw attention. Prisha assumed statue mode too.

"See anything?" asked a gravelly voice, partially masked by the wind.

"Not yet," a female voice answered.

Not *yet?* Fuck.

"I'll check the other side."

Arnold and Prisha remained immobile, Arnold's breathing fast and shallow, heart hammering hard, ready to explode from his chest like The Alien. Head and eyes to the right, he waited for a face to pop around the corner and shine the LED at him. A moment later, he saw a burly uniformed cop step to the parapet just three feet away and glance over the edge to the alley below and wash the beam of a Maglite over the convex skybridge glass roof, then swept it back and forth.

Please don't look left...

Apparently satisfied, the cop shook his head, turned away and vanished.

He and Prisha waited, listening.

"Nothing?" Arnold heard the female ask.

"Probably beat feet long before we pulled up. C'mon, let's get the hell out this shit."

Arnold and Prisha waited for what Arnold estimated to be three minutes but was too shaky to risk lifting his arm to check.

Besides, what difference did it make?

"What d'ya think?" Prisha whispered loud enough to be heard over the breeze.

"I didn't hear the door latch click."

"Probably wouldn't with that paper stuffed in there."

"Oh, right, forgot about that. Oh, man, what if they saw it and…" They'd either found it or hadn't. They'd either left the roof or hadn't. Regardless, he had to get off this freaking ledge before his legs collapsed. Besides, if caught, they'd figure out *something*. Anything was better than falling. "Let's go."

Arnold began edging back, slipped around the corner and stepped down onto the security of the dirty white membrane, Prisha dropped down next to him. He glanced around. No cops. But by now he could give a shit if they were waiting with cuffs out. No way he was going back on that freaking parapet again. Ever.

He crept to the front and leaned over enough to look down. The patrol car remained but with flashers now off. Prisha joined him but didn't bother looking.

"Probably writing up a report," Arnold muttered.

"In other words, we're stuck up here until they bounce," she said with a trace of irritation.

* * *

Ten minutes later, Arnold slid into Prisha's passenger seat, jammed his rucksack in the footwell, clicked home his seatbelt.

"What odds you give that we really got it?" he asked.

CHAPTER 48

LEFT HAND CLUTCHING the rucksack straps, right hand on the car roof, Arnold leaned closer to the open passenger window.

"I'll call the moment I know. But first, I plan on a good ten minutes under a hot shower."

"No shit, Kemosabe."

"All right then."

Straightening up, he double-tapped the roof a split second before she accelerated from the curb, clearly on a mission to get the home and into dry warmth.

Arnold turned toward his house but halted. The front door stood open an inch. Only an inch, but open, nonetheless. A giant fist clamped around his gut and squeezed.

Chance.

He bolted for the door, pushed on into the front room. Just inside the door, Chance was doing his cast-impaired happy dance at the sight of him. After giving him a perfunctory choobers, he flipped on the lights and cautiously scoped out his surroundings. Singh must've somehow broken in without triggering the security system. Then he noticed several large drops of blood on the floor trailing out the door.

That fucker!

After setting the backpack down, he dropped onto his haunches and caressed Chance's head, getting nose to nose with him.

"What is it, boy?" as if the pooch would suddenly explain the intrusion.

Then carefully checked him for any injury. Nope, unscathed. Meaning the blood must be Singh's. It suddenly slotted together as he flashed on Singh's bandaged arm when he had stormed from the bathroom. Laughing, he gave Chance some extra choobers.

"Good boy, Chance is a very good boy."

Still chuckling, Arnold locked the door, draped his wet coat on a kitchen chair, then went to the computer room to start a total system malware scan. On the second floor, he stripped off his cold soggy clothes, tossed them into the dryer, then jumped into a hot shower.

Moments later, pleasantly warm, bundled in a pair of thick fleece sweats, cup of hot chocolate on the table, he checked his security system logs.

As suspected, the system had been disarmed at approximately the same time he and Prisha had crept the parking-garage stairs. But there wasn't a stitch of evidence to suggest that Singh got further than one foot inside the house before Chance nailed his ass. Arnold changed the security code but knew this would only slow another reentry.

Clearly, Singh had discovered a clever way to defeat the system, which just upped the ante on nailing the vindictive asshole before he had a chance to return, intent on payback.

CHAPTER 49

"THING IS, HE'S got copies of confidential documents from both companies in there," Arnold said.

He and Prisha were at his kitchen table sipping Anchor beer, having polished off an order of green papaya salad, meatball satay, and fresh spring rolls from the Tamarind Tree, his favorite Vietnamese joint.

"Well, hell," Prisha said, "there's your smoking gun. I still don't understand what the issue is?"

He raked his fingers through his black hair.

"The issue is, yeah, we have evidence, but what can I do with it? Say I try to give it to Fisher. The first thing he's going do is ask how I got it? What am I supposed to say?"

With a frown, Prisha nodded slowly, Arnold gnashing his molars, thinking. There had to be a way to funnel this information to the feds so it could be legally put to use, but he couldn't see it.

After a long silence, she asked, "You're their CI, aren't you?"

"Yeah? So? They can't just give me a pass on account of that."

She shook her head.

"See, that's what I don't buy. There's gotta be a way they can cut you some slack on this."

Point taken.

Which got him thinking...

Prisha leaned forward, hands on the table.

"You know damn well that eventually you *have* to hand it over to them. You can't just sit on this and pretend you don't have it. Besides, soon as Singh gets the slightest hint of this, you damn well know he's gonna sanitize the bejesus outta that machine."

"Yeah, I know, I know...it's just that..."

Why didn't I think of this?

"Know what? I need to run this past Mr. Cain." He liked the idea even better now that he'd verbalized it. "I'm sure he can figure out a way to finesse this puppy."

* * *

Noah Cain leaned back in his chair, palm to palm, thoughtfully tapping his dimpled chin, digesting Arnold's story.

"Just to be clear, can you provide more specifics on the methods employed in obtaining your *proof?*"

The question carried enough inflection and intonation for Arnold to understand the unstated parenthetical caveat: don't include information that might be discoverable and/or considered illegal. However, if you *must* do so, do so in such a way we can engineer a legal work around.

Arnold applied equivalent prudence to formulating his answer, turning the information exchange into a tango devoid of incriminating statements just in case he ended up on the stand under oath. But to be honest, he was convinced that his method of capturing Singh's password would pass legal muster.

On the other hand, breaking into the parking-garage roof was, well...did Mr. Cain want him to explain that? So far, the topic hadn't been raised, so he opted to not mention his launch site.

"The Cliff's Notes version is, I weaponized the malware Singh illegally implanted in a Camano computer to send me his IP address," giving his best Mr. Innocent impersonation. "Then I used a radio *outside* his condo to receive and record his password that was being *broadcasted* by his router. In other words, at no time did I enter the condominium building or his unit. I used his password to, ah, peek at the contents of his computer?"

He cringed at turning that last statement into a question. He shot a sideways glance at Prisha, who appeared preoccupied with the view.

Cain pondered Arnold's summary for a good ten seconds before nodding.

"I know you specifically said this, but just for absolute clarity, at no time did you *physically enter* his residence for the purpose of gathering said information. Am I absolutely accurate about this? This is your opportunity to be completely honest with me, son."

"I'll gladly testify under oath that I've never set foot in his apartment."

Felt good to not have to manufacture a workaround on this point.

Cain's expression brightened.

"Good. But I require more detail than just provided. This is critically important to Carlos's defense."

Arnold scratched his head a moment, synthesizing their actions into a legally acceptable facsimile of the truth.

"It's complicated, but once I determined which unit was his, I flew a drone outside his front window to record the information," he said with another Mr. Innocent shrug. "I operated under the impression that broadcasted information is—in my admittedly nonlegal opinion—considered public domain and therefore legal to record. Am I incorrect?"

Cain appeared to ruminate on the question several long seconds before giving a tentative nod.

"Said signal wasn't in any way encrypted or otherwise protected?"

Arnold shook his head in wide-eyed innocence.

"Not at all."

Smiling with apparent relief, Cain said, "Then I believe we're good." He cleared his throat, his oral equivalent of a new paragraph. "Have you shared this information with either agents Fisher or Chang?"

"No. That's why we're running this by you now. I—and now, by extension, *we*—work for you and Mr. Davidson, so we consider this privileged information. Unless, of course, you want me to share it with them."

Again, Cain appeared to weigh his answer.

"I commend your judgment, son. We certainly intend to share it, but only after I've had sufficient time to consider this." Then, after another few seconds, added, "We'd have a much tighter package if we could establish a link between Carlos and Singh." His eyes brightened. "Hang on while I call him now."

"Sure."

* * *

"I'm on speakerphone with Arnold Gold. Is that acceptable?"

Cain was leaning back in his black leather chair, rotating slowly side to side, eyeing the phone.

"No problem," Lopez replied. "Hope this means good news. Hey, man, how you doing?"

"Good, Carlos, Good. Before I forget, I'd like to call you later today with a totally unrelated item to discuss."

"Yeah? Like?"

"Later." He did not want to get into it now and dilute the

main topic. "Won't take but a few minutes and I don't charge nearly as much as Mr. Cain."

Carlos laughed.

"For sure, dude, for sure."

Cain stopped rotating his chair, leaned closer to the speakerphone.

"Carlos, I'm going to ask an important question, so I want you to give a moment of close thought before you answer. Have you ever had any contact of any type with a man name of Ramesh Singh?"

Cain eyed Arnold as he asked the question, as if asking for verification on the name. Arnold nodded approval.

Lopez spoke with a note of confusion.

"Ramesh Singh?"

"That's right," Cain answered eyeing the speakerphone again.

The office fell silent except for distant street sounds.

After a pause, "No, not that I remember. Why? Is this important?"

With an affirmative nod, Cain leaned closer to the phone, both forearms on the desk now.

"Yes. He could be the person behind this mess."

Silence again, followed by, "Man, this is so strange. I mean that name doesn't sound even *vaguely* familiar."

"Are you absolutely certain about this? Think carefully, Carlos."

Cain seemed to be studying the phone hard now, as if willing Carlos to think thoroughly without leading him.

"I'm certain. The name means nothing to me. Of course, that doesn't mean we didn't brush into each other at some point in the past, but I sure don't recognize the name."

Frowning, Cain straightened up, drumming his fingers on the desk.

"In that case, that's all I have for now. Thank you,

Carlos."

His index finger was poised to disconnect the call.

"Hold on," Arnold said, suddenly remembering a potentially relevant piece of intel on Singh's computer. "Have you ever done any work for Orcas Technologies?"

"Orcas Technologies? Huh, wait one sec, yeah, as a matter of fact, I did do a job for them, oh, a year or so ago?" Another pause. "They had an issue and ah, *fuck, n*ow I remember. A hacker had been in their network. I stumbled across his access port and shut it down."

Holy shit.

"How'd you find him? I mean, he do any damage?"

This time Arnold was leaning closer to the phone, elbows on knees, numerous questions flooding his brain all at once.

"Naw, nothing like that," Carlos answered dismissively. "I was just up to some routine admin work and noticed a few things were off kilter, so got suspicious. All I found was evidence of an intrusion. Nothing more than that, but I locked down the port he'd snuck through."

Arnold was shooting Cain a knowing look. Cain returned a message-received nod.

No one spoke for several seconds until Cain asked Lopez, "Assuming this unidentified hacker was Singh, is it possible that your actions were sufficient enough motive for him to target you in an act of revenge?"

"I don't have the foggiest, Mr. Cain. I just do my job and move on. Anything's possible, I guess, especially knowing how shaky some egos are."

Lopez gave a contemptuous laugh.

* * *

Cain shook Fisher's hand before ushering him into the office where Arnold and Prisha stood to greet him.

"Glad you could make it, Agent Fisher, especially on such

short notice."

"No problem...I was happy for a break from paperwork."
Arnold introduced Prisha.

After all were seated, Cain opened the discussion by
asking Fisher, "To be clear, this discussion is off the record.
Agreed?"

Fisher shrugged.

"That's your call, counselor. All I know is what you said
on the call, that you have"—finger-quoting the next words—
"new information pertaining to the Lopez case."

He glanced from Cain to Arnold, back to Cain.

Cain cleared his throat.

"Mr. Gold has come across some very strong evidence
linking another hacker to the Camano and Curchfield
catastrophes."

Fisher chewed the corner of his lip a moment, studying
Arnold.

"Let me guess. You obtained this illegally, which explains
why this meeting is off the record."

He stated it as if it were fact.

The old, *when did you stop beating your wife* spin.
Arnold raised his eyebrows at Cain. Cain sent him a barely
discernable headshake before turning to Fisher.

"It's my understanding that when Mr. Gold advised the
Bureau of his role as an investigator for our defense team, that
you assured him he was still on the books as a confidential
informant. Isn't this true?"

More lip chewing. Fisher finally nodded.

"It is."

Cain nodded.

"Good. In this case, Mr. Gold's"—Cain cleared his
throat—"unorthodox activities on behalf of the Bureau should
be adequately covered by an OIA, are they not?"

Arnold realized that Cain was referring to an internal FBI

document approving "otherwise illegal activity."

Fisher shook his head.

"No, they're not."

Cain smiled at Fisher.

"Then I'm afraid we're unable to disclose any findings."

An unequivocal statement.

Fisher stood, smoothing his shirt in the process.

"Thanks for the excuse for a break."

"Hold on," Arnold said, raising a hand. "The hacker's name's Ramesh Singh and his primary computer's loaded with confidential files stolen from both companies."

Fisher's face suddenly turned hard.

"Spell the name, please."

He slowly sank back into his chair.

"Why? Is it important?" Arnold asked.

"Maybe. Just spell the name, Gold," Fisher said with a get-on-with-it hand motion.

For the next five minutes Arnold walked Fisher through exactly how he'd identified Singh as the hacker, captured his password, followed by a quick summary of the pertinent evidence in his computer. He explained how Singh had hacked Lopez's desktop, then used it to access the Camano and Curchfield media-relations computers, thereby craftily framing him. (Arnold was still scratching his head over how Singh was able to keep Lopez from discovering the security breach, but decided, it just goes to show you...)

Once Arnold wound down, Fisher worked on the corner of his mouth a moment, then turned to Cain.

"If I *were* to get an OIA signed off"—then, to Arnold—"would you be willing to download critical parts of that evidence for us?"

Cain gave Arnold an *it's-your-call* shrug.

Arnold smiled.

"Hey, no problem."

* * *

The group reconvened that afternoon in Noah Cain's office. Once Cain was convinced that Arnold's ass was adequately covered for a deep dive into Singh's computer at the Bureau's behest, Arnold agreed to verify that the incriminating documents remained in place.

"Here's how I want this to go down," Fisher explained. "We wait for the entry team to be in position and ready to go in with Chang and one other tech. Then, the moment you confirm the evidence is still intact, we'll seize his devices."

"Then let's get going. The longer we wait, the greater the odds he'll get rid of it."

* * *

The raid went down without a problem. When Arnold later spoke with Special Agent Chang, he learned that Singh wasn't saying diddly squat and had immediately lawyered up, but that best as he could tell, the entire setup had been a reprisal against Lopez for him having foiled a hack in progress.

When Arnold mused aloud if such a personal reprisal warranted ruining two companies, Chang said that apparently the asshole really didn't give a rat's ass. Arnold just shook his head and thanked Chang for the update.

Some people...

CHAPTER 50

"LOOK, RACH, THIS shit's gotten *way* out of hand," Arnold said when she finally answered.

"What shit, Arnold?" she asked in mock innocence.

"C'mon, Rach, I'd think we're well beyond that now. You refuse to answer my calls and texts. You made a unilateral decision to move back to your old apartment. And you threw a hissy fit over me hiring a female associate. I'm talking about this entire mess, sweetie. You've just about destroyed everything good about our relationship." He paused briefly. "If you *really* want to end it, just come out and say so and I'll find a way to move on. But this shit either ends now or *we* end. I simply won't tolerate this any longer. It's your call. Is this clear enough?"

After a beat, he added, "Oh, almost forgot. Either accept the job as our business manager or tell me no and I'll start looking elsewhere, but I think it's a terrific opportunity for you to be part of the company." He paused for a breath. "Face it, Rach...we'll never be a couple if we can't support each other. You have nursing and I have this. Please, don't destroy our relationship over this."

Silence. Arnold vowed to wait her out.

"What exactly does the job entail?"

His heart began pinballing around his chest.

Detente? A glimmer of hope?

"That's a good question. Truthfully, I haven't a clue. Guess you'll just have to figure that out while you're setting up our copy of QuickBooks. After all, we now have three employees on payroll if we count you," intentionally using the plural possessive as a way—hopefully—of making her feel like part of the team.

"That should be easy enough. How do I access it?"

His heart soared.

"I'll send the link to our Dropbox account. There's a spreadsheet of all pending as well as completed jobs. For now, we'll use it for all business-related work until we can find a more versatile and secure solution. How's that sound?"

Sounded brilliant to him, especially coming right off the cuff.

"Okay, I'll do it."

His heart exploded in a Roman candle of hope.

"Great. But, what about *us?*"

She hesitated a beat.

"I think we need to move more cautiously, sweetie. I need to think through things more. I feel like we rushed the living-together thing, so at least for now, I need my own space. Can you understand this?"

"Not really, but then again, I'm not very objective about it either. But if you're asking, will I live with this, then yes. I'm just super thrilled to be communicating again." He inhaled deeply. "Look, Rach, I love you. You know that. I'll do everything I possibly can to get us back on track, so we'll just move forward one step at a time. But since you're back in your old place and Chance is here, I should stay a few extra days to finish up several business-related items."

"Like?" she asked with a hint of suspicion.

"Well, for one thing, we're exploring the potential of expanding our service line to include pen-testing. That's going to take some planning. Yes, we *could* do some of that virtually, but long as I'm in town I think it's optimal to do as much as I can in person."

"Oh…"

"So are we good?"

"Yes, we're good," she replied with a distinct note of disappointment. "I hope you know I love you too, sweetie. I'm just disappointed you're staying there to work, but I understand. When you do get back, we need to spend some time catching up."

Ain't that the truth.

"Love you."

After the call, Arnold spent a moment savoring the sweet taste of hope that they'd taken their first step in resolving whatever precipitated this recent issue. The side effect was feeling renewed pressure to wrap things up as expeditiously as possible so he could return to Oahu.

Took a moment to reorganize his thoughts to turn his attention to figuring out just how the hell that asshole had defeated his security system.

This shit had to stop.

Like, now.

CHAPTER 51—Wednesday Morning

ARNOLD SAT AT the kitchen table sipping the last of his grandé latte, licking his fingertip to mop up crumbs from the classic Starbucks breakfast sandwich, Chance snoozing on the deck on the other side of the French doors seemingly unfazed by the glistening condensation from the November overcast on his dense winter coat. Prisha sat across the table, listening to him pitch the job to Lopez.

"What do you think?"

"How much time do I have to think about it?" Lopez sat to Arnold's right.

Good question, one he hadn't anticipated. He had hoped for a shriek of glee and an enthusiastic "yes." But in the sage words of Mick Jagger, "You can't always get what you want."

Set a time limit? If so, how much? A day? Hours?

Thought about that a moment, decided no, dude either wants it or he doesn't. Period. What's to consider?

Don't be stupid. You want and need him. Or at least you need people you know can excel at the type of work we'll be doing.

The dude slots that requisite perfectly.

"Forty-eight hours. Tops."

That seemed like a perfectly reasonable period, right?

"In that case..." Lopez drew out his answer.

Oh, Jesus-freaking-Christ, get on with it. Had he and Prisha jumped the gun?

"Of *course* I'm in, man." Lopez said with as much enthusiasm as Arnold had hoped for. "Sounds like a total blast. Was just messing with you, is all, man."

"Cool. I'm seriously amped," Arnold said, before turning to Prisha, "You?"

"Hell yeah. I'm incredibly pumped. Perfect timing too. Wow...yeah, wow."

They all slapped high-fives.

"Alright, then," Arnold said, "Looks like we've got a core team. Okay, so let's meet again at, say, sixish for our first official business meeting. I'll supply dinner. That is, of course, if you like pizza. If not, then, bring something you do like. Can Vihaan make it?" he asked Prisha.

"Far as I know, he's got nothing scheduled."

Wednesday Evening

Prisha, Vihaan, and Arnold sat around his kitchen, a large Flavio's pepperoni sausage pizza in the open box on the table, a plastic green-top container of Kraft parmesan cheese and a shake bottle of hot peppers off to the side, sweating amber bottles of Anchor Steam next to their paper plates, a roll of paper towels beside the pizza box to tear off as needed. Chance lay outside on the porch curled into a tight ball, nose to tail, snoozing, the chilly fall air crisp and clean without rain at the moment.

Arnold pulled a pizza tranche from the rapidly diminishing pie, broke an especially persistent strand of cheese with a finger, then bit off the apex, the wayward strand falling onto his chin. He wiped it off with a wad of paper towels.

Man, Flavio's. Nothing compared.

"Now that our core team's established," Prisha announced triumphantly, raising her amber bottle toward the center, "I propose a toast. To us!"

"To us!" they responded, clinking bottles.

Glowing pride warmed Arnold's chest, radiating out through his arteries into the furthest reaches of his extremities.

Gold and Associates had blown past a major milestone by transitioning from a One-Banana Show into a troupe of accomplished Teatro ZinZani trapeze artists capable— hopefully—of dazzling acts of daring.

Page One of a new chapter for his start-up.

Exhilarating, and, well, a bit intimidating. None of them had ever attempted to jump-start a business, especially in a city packed to the gunnels with seasoned talent.

Arnold asked Vihaan, "You'll start the new website design?"

"I'm already playing with some audacious ideas, so yeah, I got it covered," Vihaan answered.

"Good. We'll hammer out the exact content once you have the general layout mocked up *including* the security measures. Particularly the honeypot."

His recent experience with Singh not only underscored this particular trap's value, but mandated that it be made even more secure and functional. You never know when it might be needed. This time the redesign would include the ability to capture an invader's IP address.

"Do you have a status update on the business-manager thing?" Prisha asked, assuming the Nose To The Grindstone role.

"Hell. I knew I was forgetting something. Yeah, we're set. She accepted the offer and is in the process of setting up QuickBooks. The only reason she's not here virtually for the meeting is she's at work."

"Excuse me if this is too personal, but what's this mean for the two of you?" Prisha pointed from him and a random point in space. "Is this good news or what?"

He shrugged.

"Wish I knew. All I can say's it's better than if she'd said no. Guess I'll just have to see how things play out."

Both Prisha and Vihaan gave a *you-the-boss* nod, the kind that recognizes a statement without taking sides.

Prisha spoke with the merest hint of suspicion.

"She aware of our new service?"

"She is."

She gave him her patented side-eye squint.

"And that's not a problem? Especially considering it'll probably mean more business travel."

Arnold glanced away.

Another question I can't answer.

"We haven't actually broached that part yet."

Prisha flashed him an even more suspicious side-eye, but said nothing.

Then again, the look she gave him said it all.

"I know, I know," Arnold said, both hands raised in surrender. "One step at a time, okay?"

"I'm just sayin'..."

"What's our next step?" Vihaan, the group diplomat, cut in.

"We just keep grinding it out, which should go a lot faster now that Carlos is on board. In the meantime, I'm getting wind of a potential RFP that's being hammered out. Not sure when it'll be released, but I have my spies working on it."

"For pen-testing? Prisha asked, eyes wide open now.

"Yup," Arnold replied with a broad smile.

Thursday Evening

Mr. Davidson, Martina, and Arnold were tucked into their favorite booth at Uptown China, four platters of food edge-to-edge on the table along with a bottle of Mark Ryan Syrah, compliments of Davidson.

"Not hungry?" Mr. Davidson asked, a hunk of lemon chicken clamped between chopsticks *en route* to his mouth.

Carefully setting his chopsticks on his plate, Arnold paused to sip wine before answering. He took a quick glance at Martina. She deadpanned him, punting the decision straight back on his shoulders. Well, hell, the subject had to be broached eventually. He shook his head.

"No, not really."

"I suspected as much. You have not seemed yourself all evening. What is it, son?"

Arnold glanced at other patrons enjoying dinner, all chatting animatedly, seemingly unencumbered by personal tribulations, though he knew each one of them undoubtedly was constantly juggling issues and rolling with the punches as part of daily life; some hassles more complicated than others, but everyone was affected in some way.

"Rachael moved back into her old place and I have no idea what's going to happen to us."

Mr. Davidson slumped in the booth with a stunned and confused expression.

"May I ask why?"

Arnold debated how much to disclose and yet avoid ruining what he intended to be an enjoyable evening. He glanced at the neighboring booth a moment, realized he was only stalling the inevitable, so...

"Basically, she's pretty unhappy about how much time I spend on work."

Davidson nodded knowingly.

"Yes, she made that abundantly clear last summer during our visit. I truly am sorry."

Arnold shook his head.

Didn't realize it had been that obvious.

"Unfortunately, it's a thing with her now, and she can't seem to let go of it."

Davidson opened his mouth to respond, hesitated, looked down at the piece of lemon chicken.

"I'm sorry if Noah and I worsened the issue by asking for your help in preparing this case."

"No, see?" Arnold held up both palms. "That's exactly why I didn't want to bring it up. It's not your fault, either of you. It's something she and I need to resolve, but she's being very closed lipped about it. Hell, I'm not even sure she has a handle on it."

"Does this mean it's not completely over between you?" Martina asked hopefully.

Arnold's shoulders slumped.

"Wish I knew. She gave me the definite impression that we have a shot, but we'll see…the one thing I know for sure is I *finally* have something in life I really want to do…something that excites me, so I have to give it all I have. This doesn't mean I'm giving up my dream of marrying her, either. But we have a ton of work to do on getting our relationship back on track. I *will* find a way to do that."

"Then why're you still in Seattle?" Martina asked bluntly.

"Had a few things I needed to wrap up," he replied with a broad grin. "But they're taken care of now and I'm heading back tomorrow. That's why I wanted a family dinner tonight."

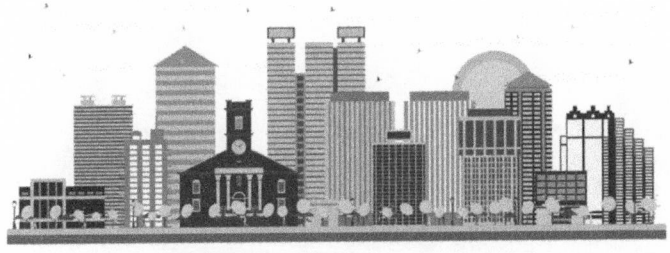

HONOLULU

ACKNOWLEDGEMENTS

I owe deep gratitude to the following patient and tolerant sources who fielded my countless questions:

Ken Roberts, Cyber Security, Qush
Jonathan Tomek, CEO and Co-Founder of MadX
Ryan Jones, Co-Founder and CTO, Digital Silence
A retired FBI agent who still wishes to remain anonymous.

CPSIA information can be obtained
at www.ICGtesting.com
Printed in the USA
LVHW100041170822
726142LV00003B/85